100 THINGS
REDS FANS
SHOULD KNOW & DO
BEFORE THEY DIE

D0027098

100 THINGS REDS FANS SHOULD KNOW & DO BEFORE THEY DIE

Joel Luckhaupt

TRIUMPH
BOOKS

Copyright © 2013 by Joel Luckhaupt

No part of this publication may be reproduced, stored in a retrieval system, or transmitted in any form by any means, electronic, mechanical, photocopying, or otherwise, without the prior written permission of the publisher, Triumph Books LLC, 814 North Franklin Street, Chicago, Illinois 60610.

Library of Congress Cataloging-in-Publication Data

Luckhaupt, Joel.
100 things Reds fans should know & do before they die / Joel Luckhaupt.
    pages cm
    ISBN 978-1-60078-794-2
    1. Cincinnati Reds (Baseball team)—History. 2. Cincinnati Reds (Baseball team)—Miscellanea. I. Title. II. Title: One hundred things Reds fans should know and do before they die.
    GV875.C65L84 2013
    796.357'640977178—dc23
                                                    2012051212

This book is available in quantity at special discounts for your group or organization. For further information, contact:
    Triumph Books LLC
    814 North Franklin Street
    Chicago, Illinois 60610
    (312) 337-0747
    www.triumphbooks.com

Printed in U.S.A.
ISBN: 978-1-60078-794-2
Design by Patricia Frey
Photos courtesy of AP Images unless otherwise indicated

To Sara, who let me turn a hobby into a career.

To Alex, who is helping me rediscover baseball as a kid again.

To Emily, whose smile keeps me grounded.

Contents

Foreword

I made it to the big leagues around the same time as the Big Red Machine. When I played for the Braves, we were looking up at them in the standings in every year but one. When I was traded to the Dodgers in 1976, all we wanted to do, all of our focus was on beating the Reds. They were the pinnacle of the sport at that time, and we knew that in order to be the best, we had to beat the best. We respected them, but we also disliked them because they were so good. That lineup was loaded, top to bottom. There were no holes.

When we finally took the division in 1977, it was even more special because the Reds were the two-time defending world champions. They motivated us to be better, to be our best. Beating them, we knew we had beaten one of the greatest teams ever assembled. That's what the Cincinnati Reds meant to us.

I was the hitting coach for the San Francisco Giants during the 1990 season. Man, we had some battles that year with the Reds. That team played us hard. Every game was a grind. I think we got the better of them head-to-head, but they took it to everyone else and didn't let up. We had some heated exchanges, but we also appreciated how hard they played. Once they got their engine going, they were hard to stop.

Those were the teams that were in my mind when I signed on to manage the Cincinnati Reds in 2008. I talked to Joe Morgan before I took the job about the rich history of the city and the franchise. Winning means everything to me, and I knew the fans in Cincinnati felt the same way. I knew that the lean years in the early part of the decade had everyone hungry for a champion—as hungry as I was. I was excited to re-establish the winning attitude, the winning feeling that I've always known Cincinnati to have. I knew what I was up against when I took the job. Let's be honest, new managers aren't brought in to take over winning teams very often. But I felt like we had the talent to get back to championship baseball and stay there.

I was impressed by Mr. Castellini's passion to return the Reds to glory. He embraced the great teams of the past, but he also wanted to add new ones to the list. When we won the division in 2010, I was so proud to be part of that moment. Winning once makes you want to win more, and I could see it in the players' eyes that they wanted to win more. Brandon Phillips, Joey Votto, Johnny Cueto, all of them want to be part of that great Cincinnati Reds legacy. That is what we play for.

Fans in Cincinnati have had a lot of reasons to be grateful over the years. So many great players have come through Cincinnati, from Frank Robinson to Pete Rose, Johnny Bench, and Joe Morgan, to Eric Davis. Being in Cincinnati for Barry Larkin's induction into the Hall of Fame made 2012 that much more extraordinary. I don't think you could have a better representative for the Cincinnati Reds than Barry Larkin. He's not just a great player, he's a great man.

I know Cincinnati has usually been known for offense, but they've had some great pitchers come through here, too. Don Gullett was a tough, tough lefty. Gary Nolan, Jack Billingham, Fred Norman, I didn't like to face any of those guys. I never could handle Mario Soto with that fastball and changeup of his. I know I got to Mario a couple of times, but it sure wasn't as much as he got to me. Jose Rijo could shut down any team in the league, and the Nasty Boys made up one of the toughest bullpens I've ever seen.

When I get the chance to talk to fans at events like Redsfest or on the Caravan, they all know that history. Those fans will appreciate a book like this. It's a book that teaches the history and celebrates it. We aren't done writing more chapters, though. The history of this team is long, all the way back to 1869, but it isn't finished. Winning once makes you want to win more, and reliving those wins only strengthens that feeling. So read this book, remember those great moments, and know that we'll keep trying to give you more great moments, more great memories on the field.

—Dusty Baker
September 2012

Acknowledgments

Books like this do not happen without some considerable help. Eric Lilly took on some of the research for me, which allowed me to focus more on the writing. Chris Eckes from the Reds Hall of Fame had some valuable input on where items belonged on the list. Reds PR Manager Michael Anderson gave me incredible support and spent an afternoon helping me get the details right on many of the Reds' key events. Jeff Brantley told me several stories that did not make it in the book and a few that did, but the conversations were always enjoyable. Finally, this book would be remarkably different without the brain trust of John Erardi, Greg Rhodes, and Greg Gajus. The combined knowledge of Reds history in the brains of those three men could—and has—filled multiple tomes. I'm honored that they felt me worthy of sharing in that knowledge.

Introduction

I was a sports fan growing up, but I didn't play much baseball. Basketball was the sport that I loved to play, though I must admit that I wasn't very good. During the fall, I attentively watched the baseball postseason, but I was also enamored with college football on Saturdays and the NFL on Sundays. College basketball and Magic and Larry got me through the winter. I was a fan of all sports with no real favorite until May 1987, just a few weeks before my 11th birthday. That's when Eric Davis went from being an incredibly gifted athlete to something close to god-like right before my 10-year-old eyes.

The month started with one of the most incredible individual performances I've ever seen in a three-game series. Davis dominated the Philadelphia Phillies over that spring weekend in Veterans Stadium with nine hits in 13 at-bats, including five home runs and 11 RBIs. He hammered two longballs in the opener and closed the series with a three home run performance in the rubber match, his second career three home run game. Davis would hit seven more home runs and drive in 25 more runs during the month of May, which included six separate games where he drove in four or more runs. Only three Reds players have ever had more four-RBI games in a *season* than Davis had in 22 games that month. Twelve home runs, including a team-record three grand slams, 36 RBIs, and 11 stolen bases—those numbers for 81 games are enough to get a player selected to the All-Star team. Davis did it all in one amazing month.

Suffice it to say that I was smitten. Eric Davis almost single-handedly made me a baseball fan—as well as a Reds fan—for life. From that point on, other sports lost their luster, and even though I continued to follow them, Reds baseball began to take up more and more of my free time with each passing year. Today, baseball is a year-long passion in large part because Eric Davis showed a 10-year-old boy the incredible things that were possible on the ballfield.

This book is for those fans who, like me, had that moment when they fell in love with the Reds. It could be the first time you saw Frank Robinson swing a bat at Crosley Field, or when Pete Rose dove head first into third base. Maybe you were at Riverfront Stadium the night that Lou Piniella showed his passion for winning while also demonstrating his skill at tossing first base. Or perhaps you are a recently born-again fan, returning after the dark decade to watch the Reds re-ascend to baseball's elite. Hopefully, this book can capture for each of you what it means to be a Reds fan through the history of some of the team's great moments and dark times. Relive the stories of your favorite players and learn about those who may have preceded your fandom.

The list of these 100 items is a subjective ranking of what I think are the most important things about being a Reds fan. Your list might be different, and in fact, my list might be different in six months. Fandom is fluid, but it is also shaped by our history and experiences. This book is full of both, and I hope you find that it covers all of the important ones. Enjoy!

[Editor's Note: Slash-line batting scores presented in this book look like this: .322/.433/.444. From left to right, the first number is the batting average, next is the on-base percentage, and the last number is the slugging percentage.]

1 The Big Red Machine

The Big Red Machine wasn't baseball's first dynasty, and it wasn't its last, either. However, it was the last great dynasty before free agency, an innovation that made dynasty-building both a baseball and business proposition. The team was also a collection of baseball archetypes. If you are a fan of the game, there is someone on this team to whom you likely feel connected. There was the hard-nosed hustler, the phenom, Mr. Clutch, Mr. Everything, the speedster, the masher, and the defensive wizards. And all of them were the best at who they were. There wasn't much that this team didn't have.

Ultimately, though, it was the sheer dominance of the Big Red Machine that will keep them in baseball's consciousness for years to come. From 1970–76, they scored 199 more runs than any other team in baseball and they scored nearly 1,000 more runs than they allowed, outscoring their opponents by 0.88 R/G over those seven years. Their .607 winning percentage during that seven-year span is the highest of any team in Reds history, and through 2012, no other Reds team had matched that number in a single full 162-game season.

The Big Red Machine was built through the combination of a fruitful farm system and a collection of shrewd trades. The first half of that formula was started by Owner/GM Bill DeWitt Sr., who was in charge when the team signed Pete Rose and Tony Perez and drafted Johnny Bench and Gary Nolan. DeWitt also signed Lee May, who would be the key piece in the Joe Morgan trade.

When Bob Howsam took over for DeWitt in 1967, he set about putting his stamp on the team, signing amateur free agents

1

Dave Concepcion and Dan Driessen and drafting Don Gullett, Ken Griffey, Rawly Eastwick, and Will McEnaney. He also made three key trades that would put the finishing touches on the world championship teams of 1975–76. First he traded for George Foster from the San Francisco Giants. Next he got Joe Morgan, Jack Billingham, and Cesar Geronimo from the Houston Astros for May, Tommy Helms, and Jimmy Stewart. Finally, he added Fred Norman in a 1973 trade, solidifying the rotation. He also made the ingenious move of hiring an unknown named Sparky Anderson to manage the squad before the 1970 season—a decision that worked perfectly for this team.

Even with all of the glory that the Big Red Machine receives today, they came dangerously close to being known as a good team that could never get over the top. In 1970 they won a franchise record 102 games, lapping the NL West by 14½ games. However, they barely made a whimper in the World Series as the Orioles won easily in five games. Two years later it was another double-digit division title, but the Oakland A's staved off an eighth-inning rally in Game 7 to beat the Reds 4–3 in the World Series. In 1973, they won 99 games but lost in the NLCS to a much weaker New York Mets team. A year later they won 98 games but couldn't topple the division-rival Los Angeles Dodgers and failed to make the playoffs.

It was May 1975 when the Big Red Machine truly turned into one of the greatest teams of all time. It was at that point when Sparky Anderson made the decision to move All-Star left fielder Pete Rose to third base so that he could get George Foster into the lineup more regularly, and at that moment the Great Eight was born. From May 21 until the All-Star break, the Reds won 41-of-50 games and turned a five-game deficit into a 12½-game lead. By the end of the year they tallied 108 victories—it was the highest total in the National League in 66 seasons.

The Reds swept through the Pittsburgh Pirates in three games, but they met their match in the World Series against the Boston

The Great Eight

When you ask a Reds fan to name the players on the Big Red Machine, more often than not the first eight names you hear will be Pete Rose, Ken Griffey, Joe Morgan, Johnny Bench, Tony Perez, George Foster, Dave Concepcion, and Cesar Geronimo. Known collectively as the Great Eight—they were so good that just being called the Big Red Machine wasn't enough—these eight men were nearly unbeatable when they were on the field together.

Of course, manager Sparky Anderson thought highly of them. "I'm not going to sit here and tell you that the starting eight of the Big Red Machine is the greatest of all time," he said. "But if somebody else has a better one, I want to sit and watch it. If they're better than the starting eight in 1976, oh my goodness."

The funny thing is that these eight men only started a game together 80 times in all the years of the Big Red Machine. They first took the field together on May 9, 1975, shortly after Rose moved from left field to third base, but Anderson didn't stick strictly with that lineup. He regularly mixed in Dan Driessen and Merv Rettenmund in the outfield and Bill Plummer at catcher. By the end of the season, the Great Eight had started only 21 games. But they were the only starters used throughout the playoffs as the Reds took home their first title in 35 years.

In 1976, Anderson used the Great Eight more regularly, but they only saw 42 games as a unit in the regular season. However, with Driessen as the designated hitter they once again were the only starters throughout the playoffs as the team swept the NLCS and World Series.

Overall, the group had an incredible 64–16 record when they started together, outscoring their opponents 489–312 in those games. That .800 winning percentage translated to nearly 130 wins during a 162-game season.

Red Sox. The two teams battled in a fierce seven-game competition that is considered by many to be the greatest World Series of all time. After five innings of Game 7, it once again looked as if the Reds might choke away a chance at a championship, but a sixth-inning two-run home run by Mr. Clutch, Tony Perez, put the Reds on the board, and a run-scoring single in the seventh from

Rose tied it up. In the ninth inning, NL MVP Joe Morgan singled home Ken Griffey to give the Reds their first lead of the game. A 1-2-3 ninth inning by Will McEnaney brought home the victory and Cincinnati's first title in 35 years.

With the monkey of missed expectations off their back, the Big Red Machine repeated as champions in 1976, once again winning the NL West by double-digits and sweeping through the NLCS. The World Series versus the New York Yankees was also a sweep as the Reds became the first team in the divisional era to win all seven games of a postseason. At this point there was no question that the Big Red Machine was among the greatest teams that the game had ever seen.

The second championship also marked the beginning of the end for the Big Red Machine. Free agency was here, and the price of doing business was starting to rise. The Reds, fearing that they couldn't afford all of their stars, dealt away Will McEnaney and Tony Perez to the Montreal Expos. The team still remained competitive though, and even traded for superstar Tom Seaver during the 1977 season. Back-to-back second-place finishes in 1977–78 preceded the firing of Sparky Anderson and Pete Rose's departure via free agency. A year later it was Joe Morgan who left, and despite a division title in 1979, it was clear that the Big Red Machine was no more. Just three years later the franchise would be a shell of its former self.

All in all, it's hard to imagine what else the Big Red Machine could have accomplished during the 1970s. Sure, they could have won a couple more championships, but it is in falling short that we learn to appreciate when we ultimately reach our goal. And six division titles during a decade when the Dodgers were very competitive every year is nothing to shake your head about. Add in six league MVPs for a roster that had five legitimate Hall of Fame candidates, and you understand that a team like the Big Red Machine may never be seen again.

2 Joe Nuxhall

During World War II, the draft and war efforts drained Major League Baseball of many of its great stars. Teams often scrambled to fill rosters, leaving no stone unturned while trying to draw fans to the park. Sometimes that meant doing something dramatic like signing a 15-year-old left-handed pitcher and sticking him on the mound. By his own account, Joe Nuxhall was not ready to pitch in the big leagues as a teenager—but in 1944, he gave it a try anyway. "I was pitching against seventh-, eighth-, and ninth-graders, kids 13 and 14 years old," Nuxhall recalled. "All of a sudden, I look up and there's Stan Musial and the likes. It was a very scary situation."

Nuxhall pitched one game that year, getting two outs while walking five batters and surrendering five runs. The one outing put him in the record books as the youngest player ever to appear in a big-league game. It also kicked off a career in baseball that lasted more than 60 years, almost all of those years with the Reds organization. Nuxhall spent 16 seasons in the big leagues, mostly as a slightly above-average pitcher. He was battler, though—someone Pete Rose called the "most competitive SOB" he ever played with. That fighting spirit carried Nuxhall to a career-high 17 wins and a league-leading five shutouts in 1955. It also got him selected for the NL All-Star team in 1955 and 1956.

Nuxhall's career with the Reds spanned three decades, and he went 130–109 with a 3.80 ERA for his hometown team. He pitched in Cincinnati in all but one of his seasons in the majors, and sadly for Nuxy, that one season he missed was 1961, the only year the Reds won the NL pennant during his career. Nuxhall retired in 1966, and two years later he was elected to the Reds Hall of Fame. Yet that was hardly the end of the line for Hamilton Joe.

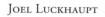

Joe Nuxhall, age 15, is shown in his Cincinnati Reds uniform in this June 10, 1944, file photo before he pitched two-thirds of an inning to become the youngest player to ever participate in a major league game. (AP Photo)

The year before Nuxhall was put in the Reds' Hall, he took a seat in the Reds' radio booth, and he passionately held on to that seat for the next 37 years. Seven years into his tenure in the booth, he was joined by the man he called "Little Buddy," Marty Brennaman. Marty and Joe became staples on Reds radio for three decades, with Nuxhall's folksy charm and unabashed fandom balancing Brennaman's straight-shooting, no-nonsense style. Fans adored Nuxhall's quirky approach to play-by-play, often letting the crowd tell the story. And many of the greatest calls during the Reds' golden era are punctuated by the sound of Nuxhall cheering passionately in the background.

When it comes to Joe Nuxhall the man, there is simply no way to describe him that does not sell him short in some fashion. He spoke to everyone as if he cared deeply because somehow, he did. A man with a heart as big as the city, Nuxhall treated everyone he met with respect and dignity. After Nuxhall's death in 2007, Dave Armbruster, the long-time engineer for Reds radio broadcasts, summed up Nuxy well when he said, "He's like the best uncle you ever had. I thought of him like that. I thought of him as almost a father figure later. He was the cool uncle who would talk to you the way most grownups wouldn't talk to you."

Many Reds fans felt as though they had lost a family member when Nuxhall passed away, even if they had never met the man. He was the patron saint of the Cincinnati Reds, the man who expressed what most fans were feeling. Nuxhall was their joy when things went well, and he was their agony in times of heartbreak. Nobody loved the Reds more than Nuxhall, and his genuine affection came through in every broadcast.

Nuxhall's legacy lives on still today through his sons, Phil and Kim, and through the multiple charitable organizations that carry his name. For Nuxy, it was always about others first, so it's fitting that his name lives on to serve handicapped children with the Joe Nuxhall Miracle Fields, to build leaders through the Joe Nuxhall

Character Education Fund, and to provide scholarships through the Joe Nuxhall Open charity golf outing.

A good ballplayer, a beloved broadcaster, and an outstanding humanitarian there will never be another Joe Nuxhall.

3 Opening Day

If you've never been to the first baseball game of the year in Cincinnati, then you've never truly been to Opening Day. In Cincinnati, Opening Day is spelled with a capital "O" and a capital "D" because it truly is a holiday celebration in the Queen City. For years businesses have closed and schools have looked the other way if a child with a ticket happens to be absent that day. The game regularly sells out months in advance, and while fans of most teams check out where they will open the season when the schedule comes out, Reds fans simply need to check the team they open against. They already know the game will be at home.

Many believe that Cincinnati's standing as the home of the first professional franchise has earned it the honor of being the home for the Reds' opening game every season. There is little historical evidence to defend that belief. It is most likely that the Reds opened at home every year because at one time they were the southern-most city in the league, a theory promoted by John Snyder, author of *Redleg Journal*. The southern location improved the chances of warmer weather, and in the early twentieth century, the Reds opened nearly every season versus their more northerly neighbors from Pittsburgh or Chicago.

During the last decade of the nineteenth century, business manager Frank Bancroft used some opportunistic marketing and a fortunate string of good weather to transform Opening Day into a citywide event and a huge money maker. So when schedule makers threatened to move the Reds on the road for their opening game in 1935, the team argued that the move would be costly for the franchise given the long tradition that had already been established. The league relented, and the tradition has protected the home opener from the schedule makers ever since.

The Reds were right to defend their home opener. Time has shown that, in the few cases where circumstances required the Reds to open on the road, the luster of Opening Day was lost and the event was much less of a draw for fans. The only two times since the mid-1980s that the Reds have not sold out Opening Day were 1990, when a labor dispute forced the team to open on the road, and 1995, when the 1994 strike delayed the start of the season and left a bitter taste in fans' mouths.

One of the big highlights of Opening Day is the Findlay Market Parade, which winds its way through downtown Cincinnati during the morning before the game. At the turn of the twentieth century, parades of players used to be a standard for opening games around the league, but that tradition was short-lived. In Cincinnati, the player parade was replaced by "rooter parades" where groups of fans dressed in costumes and riding in decorated vehicles paraded through downtown. These rooter parades eventually evolved into the Findlay Market Parade, which dates its initial run back to Opening Day 1920. For many years, the parade finished its route on the field, both at Crosley Field and at Riverfront Stadium, but that tradition was stopped in the early 2000s when the Reds changed the playing surface to grass at Riverfront/Cinergy Field. Many traditionalists feel that the spirit of the parade has been lost because of that move, essentially making the game and the parade two parallel but unconnected events.

It's hard to say that the change has dampened the energy of either event as crowds swarm to downtown every Opening Day to be part of the annual celebration. The team still rolls out the red carpet for the event, too, bringing in local and national VIPs to help celebrate the day. In recent years, the Reds have expanded the celebration to Opening Night, bringing special attention to the first night game each year (usually the second game of the season). The success of Opening Night just goes to show how high enthusiasm is for baseball once the season starts, and also how much Cincinnatians love a good party.

4 Pete Rose

Ask a non-Reds fan over the age of 40 to name a Cincinnati Reds player, and more often than not he'll say, "Pete Rose." Born on the west side of Cincinnati, Rose was the epitome of the hometown kid who made good. He was a good athlete, but he was small for his age, which stunted his progression as a running back in football. He continued to excel at baseball, and with the help of his uncle, Buddy Bloebaum, who was a bird dog scout for the Reds, Rose was able to convince the Reds to give him a contract once he graduated from high school.

Rose hit well throughout the minors, and in spring training 1963 he got his shot to make the team out of camp. An injury to Don Blasingame opened up a spot at second base, and Rose took advantage, winning the starting job outright and never relinquishing it. That same spring, Whitey Ford of the New York Yankees gave Rose the nickname "Charlie Hustle" for the over-the-top effort the youngster exerted on the ballfield. Intended as a derisive nickname, Rose wore it as a badge of honor, eventually turning it into a positive validation of his hard-nosed style of play.

The 22-year-old Rose easily won the Rookie of the Year Award in 1963, and two years later he was selected for the first of 17 career All-Star Game appearances. He finished sixth in MVP voting in 1965 after leading the league with 209 hits. He would receive MVP votes in 15-of-17 seasons starting that year, an unheard of string for a player who only topped 80 RBIs twice in his career. It goes to show that a player can be valuable to his squad even when he's not one of the boppers. He topped 200 hits 10 times during his career, and he led the NL in that category seven times. As the table-setter for the Big Red Machine, he scored more than 100 runs in 10 seasons, pacing the NL for four of those years.

His finest individual season was 1973 when he won the batting title with a .338 average and led the league with a career-high 230 hits, all while playing excellent defense in left field. Rose was rewarded with his only NL MVP Award as the Reds coasted to their third division title in four years. The Machine dropped a five-game series to the New York Mets that year in a matchup that featured a violent brawl at second base between Rose and the Mets' Bud Harrelson in Game 3.

The fight demonstrated something about Rose that endeared him to many in Cincinnati—a burning desire to win at all costs. Rose frequently reminds people of how he played in more winning baseball games than any player in big-league history (though he usually leaves out that he also played in the most losing games in NL history). Winning was the most important thing to Rose, and fans appreciated that about him. When the Big Red Machine finally won its first title in 1975, nobody enjoyed it more than Charlie Hustle.

He would win two more titles, one in 1976 with the Reds and one in 1980 with the Philadelphia Phillies. Along the way he would set multiple NL and MLB records. In 1978, he matched Wee Willie Keeler for the NL record for longest hitting streak at 44 games. In 1985, he passed Ty Cobb as the all-time hits leader,

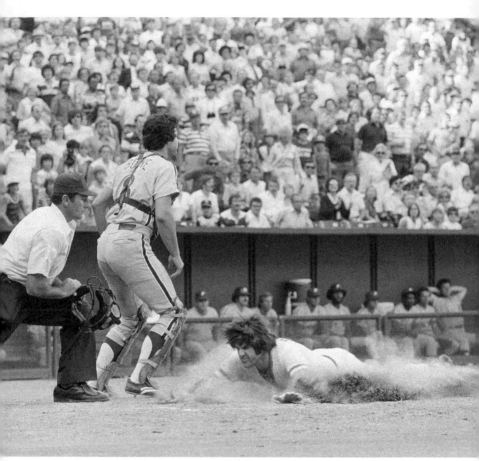

Pete Rose goes across home plate headfirst to score in the third inning of the first game of a doubleheader with the Philadelphia Phillies in Cincinnati on Friday, July 28, 1978. Rose made the diving headfirst slide his trademark. Rose had doubled earlier in the inning to give himself a hit in his 40th consecutive game. (AP Photo)

finishing his career with 4,256 base knocks. He played in more games than any major leaguer in history, which is fitting since no one has ever had a passion for baseball like Rose, who famously said, "I'd walk through hell in a gasoline suit to play baseball."

Like most tragic heroes, it was that passion and competitive spirit that led to Rose's downfall. In 1984, he took over as the Reds' manager and led the team to a fifth-place finish followed by second-place finishes from 1985–88. While he was doing that, Rose was also compulsively gambling on baseball and on the Reds—the biggest taboo in the sport. When Major League Baseball caught wind of Rose's transgressions, commissioner Bart Giamatti brought down swift justice and banished Rose from baseball for life, though he would be able to petition for reinstatement in the future. In a situation akin to Greek mythology, Rose is now treated as a pariah by the one sport he cherished above all else. His self-inflicted wounds have left him on the outside of many great honors. Banished from the game's Hall of Fame, the Reds Hall of Fame and, most importantly, from ever participating on a major league field, Rose is forced to ask for special permission to even be honored at events like the All-Century Team, to which he was elected in 1999.

Whether or not Rose will live to see enshrinement in the Hall of Fame remains to be seen. At this point, the commissioner's office shows no sign of any desire to change Rose's status. The evidence shows that Rose is far from innocent, as do his later admissions, but it would be a shame if one of the most beloved sports figures in history is left on the outside looking in until the very end.

Johnny Bench

The early days of the amateur draft were much less scientific than they are today. They didn't have the breadth of scouting and reporting that teams now utilize, and kids were not being scouted for years leading up to the draft like they are now. Even with all that in mind, it is hard to figure out how Johnny Bench wound up as a second-round pick in the 1965 draft and the eighth catcher taken. It would not take long before at least seven other franchises kicked themselves for that mistake.

Johnny always knew that he wanted to play baseball, but he spent most of his American Legion days on the mound, not behind the plate. His father, Ted Bench, was a semi-pro catcher in his day, and he convinced his son that catching was his fastest ticket to the big leagues. Johnny started catching regularly as a 17-year-old, and it was not long before he revolutionized the position in the majors.

Two years after he was drafted, Bench made his debut with the Reds, but he struggled at the plate as a late-season callup. A year later, he took the baseball world by storm, batting .275/.311/.433 in 154 games, edging out Jerry Koosman for the Rookie of the Year Award. Bench's bat was impressive for a 20-year-old, but it was his defense that caused chins to drop. A gifted thrower, Bench shut down the opposing running game not just with a strong arm but with impeccable footwork and technique that slammed shut the window of opportunity for base runners. That season he won the first of a record 10 consecutive Gold Glove awards at catcher, quickly establishing himself as the greatest defensive catcher of all time.

The young man from Binger, Oklahoma, was just getting started with that great rookie season. He improved his home run and RBI totals in each of the next two seasons, and in 1970 he put up one of the best offensive performances by a catcher in history, walloping 45 home runs and driving in a then franchise record of 148 RBIs. A fantastic athlete, Bench played five other positions besides catcher that year, including two starts in center field. He easily walked away with the first of his two MVP Awards as the Reds galloped to the NL pennant for the first time since 1961.

Bench was not only a great player at and behind the plate, but he was an innovator, as well. He is the first big-league catcher to use the one-hand reach-and-grab style behind the plate, a change that helps catchers more easily handle balls in the dirt. He's also credited

Pittsburgh Pirates left fielder Willie Stargell is tagged out by Reds catcher Johnny Bench as he tries to score from second base on a hit by Manny Sanguillen in the sixth inning during a game in Pittsburgh on August 15, 1973. The throw came from Reds center fielder Cesar Geronimo. (AP Photo/ Harry Cabluck)

as the first catcher to use a helmet instead of a cap while catching. And even veteran pitchers like Jim Maloney felt that Bench was one of the best at calling a game from the day he arrived. "Every time I'd think, *Gee, I hope he'll call a curve,*" Maloney remembers, "boom, he'd drop down two fingers for the curve."

Manager Sparky Anderson trusted Bench so much that he'd often let Bench decide when a pitcher was through. "If I'd glance over at Sparky in a certain way," Bench said, "he'd know it was time to get somebody up in the bullpen. We'd go to the mound, and he'd look at me, and I'd tell him whether the guy was okay or not."

The man known as "Little General" would go on to have a 17-year career with the Reds, and not coincidentally, all of it spanned the golden era of Reds baseball. His success as a member of the Big Red Machine turned Bench into a national celebrity. Whether it was a glamorous wedding to a model or a regular gig hosting the *Baseball Bunch* on Saturday mornings, Bench has always been comfortable in the spotlight. Even today he is sought after for speaking engagements and public events.

In 1989, Bench was elected to the Baseball Hall of Fame in his first season on the ballot. A decade later, he was voted by the fans to be the catcher on the All-Century Team, joining Big Red Machine teammate Pete Rose. He's had every possible honor heaped upon him by the Reds organization. His No. 5 jersey was retired in 1984, a year after he retired. In 1986, he was inducted into the Reds Hall of Fame. Twenty-five years later, on the 28th anniversary of the last time he played catcher for the Reds, a statue of Bench throwing out a runner was unveiled outside of the Reds Hall of Fame and Museum. That same night, the city of Cincinnati renamed a portion of Broadway Street immediately outside Great American Ball Park to Johnny Bench Way. All Bench could say in response is, "It just doesn't get any better than that."

The same could be said about the greatest catcher who ever played the game.

6 The 1869 Cincinnati Red Stockings

The story of the first professional baseball team in 1869 actually starts in 1866 when a group of lawyers formed a squad known as the "Resolutes" that would later become the Cincinnati Base Ball Club. This team was not made up of paid players, at least not above the table, but it was this organization that would eventually become the Cincinnati Red Stockings, baseball's first club of salaried players.

The Red Stockings were managed—or captained as it was called in that day—by Harry Wright, who was also the team's center fielder and "change pitcher," what we now call a relief pitcher. Wright had been a member of the Cincinnati Base Ball Club from its inception, the only member of the 1869 squad that can make that claim. Having Wright was a fortuitous break for the Red Stockings since it enabled the team to also bring in his brother, George Wright, prior to the 1869 season. George was a heavy hitter and an excellent defensive shortstop, and he was the team's best all-around player during the 1869 season.

One would think that the first team made up of salaried players would be an All Star team of sorts, but that wasn't the case with this squad. In fact, prior to the 1869 season, the Red Stockings had lost one of their best players, John Hatfield, who went to play in New York. Several other players refused to give up their amateur status, leaving the squad with a new lineup in 1869. Charley Sweasy and Andy Leonard were added from the rival Cincinnati Buckeyes, and an 18-year-old named Cal McVey was signed from the Indianapolis Actives. The team's best pitcher was Asa Brainard, a 5'8" 150-pound right-hander from Albany, New York, who had been with the team since early 1868. The Cincinnati nine were paid anywhere between $800 and $2,000 for their services with Harry and George Wright as the top paid players.

On May 4, 1869, the club played its first official match, defeating the Great Westerns of Cincinnati 45–9. The game in that era was a high-scoring affair with pitchers throwing underhand from 45' away. Parks were spacious, and the lack of fielding gloves led to a lot of hits and errors. It was not uncommon for hitters to swat multiple inside-the-park home runs in a game.

Teams were not organized into leagues yet, so clubs often scheduled whoever they could find to play, leading to many lopsided affairs. A few weeks after their first match, the Red Stockings departed on a month-long tour of the East Coast to play many of the best teams in the country. The Cincinnati club saw large crowds and exciting matches as they faced teams like the New York Mutuals, the Washington Nationals, and the Philadelphia Athletics. The club also had the honor of meeting President Ulysses S. Grant, an Ohio native, at the White House, making them the first championship team to be received by a president. The squad returned home on July 1 to a large parade of fans celebrating the completion of a perfect 20–0 road trip.

The team continued to dominate opponents for the remainder of the summer, including a 103–8 drubbing of one-time rivals, the Cincinnati Buckeyes. In mid-September, the team traveled to California for a tour of games and was met with much fanfare upon its arrival. There were not many first-class teams on the tour, and the Red Stockings won every match handily. The team returned home to Cincinnati with a perfect record intact, a tribute to the success of its manager, Harry Wright, who was able to get a lot out of his young team. The team finished the year with an undefeated record in 57 games.

The same nine players were brought back in 1870, but financial issues troubled the team throughout the year. In June, the squad's 81-game win streak was broken with a defeat at the hands

A Nineteenth-Century Timeline

Inside Great American Ball Park is a sign that reads, "Cincinnati Reds Est. 1869." This is only partly true. Yes, Cincinnati had the first professional baseball team, but in an era where leagues were popping up and dissolving every year, the line from the Reds back to that 1869 squad isn't a straight one.

1866—A baseball club called the Resolutes is formed by a group of lawyers in Cincinnati. During that summer, the name is changed to the Cincinnati Base Ball Club. The club was one of three to form in Cincinnati that year. The other two were the Buckeyes and the Live Oaks.

1868—Fans start calling the club the Red Stockings because of the long red socks they wore beneath their white knicker pants.

1869—With Harry Wright at the helm, the Red Stockings form the first all-salaried club and roll to a 57–0 season.

1871—The Cincinnati Base Ball Club hires no professional players for the season and returns to amateur status. Wright takes several of the players to Boston and forms the Boston Red Stockings, who eventually became today's Atlanta Braves.

1875—The club hires nine professional players once again but does not join a league, choosing only to play amateur teams and exhibition matches.

1876—The Cincinnati Base Ball Club, now owned by meat packer Josiah Keck, joins the National League in its inaugural season.

1877—Suffering through financial trouble, the Reds disband midway through the season. They reform under new ownership and resume the season three weeks later.

1880—The Reds are kicked out of the National League at the end of the season for their refusal to abide by new rules that banned the sale of alcoholic beverages and the renting of parks for use on Sundays. Financially strapped, the Reds needed both to remain solvent.

1882—The Reds join the American Association, winning the league championship easily.

1890—The Reds are re-admitted to the National League, where they have remained ever since.

Source: *Redleg Journal*

of the Brooklyn Atlantics. The team would lose six games during the year plus one tie. While a 67–6–1 record is impressive, it was considered a bit of a disappointment in Cincinnati. Interest in the professional squad waned, and by the end of the year the Cincinnati Base Ball Club decided that it would no longer field a team of salaried players.

The original nine dispersed among the Boston Red Stockings and the Washington Olympics, two teams in the newly formed professional league. The two squads played an exhibition match in Cincinnati in July 1871, with the former members of the Cincinnati Red Stockings reforming as a squad one last time.

It would be another four years before the Cincinnati Base Ball Club would assemble a professional nine again, but that team in 1869 was the ultimate precursor to our national pastime, establishing legitimate professional baseball as an entertainment option for the American people.

7 Sparky Anderson

When George Lee "Sparky" Anderson was hired by the Reds after the 1969 season, all the local paper could think to say was "Sparky Who?" The 35-year-old, prematurely gray, failed second baseman had never managed above Triple A before general manager Bob Howsam handed him the keys to the burgeoning Big Red Machine. At the time, it looked like a foolish decision. A decade later, it would have seemed foolish not to have hired Sparky.

As a player, Anderson was a light hitter with a short temper. That short temper is what earned him the nickname "Sparky," as he explained in his biography, *Sparky*. "There was an old radio announcer whose name I don't remember. 'The sparks are flying tonight,' he'd say after I charged another umpire. Then I'd do it the next night—and the next. Finally he got to saying, 'And here comes Sparky racing toward the umpire again.'"

Anderson begrudgingly took on the nickname at first, but he soon learned to accept it as if it were his given name. By the time the Reds hired him, he had his temper much more under control, though he could be counted on for an outburst from time to time. Mainly he reserved it for moments when players needed a wake-up call or an umpire needed a reminder that he was in the dugout.

Sparky's best skill as a manager was his understanding of people. The Big Red Machine was a team full of big egos and large personalities, but Anderson deftly balanced the needs of the individuals with the needs of the team. It was no easy task.

"Sparky makes you feel like a professional," catcher Johnny Bench explained. "He treats you like a man, a professional. He asks things of you, sure, but not things you aren't capable of. With him, rookies and veterans are veterans."

His craftiest maneuver came during the 1975 season. With the team struggling and Sparky feeling the pressure to win a championship more than anybody, the manager knew that something needed to be done to generate more offense. He had an idea of what to do, but he needed the buy-in from his superstar left fielder.

Anderson knew that if he could get George Foster into the lineup more regularly, the middle of the Reds lineup would become even more formidable, but he already had Pete Rose playing in left field. So he went to Rose and humbly asked the All-Star to give third base a try. Rose had played third nearly a decade earlier, but it wasn't a good experience, and he blamed his then manager, Don Heffner, for making it worse. Sparky was different. While Heffner forced the move on Pete, Anderson made it Rose's decision. And

Rose, who regarded Anderson as highly as anyone short of his father, obliged by making the move. From that point forward, the Reds were an unstoppable machine.

"Sparky was, by far, the best manager I ever played for," Rose said. "He understood people better than anyone I ever met. His players loved him, he loved his players, and he loved the game of baseball. There isn't another person in baseball like Sparky Anderson."

Anderson wasn't just a master psychologist, he was an intelligent game tactician, and he revolutionized the role of the relief pitcher during the 1970s. He rightly earned the nickname "Captain Hook" for his tendency to pull a starting pitcher at the first sign of trouble. By the end of the 1975 season, only one National League team had fewer complete games in history than the Reds' 22 that season. No team had ever gone 45 straight games without a complete game like the Reds did that year. Sparky helped usher in a new era of reliever specialization that has become the norm in today's game.

The Reds won two world championships under Anderson, who finished first or second in eight of the nine seasons he managed in the Queen City. He was let go by the organization after a second straight second-place finish in 1978, but the decision came not from disappointment in Sparky. Rather, it stemmed from his loyalty to his coaching staff as general manager Dick Wagner had asked Anderson to fire three of his coaches, which Sparky refused to do. Wagner felt he had no other choice but to fire Sparky as well, thereby parting ways with the winningest manager in franchise history.

Anderson would win another title with the 1984 Detroit Tigers, an organization with which he would spend 17 seasons. However, when the time came for his induction into Cooperstown in 2000, there was only one real choice for which hat Sparky, would wear. Anderson knew that he had to go in with a Reds cap as a tribute to

Bob Howsam. As he said, "Without Bob Howsam, I don't ever get to Detroit."

It is that level of humility that defined the life of Sparky Anderson, who passed away in November 2010. He was not only a great manager; he was a great human being beloved by all who knew him. There was great sadness in the city when he was fired in 1978 and even more when he passed away, but ultimately his legacy is one of the joy that he brought out in others through his great passion for baseball.

8 Marty Brennaman

The first game that Franchester Martin Brennaman ever called for the Cincinnati Reds was historic—but not because Marty was behind the mic. On that Opening Day in 1974, Hank Aaron tied Babe Ruth's record with his 714th career home run. It was a fortuitous start for Brennaman, who replaced Al Michaels in the Reds booth and had the great fortune of calling games for the franchise's greatest team right from the get-go.

For 31 seasons, Brennaman worked side-by-side in the booth with Reds Hall of Famer Joe Nuxhall. The two men worked fabulously together, mixing a down-to-earth style with a light-hearted atmosphere. "It works in Cincinnati," Brennaman said of the duo's schtick in 2000. "It might not work somewhere else, but we're able to laugh at ourselves and talk about our golf game and my tomatoes and everything else under the blasted sun."

Marty and Joe, as they were known around Reds Country, were beloved among fans in part because Brennaman never pulled any punches about the team. When things were going bad, he was the first to be critical. It's a unique position that he holds among sports broadcasters. "I've been lucky because I don't think there's an announcer in baseball that has the freedom to say what he wants to say like I do," he said.

That doesn't mean that Brennaman has avoided controversy over the years. In 1988, he and Nuxhall were pulled into the National League president's office for their perceived role in inciting a riot when manager Pete Rose was ejected for bumping umpire Dave Pallone. He's also been called out and criticized by players, their wives, and even the team's owners during his tenure with the team. He has weathered all of the criticism, however, and in 2013 he will begin his 40th season with the organization.

During those 40 seasons, he's been a part of many great moments for the franchise. He's made the call for three World Series and seven postseasons. He's been on the mic for some great personal milestones like Pete Rose's 4,192nd hit and Ken Griffey Jr.'s 500th and 600th career home runs. He said his favorite calls are the ones that catch him off guard, like his call of Jay Bruce's division-clinching, walk-off home run in 2010. That call, like so many others before it, was handled with near perfection, and Brennaman ended the victory with his trademark, "This one belongs to the Reds."

For all of the great calls that Brennaman has made through the years, the one event that may demonstrate more than any other what he means to the fans happened outside of the broadcast booth. On the team plane during the 2012 season, Brennaman made an off-the-cuff bet with bench coach Chris Speier that if the Reds won 10 straight games that season, he would shave his head. Sure enough, the Reds obliged with a 10-game winning streak shortly thereafter. Always a man of his word, Brennaman did not back out, despite acknowledging that, "There is no man on earth who has had a more passionate love affair with his hair than I have."

Brennaman did not stop at just shaving his head, however, as he used the moment for a bigger cause. He told fans that if they could raise more than $20,000 for the Reds Community Fund in a week, he would have his head shaved on the field for all to see. Fans came through in a big way, raising $50,000 (a number that was later doubled by actor Charlie Sheen) and Brennaman went through with the ceremonial shaving on the field in front of a packed house at Great American Ball Park (GABP). He showed his humanity during the event as he donned a shirt with the words, "I'm Still Me," on it, and he became choked up talking about the children fighting cancer that would be helped by donations because of this event. It was a different side to a man that happy-go-lucky Sean Casey described as "cantankerous."

In 2000, Brennaman was given the Ford C. Frick Award by the Baseball Hall of Fame, putting him on stage with both Sparky Anderson and Tony Perez during their induction ceremony. Five years later, Brennaman was inducted into the National Sportscasters Hall of Fame and the National Radio Hall of Fame. For many in Cincinnati, it's hard to imagine what baseball would be like without Marty behind the mic. He has become synonymous with Reds baseball throughout the country.

As Brennaman would say, "Ain't that somethin'?"

4,192

When manager Pete Rose decided at the start of the 1985 season that player Pete Rose was going to be the Reds' starting first baseman, he knew he had a pretty good shot to break one of the most storied records in sports history. He started the 1985 season needing just 95 base hits to pass Ty Cobb for the all-time hits record. Rose didn't feel any added pressure during the year because he knew it was only a matter of time before the record would fall. Even at 44 years old, Rose knew he could stumble out of bed and get 95 hits in a full season.

Fifty-four games into the season, he was already halfway to his goal. To Reds fans, it looked like the record might tumble before the end of July, but a cold streak in July left fans wondering if Rose was going to be able to get the record before the season ended. Rose always remained confident. August brought a familiar hit streak, and by the end of the month he was eight hits shy of the record.

Rose had been a switch-hitter his entire career, but by 1985, he knew that he didn't have the stamina to play everyday. So he started strictly versus right-handed pitchers that year, which still got him 110 starts but also allowed him to rest and focus on managing the team as it tried to win its first NL West title in six years. The platoon with Tony Perez became significant on September 8 as Rose sat three hits shy of breaking the record. On that day, the Chicago Cubs were supposed to start left-hander Steve Trout, meaning Perez would be in the lineup. Rose had already sent his family back to Cincinnati where the Reds were due to start a 10-game homestand the following day—since he wouldn't be playing, there was little chance the record would be broken in Chicago. However, a bike accident by Trout meant that rookie right-hander Reggie Patterson would be on the mound, and suddenly Rose was thrust into the lineup.

A first-inning single put Rose one hit short of Cobb. A ground-out in the third was followed by a single in the fifth, tying Cobb and bringing a standing ovation from the Wrigley faithful. Rose was touched by the gesture and tipped his cap to the crowd. In Cincinnati, owner Marge Schott was frantically trying to reach someone in the Reds clubhouse to try to convince Rose to pull himself from the game and break the record at home. Schott felt that Rose owed it to Cincinnati fans. Rose, as always, was only focused on winning the game. Pete stayed in, grounding out in the

Pete Rose slams his 4,192nd hit on September 11, 1985, in Cincinnati to break Ty Cobb's all-time hits record. (AP Photo/Mark Duncan)

seventh and then striking out in the ninth after a two-hour rain delay. The game would eventually be called because of darkness with a 5–5 tie, meaning all records were official. Rose had tied Ty, and now he was going back to Cincinnati to pass him.

It's funny to think about now given the dark times that lay ahead for Rose just four years later, but the chase for the hit record was actually a bright distraction during a dark time for baseball. While Rose was inching closer to history, players were being called to the witness stand to testify about a cocaine scandal that was threatening to tear apart the sport. As if trying to make history wasn't enough pressure, Rose was tasked with reminding fans how great the sport really is. If there was anyone who was up to the challenge, it was Rose.

With the lefty on the opposing mound on September 9, Pete the manager held Pete the player out of the lineup at the start of the homestand. The following night, Rose took the collar against LaMarr Hoyt and had one at-bat against reliever Lance McCullers as the San Diego Padres toppled the Reds 3–2. It would be Eric Show on the mound for the Padres on Wednesday, September 11, and there was a feeling in the air for many that this would finally be the night. Rose penciled himself in the No. 2 spot in the order and came to the plate to face Show with one out in the bottom of the first. On a 2–1 pitch, Rose slapped a blooper into shallow left field as radio announcer Joe Nuxhall screamed, "Get down! Get down!" The ball bounced in front of the left fielder, and Rose rounded first base with all 47,237 fans in attendance standing on their feet and screaming at the top of their lungs.

Rose said he never felt so lonely on a ballfield as he did in that moment, standing on first base, and when he looked up in the sky and saw his father and Ty Cobb staring down at him, his emotions overcame him and the tears started flowing. His teammates gathered around as he hugged his son, Pete Rose II, and wept. For a hardscrabble player like Rose, it was a rare showing of a softer side that touched many in attendance. For people in Cincinnati, it will always be a, "Remember where you were when…" moment.

Rose played part of the 1986 season with the Reds before hanging up his cleats to focus on managing full-time. He finished his career with 4,256 hits in 24 big-league seasons. When he retired, he held 18 other major league records, but none will ever top the night when he became baseball's hit king.

10 Frank Robinson

For many fans, especially those who discovered baseball after 1965, Frank Robinson is a Baltimore Oriole, or a former manager, or a baseball executive. His days with the Reds are often left as a footnote or just mentioned in passing when talking about the fact that the Reds made a regrettable trade to deal him away. If this book were simply about ranking the greatest players in Reds history, it would be hard to imagine Robinson not falling in the top four or possibly the top two. He was a fierce competitor and a great hitter. He's still holds the Reds single-season record for runs and doubles, and he's the only Reds player to have 10 consecutive seasons of 20 or more home runs.

Born in Beaumont, Texas, the same hometown of Reds right fielder Jay Bruce, Robinson moved to Oakland and attended the famed McClymonds High School, where he played basketball with Celtics great Bill Russell and baseball with future major leaguers Curt Flood and Vada Pinson. When he signed with the Reds in 1953, he wasn't quite 18 years old yet, but his athleticism was obvious, and he dominated the minor leagues for three seasons. He made his major league debut at the age of 20 and was unstoppable from the start. During that 1956 season, he led the NL in runs scored and set the rookie record for home runs with 38. His presence was a sparkplug for a Reds team that tied the major league record for home runs and won 91 games, the franchise's first winning season in 12 years. Robinson was the unanimous winner of the National League Rookie of the Year award, becoming the first Reds player to win the award.

Chuck Harmon had broken the color barrier for the Reds in 1954, but it was Robinson who became the team's first African

American star. He made the All-Star team in six of the 10 seasons he was with the Reds—no easy task given the depth of outfielders in the National League in the 1950s and '60s. He received MVP votes in all but one year with the Reds, and won the award easily in 1961 as the Reds returned to the World Series for the first time in two decades. Robinson was durable, never missing more than 15 games in a season, and powerful, leading the NL in slugging in three straight seasons from 1960–62. In short, he was everything a Reds fan could ask for in a player.

That's why it was so confusing when general manager Bill DeWitt traded Robinson after a very good 1965 season. The problems between DeWitt and Robinson started early. "I really had no problems at Cincy until DeWitt came along in 1960," Robinson recalled. "The first time I met the man, I was stunned. I had a good relationship with Gabe Paul, walking into his office and chatting. But the first thing DeWitt says to me is, 'I understand you don't hustle,' and he offers me a $1,200 cut."

From that point forward, Robinson, who was a very proud man, felt like he constantly needed to prove himself and often felt underappreciated. When former high school teammate Vada Pinson joined the Reds, he and Robinson became fast friends. Murmurs spread throughout the media of the two players forming a "negro clique," even after the two men took rookie Pete Rose under their wings. Frank took the accusations very personally and felt that may have been part of the reason why he was traded. Famously, DeWitt claimed the deal was because Robinson was an "old 30," but Robinson showed that he was no such thing, winning the AL MVP and Triple Crown in 1966, the year after he was dealt. He appeared in five All-Star Games and won two World Series with the Baltimore Orioles, and he was a productive player even at the age of 38. When he retired, he had the fourth-most home runs in major league history, behind only Hank Aaron, Babe Ruth, and Willie Mays.

It took a long time for Robinson to get over the hurt of how things ended in Cincinnati, if he ever truly got over it. In 1982, he was elected to the Baseball Hall of Fame in his first year on the ballot. Despite playing more than half of his games with the Reds, Robinson chose to wear an Orioles hat on his plaque.

The Reds, for their part, have done their best to honor Robinson for his greatness in a Reds uniform. In 1978, he was inducted into the Reds Hall of Fame. Twenty years later, his No. 20 was retired, never to be worn by a Red again. Then in 2003, when Great American Ball Park opened, Robinson was honored with a statue in Crosley Terrace, standing at home plate and undoubtedly ripping a double down the line or a home run to deep center field. Robinson may not always be recognized as a Red, but that statue will ensure that he's always remembered as one.

11 Joe Morgan

When the Reds traded Lee May for Joe Morgan and others, many fans were confused. Here they were giving up a slugger who had three straight years of at least 34 home runs, and the primary piece they were getting in return was a 5'7" second baseman who had never hit more than 15 home runs and had never batted higher than .285. On the surface it looked like a foolish deal, but the surface hid a lot of things about Joe Morgan.

For one thing, even though he was a two-time All-Star, Morgan was undervalued in large part because of his home stadium, the Astrodome. No park in that era stifled a player's power more than the cavernous dome in Houston. The large gaps and Astroturf did

Joe Morgan watches the ball fly as he hits a home run in the first inning of the All-Star Game at Yankee Stadium in New York on July 19, 1977. Morgan was the NL's first batter. (AP Photo)

allow the second baseman to show off his speed, but otherwise, the park did little to help him demonstrate his skills.

Morgan's other great talent, the ability to get on base, was also mostly hidden by the fact that few fans who followed baseball at the time really understood the value of a good on-base percentage. Of course, one man who did understand it was Reds GM Bob Howsam, which is why he did whatever it took to bring Morgan into the Big Red Machine.

According to Morgan, he needed the Big Red Machine, too. Not only did their success give him the opportunity to shine on the big stage, but he learned how to make himself into a great ballplayer from the other greats in the clubhouse like Pete Rose, Johnny Bench, and Tony Perez. Manager Sparky Anderson purposely put Morgan's locker next to Rose's because, as Morgan recalls, "[Sparky] wanted me to see a guy who knew how to go about his business."

Always a very good player, Morgan blossomed into a superstar with the Reds. He made the All-Star team in all eight seasons he played with the Reds, starting at second base in seven of the eight games. He won five consecutive Gold Gloves at second base starting in 1973, helping to solidify one of the greatest up-the-middle defensive teams in major league history. And of course, there are the back-to-back MVPs in 1975–76. Morgan is the only Reds player to pull off that feat.

An argument can be made that not only was Morgan the best player in the National League from 1972–76, but those five seasons could be the greatest run of five years in Reds history. A statistic from the site Baseball-Reference.com called Wins Above Replacement (WAR), which attempts to evaluate everything a player does on the field and quantify that into the number of wins a player contributes to his team, ranks Morgan's years from 1972–76 as five of the six best seasons in Reds franchise history.

It's not a coincidence that Morgan's top two years with the Reds coincided with arguably the two greatest seasons in franchise history. In 1975, Morgan led the NL in OPS and set the Reds' franchise record in OBP with a league-leading mark of .466. A year later, he once again led the NL in OBP and this time also led the NL in slugging percentage, becoming the first NL second baseman to accomplish that since Rogers Hornsby in 1929. Morgan did it all in 1976, finishing fifth in the NL in home runs; second in RBIs, walks, and stolen bases; and first in sacrifice flies. Amazingly, despite 139 opportunities to do so, Morgan only grounded into two double plays the entire 1976 season.

If there is one knock on Morgan, it's that he never hit particularly well in the postseason. In 50 postseason games, Little Joe batted just .182, but he'll be remembered by most Reds fans for his clutch ninth-inning, go-ahead single in Game 7 of the 1975 World Series that all but clinched the Reds' first title in 35 years. He also hit very well in the 1976 sweep of the Yankees in the World Series, batting .333 with a double, triple, and home run in the four games.

Morgan would stick around with the Reds through the 1979 season before going back to Houston as a free agent. He retired four years after that, and in 1990 he was inducted into the National Baseball Hall of Fame, joining fellow Big Red Machine alum Johnny Bench. His No. 8 was retired by the Reds franchise in 1987, the same year he was inducted into the Reds Hall of Fame. After a long and successful career as a broadcaster with ESPN, Morgan rejoined the Reds as a special advisor to the general manager in 2010, working with baseball operations as well as community outreach.

12 Joey Votto

Growing up in Toronto, Joey Votto thought of baseball more as an escape and a way to stay out of trouble than as his future job. Like so many Canadian athletes, he tried hockey first, but it didn't work out. Baseball stepped in as a way for Votto to focus his energy. And focus he did.

"I remember I said to Joey, 'Swing the bat 500 times a day. And when you get through doing that, swing it another 500,'" Votto's high school coach Bob Smyth said. "I think he took it [literally].... He worked and worked and worked."

That work paid off when Votto was drafted by the Reds in the second round of the 2002 draft, but there was still more work to do. Coming from Canada, he did not have the benefit of being a highly touted prospect. He progressed station-to-station through the minor leagues, spending a full season at each level from Class A through Triple A. As he moved up, his bat started to get some attention, but the scouting publication *Baseball America* never ranked Votto higher than No. 44 on its top 100 prospect list (that same season, 2008, Jay Bruce was the No. 1 overall prospect in baseball).

It turns out that lack of attention suited Votto's personality just fine. He made his debut in 2007 and the following season was installed as the starting first baseman, finishing second in the NL Rookie of the Year Award voting after an impressive season where he batted .297/.368/.506 with 32 doubles and 24 home runs. The season was not a joyous one for Votto, however, as his father, Joe, died suddenly of a heart attack at the age of 52.

His father's death deeply affected the highly introspective Votto, and 2009 was a turbulent year for the Reds' first baseman.

First baseman Joey Votto fields a ground ball against the St. Louis Cardinals during a game on Thursday, June 12, 2008, in Cincinnati.
(AP Photo/Al Behrman)

Struggling with depression and anxiety over his father's passing, Votto missed three weeks during June as he tried to sort out his life. When he went on the disabled list, he was having a spectacular start to the season, ranking second with a .357 batting average, first in on-base percentage (.464), and third in slugging (.627). Many fans could not understand how a player could perform at such a high level with so much anxiety in his life, but as he would demonstrate, Votto is no ordinary player.

The 2010 season was cathartic for the 26-year-old as he led the league in on-base and slugging percentages and helped the Reds to the postseason for the first time in 15 years. He was rewarded for his efforts with the National League MVP Award. The postseason and the MVP were validation of all of his hard work, and Votto was very emotional about it. "Not to be dramatic or anything," he told reporters, "but after I was told [of the MVP win], I couldn't help but cry. Because I knew how much something like this meant to me and would have meant to my father."

With the title of MVP, Votto was on every team's radar the following season. He still posted an impressive .309/.416/.531 line, once again leading the league in on-base percentage. The Reds rewarded their superstar with the largest contract in team history—a deal that put Votto under contract for 12 more years and would pay him more than $250 million during that span. For Votto, the money was nice, but it was more about being where he worked to be. "The bottom line is I like it here," he said after the contract was announced. "I like the momentum that we're building with the fans. That was big for me."

With the pressure of the new deal behind him, Votto mostly answered the bell in 2012. He looked like he was on his way to another MVP before a torn meniscus put him on the DL for two months. He was still impressive when he was on the field and posted an all-time franchise high for on-base percentage. He also came close to winning a batting title and leading the league in doubles despite missing 50 games.

Coach Smyth does not think that Votto is done improving. "I don't think Joey has overachieved," Smyth said. "I think he's at his potential, and I even think he'll do better. He'll figure it out even more.... He's very dedicated at what he does. He's always very inquisitive, always asks questions. That's the sign of somebody who wants to get better. Mostly, it's the hard work."

13 The 1975 World Series

When the Cincinnati Reds faced the Boston Red Sox in the 1975 season, one thing was certain, somebody was going to end a long drought without a World Series championship. The Big Red Machine had been to two Series in the previous five seasons, but they'd come up empty both times and hadn't hoisted the trophy in 35 years. The Red Sox last reached the Series eight years prior, but they had only had one other shot at the title since they last won it in 1918. Both teams swept through their respective League Championship Series, leaving both confident in their ability to win the title.

Game 1 was played in Boston on a chilly, damp afternoon. After six innings worth of a pitchers' duel, the Red Sox plated six runs in the bottom of the seventh and Luis Tiant shut out the Reds for a complete-game victory. Game 2 brought more miserable weather, and the Red Sox led from the outset. They took a 2–1 lead into the ninth inning when Johnny Bench led off the inning with a double. Two outs later the Reds were in danger of going home with a 2–0 deficit, but Dave Concepcion singled to score Bench, tying the game. Ken Griffey followed with a double to score Concepcion, and the Reds snatched a 3–2 victory.

Game 3 was back in Cincinnati, and it was the Reds who blew the lead in the ninth this time. After trailing 5–1 to start the sixth, the Red Sox battled back, tying the game on a ninth-inning, one-out, two-run home run from Dwight Evans. Controversy showed up in the bottom of the 10th inning when a sacrifice bunt by Ed Armbrister led to a collision in front of home plate by Armbrister and Red Sox catcher Carlton Fisk as Fisk tried to make a throw to second base. The Red Sox argued for an interference call, but the umpires refused and the Reds ended up with runners at second and third base. Three batters later, a sacrifice fly by Joe Morgan sealed the 6–5 Reds victory.

The Red Sox took Game 4 with Luis Tiant on the mound once again. The Reds had an early 2–0 lead, but a five-run fourth by the Sox was all that El Tiante would need as the Sox evened the Series with a 5–4 victory. The largest crowd in Cincinnati baseball history was on hand to watch Game 5, and the Reds' bats didn't disappoint. Led by two home runs from Tony Perez, who was 0-for-14 in the Series coming into the game, the Reds easily won the game 6–2 and found themselves one victory away from their first championship since 1940.

The team would be forced to wait for that victory as a rain storm swept the New England coast. The Series was put on hold for three days, but the Series restart would be worth the wait. Game 6 would go down as one of the greatest games ever played as each team battled back from separate three-run deficits. The Red Sox started off the scoring in the first inning on a three-run home run by Fred Lynn. The Reds were shut down by Tiant again until the fifth inning when a triple by Griffey drove in two runs and a Bench single scored Griffey to tie the game. George Foster gave the Reds a two-run lead with a double in the seventh, and Cesar Geronimo extended that lead with an eighth-inning home run, leaving the Reds six outs away from the championship.

A former Red came back to haunt them in the eighth inning when Bernie Carbo, the first ever draft pick by the Reds in the 1965 amateur draft, blasted a two-out, three-run home run to deep center field—his second dinger of the Series. The game was tied, and the Red Sox were revitalized. The Reds went quietly in the ninth while the Sox loaded the bases with no outs to start their half of the inning. That's when Foster caught a fly ball off the bat of Fred Lynn and fired a laser into home plate, gunning down Denny Doyle before he could score the winning run. The Red Sox rally fizzled, and the game went into extra innings.

The Reds put runners on base in each of the three extra innings, but were not able to score. Their 11th inning ended on a dramatic leaping catch by Evans to take away an extra-base hit by Morgan, doubling up Griffey at first base. An inning-and-a-half later, Fisk led off the bottom of the 12th with one of the most memorable home runs in baseball history, waving the ball fair as he hopped down the first-base line and tying the Series at 3–3.

The Red Sox jumped out to an early 3–0 lead in Game 7, scoring three runs—two on bases-loaded walks—in the third inning. And once again, the Reds battled back. A two-run home run by Perez on a Bill Lee Eephus pitch in the sixth cut the deficit to one run. An inning later, Griffey scored on a single by Rose to tie it. Griffey walked again to lead off the ninth, and after advancing on a sacrifice, he scored on a single to shallow center field by Morgan, giving the Reds their first lead of the game. Will McEnaney closed it out in the ninth, and the Reds won their third World Series title in franchise history.

In all, the Series saw five one-run games, five come-from-behind victories, and another match where the Red Sox erased a four-run deficit only to lose in extra innings. The winning run was scored in a team's final at-bat four times. Many people consider this Series to be the most exciting ever played. It's hard to imagine one that is better.

14 Tom Browning Has Pitched a Perfect Game!

September 16, 1988, was a rainy night in the Queen City. The 7:35 PM start time for the game that night at Riverfront Stadium blew by without the tarp moving an inch off the field. It was a Friday night, so many of the 16,591 ticket holders tried to hang around to watch the tilt between the third-place Reds and the first-place Dodgers, but by the time the rain delay entered its third hour, only a sparse crowd remained. Can you blame them? It's not like they knew they were going to miss out on history.

And did they ever miss out on some history. The game finally kicked off at 10:02 PM after a two-hour 27-minute delay. On the mound for the Reds that night was left-hander Tom Browning, who earlier in June had come within two outs of throwing the team's first no-hitter since Tom Seaver did it a decade earlier. He faced Tim Belcher, the pitcher who had homered off Browning just five days prior in the Dodgers' 5–3 win in Los Angeles.

Browning, who was always an incredibly fast worker, got going on this night like he was still trying to make his dinner reservations. He quickly dispatched the first 18 Dodger batters in a breezy 68 pitches. The only close play in the bunch was a shot to third base by Mike Marshall to lead off the fifth inning that Chris Sabo quickly gathered in and threw across to first base, beating Marshall by a half-step.

To his credit, Belcher nearly matched Browning's dominance. His only blemish in the first five innings was a walk on a 3–2 pitch

Pitcher Tom Browning tips his hat to the crowd at Riverfront Stadium in Cincinnati, Ohio, on September 16, 1988, after he threw a perfect game against the Los Angeles Dodgers. Cincinnati won 1–0. (AP Photo/Mark Lyons)

to Eric Davis to lead off the second inning. The game's first hit didn't come until there were two outs in the bottom of the sixth. Barry Larkin doubled down the right-field line to break up the no-hitter, and Sabo followed with a single to drive in what would end up being the game's only run.

Now that he had the lead, Browning set forth to finish off the Dodgers.

"His concentration was intense the entire time," pitching coach Scott Breeden said. "He had the type of control that he could put the ball where he wanted. As a result, he didn't make any mistake pitches."

The memories of the lost no-hitter in early June, as well as teammate Ron Robinson's near perfect game in May that was lost with two outs in the ninth, were nowhere near Browning's mind. He simply kept reminding himself to keep his composure and keep moving the ball in and out.

Just 24 more pitches to get through the seventh and eighth innings. Not a single Dodgers batter would see a three-ball count on the night. Only one of them saw more than five pitches in any at-bat. The lefty was in full control.

Catcher Rick Dempsey led off the ninth inning with a lazy fly ball to right field. Swinging at the first pitch, Steve Sax grounded out to Larkin at shortstop. Tracy Woodson then pinch hit for Belcher and stood as the man blocking Browning's date with history. With those who were left in the crowd standing and screaming at the top of their lungs, Woodson swung and missed at a high fastball on a 2–2 count. Browning had just enough time to pump his fist a couple of times before being mobbed by his teammates in a pile just off the mound.

It was the first perfect game in the National League since Sandy Koufax did the deed versus the Cubs in 1965. It took all of one-hour 51-minutes for Browning to finish off the Dodgers. That's 36 minutes shorter than the rain delay that preceded the game.

Browning will tell you that those two hours changed his life probably more than any other two hours he's had. Since that day, he is introduced as "Mr. Perfect" just about everywhere he goes, and hardly a day goes by when he isn't asked about that night.

As Sabo summed it up afterward, "We're all little boys at heart. It's something dreams are made of. He got a dream tonight."

Barry Larkin

Every player who reaches the big leagues is an athlete in one form or another, but it is the rare player who is truly gifted in all facets of the game. Barry Larkin was one of those, a true five-tool star who could have just as easily ended up on an NFL field as he did in a major league ballpark. He was recruited to the University of Michigan to play football, but when head coach Bo Schembechler redshirted Larkin as a freshman, he focused solely on baseball and never looked back. Three years later he was a first-round draft pick by his hometown Cincinnati Reds, and 27 years after that he was inducted into the Baseball Hall of Fame in Cooperstown.

Larkin, who was born in a Cincinnati suburb and attended Moeller High School, was coached by his father, who drove him to achieve greatness. "If we were going to do something, we were going to do it right," Larkin said. "Growing up, [my father] challenged me. That was so instrumental."

By the time he fully committed to baseball in college, he had every intention of playing in the majors. "I've expected all along that I was going to get to the big leagues," Larkin said. "I've got an aggressive attitude, and I want to prove to myself that I can play at this level." He made his major league debut in 1986, just more

Barry Larkin holds his plaque after his induction into the National Baseball Hall of Fame during a ceremony on Sunday, July 22, 2012, in Cooperstown, New York. (AP Photo/Tim Roske)

than 14 months after he was drafted by the Reds. A year later he made the team out of spring training and ripped the starting short-stop position away from Kurt Stillwell, another first-round pick taken two years before Larkin. He would hold on to that shortstop position for 18 years, playing more games there for the Reds than anyone but David Concepcion.

Concepcion played a big role in acclimating Larkin to the big leagues. Teammates for three seasons, Larkin spent those years picking the brain of his boyhood idol, the last remaining member of the Big Red Machine. It wouldn't be long before Larkin would surpass his idol, though. He made his first All-Star Game in 1988, backing up Ozzie Smith. Larkin was selected to 12 All-Star Games in all and started in five of those contests. He also won his first Silver Slugger award in 1988, an award that he would take home nine times in his career—more than any other shortstop in history.

In 1990, Larkin was the best player on the world champion Wire-to-Wire squad. In 1995, he was the best player in the National League, becoming the first shortstop to win an NL MVP since Maury Wills in 1962. As good as Larkin was in 1995—he batted .319/.394/.492 with 15 HR and 51 steals while winning a Gold Glove at shortstop—he was even better in 1996. That season he became the first shortstop in history to hit 30 home runs and steal 30 bases in the same season, and he did it while once again playing Gold Glove defense.

Larkin's impact on the team came from more than just the numbers that he put up. A natural leader, prior to the 1997 season he was named the fourth captain in team history, following in the footsteps of Billy Myers, Pete Rose, and David Concepcion. Manager Davey Johnson appreciated Larkin's versatility, calling the shortstop his best leadoff hitter, best two-hole hitter, and his best three-hole hitter. And history showed that when Larkin was in the lineup, his team was successful. During his tenure, the Reds were

1,075–982 (.523) when Larkin started, and 377–452 (.455) when he didn't. That last number is the one downside of his memorable career. In his 19-year career, he only played 140 games seven times, which is the same number of times that he played in less than 110. Larkin's health frequently sabotaged a brilliant season, leaving the Reds scrambling to find a reasonable facsimile of Larkin's performance to fill the void.

Nevertheless, when all was said and done, Larkin was recognized for his outstanding achievement more than his missed time. Bill James, the father of Sabermetrics, rated Larkin as one of the 10 most complete players in all of baseball history. It took three years on the ballot, but the Baseball Writers Association of America concurred about Larkin's greatness and voted him into the Baseball Hall of Fame in 2012. He is also a member of the Reds Hall of Fame (2008), University of Michigan Hall of Honor, and the Moeller High School Hall of Fame. In 2012, Larkin's No. 11 was retired by the Reds and was only the 10th number retired in team history. Truly a great honor for a hometown kid who was always just trying to be the best player he could be.

16 Reds Trade for Speed and Get So Much More

A year removed from the World Series loss of 1970, the Big Red Machine was at a crossroads after the 1971 season. The team had just completed its first full year in a sparkling new ballpark with a fourth-place finish and a 79–83 record, only the second losing season for the franchise in a decade. General manager Bob Howsam knew something had to be done. And he had a plan on how he was going to do it.

Howsam prided himself on knowing opposing franchises better than they knew themselves. When he set his sights on a player, he knew exactly what it would take to get him. And in 1971 the player he locked in on was Joe Morgan from the Houston Astros.

The Reds GM knew the Astros needed a first baseman, so he offered up his big bopper, Lee May, who had hit 39 home runs for the Redlegs in 1971. Howsam hated to give up such a valuable player, but he knew, "You can't expect to trade a bucket of ashes for a bucket of coal." He also knew that although May was a great player, Morgan was perfectly equipped with what his ballclub needed—speed.

That's not to say that Morgan didn't come with question marks. There was some concern about Morgan's attitude as there were reports of confrontations between him and manager Harry Walker, but those concerns were put to rest by the tireless efforts of super scout Ray Shore, who learned just about everything there was to learn about Little Joe. He knew Morgan wouldn't be a problem in the clubhouse, and Shore had a hunch that there was much more to the player than what they had seen in Houston.

The deal took some time to materialize after Howsam initially contacted the Astros in September 1971. As discussions carried on, the Astros added third baseman Denis Menke and the Reds countered with second baseman Tommy Helms. By this point, though, the Reds felt they needed more in return as both May and Helms were All-Stars who had more perceived value. That's how Jack Billingham and Cesar Geronimo were added to the deal. To round things out, the Reds added pinch-hitter extraordinaire Jimmy Stewart and the Astros tossed in minor leaguer Ed Armbrister. By the Winter Meetings in November, the eight-player deal was ready to be announced.

Once it was announced, it was immediately panned by the Cincinnati media. *Enquirer* reporter Bob Hertzel wrote, "For Lee May you'd expect a Willie Mays, not just a guy named Joe."

Fans wondered if Howsam had been hypnotized and bamboozled. Even Howsam himself had some second guesses, telling his people that while the trade was good for the Reds' future, "I've just given the pennant this year to Houston."

One person vehemently disagreed with his boss's opinion. After the deal was announced, Sparky Anderson told Howsam, "You have just [secured] the pennant for the Cincinnati Reds."

Ultimately, Anderson was correct as the Reds won the pennant in 1972 and again in 1975 and 1976. While many fans were unhappy with the deal when it was made, it ended up being a highly lopsided deal in the Reds' favor. Lee May continued to be a very good player and Tommy Helms had some decent years for the Astros, but Joe Morgan became one of the greatest second basemen of all time, and Billingham and Geronimo are both enshrined in the Reds Hall of Fame (as are May and Helms). The deal now goes down as the greatest in Reds history and one of the biggest feathers in Howsam's cap.

17 Vander Meer's Back-to-Back No-Hitters

On June 22, 1938, heavyweight champion Joe Louis was scheduled to fight Max Schmeling in the rematch of an epic bout from two years earlier. It was the most anticipated sporting event of the summer, even more so because a week prior to the fight, Louis predicted that he would knock out the German as payback for his only defeat in the ring. It would take a special accomplishment for an athlete to break through the national coverage of that fight.

Twenty-three-year-old Johnny Vander Meer did exactly that.

Johnny Vander Meer on June 21, 1938, at practice. (AP Photo)

A handsome young lad from Midland Park, New Jersey, Vander Meer played the part of a typical American boy getting a baseball tryout for a newsreel short when he was 17 years old. From there the Brooklyn Dodgers signed him and sent him to pitch in Dayton, Ohio. Vander Meer then bounced around from Scranton to Nashville to Durham, passing through the Boston Braves organization for a short time. In 1937 he finally got the call up to the big leagues for the Cincinnati Reds, where he spent part of the season pitching in 19 games with a 3.84 ERA in 84.1 innings.

Vander Meer made the Reds rotation at the start of the 1938 season and put together a stellar string of outings leading up to his 20th big-league start on June 11 versus the Boston Bees (as the Braves were known at the time) in Cincinnati. The lefty fireballer had thrown complete games in four of his previous five outings, and only once had he surrendered more than one run.

The Bees did not put up much of a fight on that June day as Vander Meer faced one batter over the minimum despite three walks. He briskly finished off the Beantown squad in one-hour 48-minutes giving the Reds franchise its sixth no-hitter and its first since 1919.

"I had a pretty good sinker that day," Vander Meer recalled. "I wasn't real quick, didn't have my real good stuff, but it was one of my few days I had control. I think there were only about five fly balls in that game. They were hitting the ball into the ground."

The Reds finished off the series with the Bees the next day with a double-header and then traveled to Brooklyn to play the Dodgers on the 14th. That game was postponed though as the Dodgers train from Grand Rapids, where they were playing an exhibition, had been delayed by five hours. This left the timing of Vander Meer's next start up in the air. As a matter of fact, Vander Meer didn't know he would be pitching on June 15 until about an hour-and-a-half before game time.

Double No-Hitters

While certainly the most famous, Johnny Vander Meer's consecutive no-hitters were not the first pairing of no-hitters in Reds history, nor were they the last.

On May 2, 1917, the Reds took on the Chicago Cubs at Weeghman Park, the name given to Wrigley Field before the friendly confines took on the now-famous moniker. Each team had its ace on the mound, which was apparent by the dearth of hits. Fred Toney of the Reds and Hippo Vaughn of the Cubs walked two batters, and the Reds managed another base runner via an error, but that was it. Through nine innings, neither team could muster even a single base hit, the only time in major league history that a full nine innings of baseball was played without a hit by either team. And since neither team scored, the game headed into extra frames.

In the top of the 10th with one out, Larry Kopf of the Reds singled to right off Vaughn, breaking up the lefty's bid for history. One out later, a fly ball off the bat of Hal Chase should have ended the inning, but center fielder Cy Williams muffed the play and the Reds had runners at first and third. Jim Thorpe followed with a chopper in front of the plate that scored Kopf for the game's only run. Toney then closed out the bottom of the inning without allowing a hit, completing the fourth no-hitter in franchise history and the first spun on the road. Although it was only May 2, it was the third major league no-hitter of the season. Two more were thrown within the next four days. There must have been something in the water in 1917.

The other tandem of no-hitters involving the Reds came 52 years later. On April 30, 1969, right-handed fireballer Jim Maloney struck out 13 Astros en route to his second complete-game no-hitter. Maloney pitched as if throwing a no-hitter was old hat for him, even when his 21-year-old catcher, Johnny Bench, was shaking so much behind the plate that Maloney had a hard time reading the signs. And why shouldn't he be relaxed, the two previous times he no-hit a team for nine innings, his Redlegs failed to push a run across the plate. This time, Maloney was staked to an eight-run lead after four innings and was able to coast into the ninth, comfortable that the victory was in hand.

Of course, that didn't prevent a little drama when the pitcher strained his groin in the bottom of the eighth inning as he scored to extend the Reds' lead to 10–0. He pitched through the pain in the ninth and was able to work around his fifth walk of the game by striking out Doug Rader to close out the historic victory.

The following day, right-hander Don Wilson of the Astros returned the favor to the Reds as he too struck out 13 batters for his second career no-hitter. Wilson despised the Reds and he came out as a man possessed. Less than a year earlier he tied a big-league record with 18 strikeouts in a nine-inning game versus the Reds, but on this day he was even more unhittable. He did walk six and also hit Bench with a pitch, but the Reds couldn't generate much else on offense and dropped the game 4–0. It was the first time the team had been no-hit at Crosley Field in 28 years. More importantly, it was only the second time in history that teams had exchanged no-hitters on consecutive days. The first instance coming more than seven months earlier between the St. Louis Cardinals and San Francisco Giants.

"Of course," Vander Meer explained, "I suspected it. But Mr. McKechnie doesn't tell us until an hour or two before the game."

The excitement leading into Vander Meer's follow-up start was less about his prior no-hitter and more about the first night game ever at Ebbets Field. More than 38,000 fans were on hand to be part of history, though not in the way they expected. Five hundred of those fans were from Vander Meer's hometown of Midland Park, New Jersey, making the trek up to see the local boy pitch after reportedly petitioning his manager, Bill McKechnie, to let him start. Included in the crowd were Johnny's mother and father, who would be seeing their son pitch for the first time as a big leaguer.

Vander Meer's pitching motion was quite involved, including a high leg kick that one newspaper described as "the schoolboy's idea of what a fastball pitcher should look like." Coupling that leg kick with a fastball that rivaled the great Bob Feller's and the dim lights of nascent night baseball, and Vander Meer was a recipe for trouble for the Brooklyn hitters.

The lefty was effectively wild through the first eight innings, striking out seven while walking five. The Dodgers were unable to get a runner to third base in those first eight, and the only close call for a hit came when Buddy Hassett hit a line drive back through the box that Vander Meer knocked down and scurried to get the batter at first base.

The Reds on the other hand hammered out 11 hits and six runs, including a big blast from Vander Meer's former Durham teammate, Frank McCormick.

It was around the fourth inning when Vander Meer started to think that a second no-hitter was possible, but it wasn't until the ninth inning when the pressure started to get to him. He gave all credit to his teammates for getting him through.

"The fielders behind me really made it possible, anyway. I had every possible confidence in them all the way through [that] night. Take that ninth inning now. The bases were loaded and two were out. With the count two strikes and one ball on Leo Durocher, I tightened up. Ernie Lombardi, my catcher, came out and told me to throw a curve. I did but it was outside. Then Ernie told me to give him the fastball down the middle. And when he hit it, I knew right away that Harry Craft would catch it."

Craft did catch it. And the man who became known as the Dutch Master went into the history books. Not only had Vander Meer thrown a second consecutive no-hitter, but he had broken the NL record for most consecutive no-hit innings set by Dazzy Vance in 1925. Vander Meer would extend his record another 3⅓ innings in his next start as he held the Bees hitless until the fourth inning when Debs Garms singled to end his shot at a third straight no-no. To this day, Vander Meer's 21⅔ straight no-hit innings stands as the NL record. Cy Young holds the MLB record at 23 straight innings, some of which came in relief.

Vander Meer pitched 11 up-and-down seasons with the Reds, and when he left the team after the 1949 season, he was the franchise leader in strikeouts with 1,251. He's since been passed on that list, but his record back-to-back no-hitters is unlikely to ever be bettered.

18 The Wire-to-Wire Reds

When a team leads its division from the first day of the season until the last, the common perception is that it dominated for the entire year, but that was not exactly the case with the 1990 Cincinnati Reds. Yes, the Reds started out 9–0, the best start in franchise history. And yes, their 33–12 record gave them a 10-game lead on June 3, but they only went 58–59 after that point for the 12th-best record in baseball over the season's last four months.

During those last four months, the Reds had three separate five-game losing streaks, including one that reached eight games. But building a large lead early gave the team some luxury to stumble. Although the Los Angeles Dodgers and San Francisco Giants played much better than the Reds those last four months, neither team got closer than 3½ games over the remainder of the season.

Despite the sputtering second half, the 1990 regular season was full of some vibrant memories. The Nasty Boys were dominant all year out of the bullpen, cutting the game to a six-inning affair on most nights. One of those Nasty Boys, Norm Charlton, garnered national attention when he barreled through catcher Mike Scioscia of the Dodgers during an ESPN *Sunday Night Baseball* game. Manager Lou Piniella gave the fans a chuckle when, in a fit of rage, he threw first base not once but twice as he emphatically tried to make a point to the umpires.

The team was a balanced squad but not a dominant one. It didn't have a single player finish higher than seventh in MVP voting. Closer Randy Myers was the only pitcher to receive a Cy Young Award vote. When the Reds finally reached the playoffs, they faced two teams that were dominant, both in their divisions and in the awards.

The Pittsburgh Pirates had the top two MVP vote-getters in Barry Bonds, who won the first of seven awards, and Bobby Bonilla, as well as the Cy Young Award winner in Doug Drabek. Many within the Reds considered the Pirates to be their biggest challenge to a title. The two teams battled through a six-game series that saw some dramatic hits and incredible defense. The Reds sealed their series win at home in Game 6 when right fielder Glenn Braggs took a go-ahead home run away from Carmelo Martinez in the ninth inning, preserving a 2–1 Reds win.

In the World Series, the Reds faced the defending world champion Oakland A's. The A's were a powerful squad featuring AL MVP Rickey Henderson and the Bash Brothers, Jose Canseco and Mark McGwire. Their pitching staff was tough with AL Cy Young Award–winner Bob Welch, the intimidating Dave Stewart, and relief ace Dennis Eckersley. The A's came into the series cocky, almost assured that the Series would be a cakewalk. And it was, just not in the way they expected.

The Reds were also confident coming into the Series. They knew their powerful pitching from staff ace Jose Rijo and the Nasty Boys could shut down the vaunted A's offense. And their hitters were not afraid of the A's tough pitching, as evidenced by a first-inning home run in Game 1 by Eric Davis off Stewart. That home run set the tone for the Series as the Reds comfortably swept the A's in four games, twice coming back against the A's supposedly unbeatable pitching staff. Billy Hatcher led the hitting attack for the Reds with nine hits in 12 at-bats, reaching base in his first nine plate appearances, a Series record. Rijo dominated the A's bats, allowing just one earned run in 15.1 innings to take home the series MVP.

The Series did end on a somber note as Davis, the team's spiritual leader, had to be taken to the hospital during Game 4 with a lacerated kidney after trying to make a diving catch in the first inning. Not having Davis at the celebration was bittersweet for many guys on the team, and when owner Marge Schott refused to pay for a private plane to bring Davis home after the Series, many of the players and fans were angered. Eventually, Davis and Schott made up, but the situation did put a bit of a damper on the celebration. It did not ruin the memory of a group of men who played as a team and surprised everybody with the fifth championship in franchise history.

19 Powel Crosley and Larry MacPhail

When Larry MacPhail took over as team president in November 1933, the Reds franchise was in dire financial straits. Owner Sidney Weil was bankrupt, and attendance was down nearly 70 percent compared to the total just seven years prior. MacPhail was a high-energy, enthusiastic promoter who had been involved with the Columbus Red Birds before joining the Reds. The son of a successful banker, MacPhail had drifted from one career to the next before finding a home in baseball. The Central Trust Company that hired MacPhail gave him the reins of the team and also the task of finding a new owner.

MacPhail turned to local businessman Powel Crosley, who he convinced to buy the team in order to protect it from a potential move if an outsider purchased it instead. Crosley made a fortune in automobile supply, but he was also a pioneer in the radio industry. He started one of the first companies to manufacture radios for the home, and in order to supply content for those radios he founded and built WLW into a 500,000-watt behemoth that became known as "the nation's station." Crosley liked the idea of buying the Reds as another avenue to promote some of his more lucrative brands.

The first step in that promotion was renaming Redland Field to the now more familiar Crosley Field. Crosley put a considerable sum of money into renovating the ballpark, including adding two large radios on either side of the scoreboard, each tuned to Crosley's own WLW.

The innovation didn't stop there for Crosley and MacPhail. Some things they tried worked, such as the hiring of Red Barber to do play-by-play even though the 26-year-old had never seen a major league game in person. Barber would become one of the most beloved broadcasters the sport has ever seen, mostly from time spent later on with the Brooklyn Dodgers and New York Yankees.

Some of the men's innovations were not quite as successful, however. It didn't take long to see that having PA announcer Harry Hartman communicate ball and strike calls over the loud-speaker was more of a distraction than anything. Also MacPhail's addition of comely cigarette girls roaming around the stands, much like those seen at nightclubs, didn't last long with the franchise, either.

At times though, Crosley and MacPhail were simply just too far ahead of their time. On June 8, 1934, the Reds became the first team to travel by airplane to their next game as they boarded a flight from Cincinnati to Chicago to take on the Cubs. The event was even broadcast live by Barber on a radio transmitter that Crosley had installed in one of the planes. It was more spectacle than practical at that point, and teams—including the Reds—didn't regularly use air travel until the 1950s.

The one innovation that put MacPhail on the map was night baseball. As an attempt to boost sagging attendance, he petitioned the league to allow teams to host night games in their ballparks, something that was done regularly in minor league parks around the country. The league resisted at first but eventually relented and allowed all teams to have as many as seven night games per year. The Reds were the first team to take advantage of the new opportunity, and Crosley spent around $50,000 to install eight separate light towers around the ballpark. On May 24, 1935, the Reds flipped the switch on the lights, and nighttime baseball has been part of the major leagues ever since.

MacPhail only spent three seasons with the Reds before moving on to the Brooklyn Dodgers and New York Yankees where he continued to innovate, most notably with the introduction of televised baseball with the Dodgers in 1939. He was elected to the National Baseball Hall of Fame in 1978 and his son, Lee MacPhail, joined him there 20 years later. They are the only father and son enshrined in the Hall.

Crosley owned the team until his death in 1961, the longest continuous ownership in team history. He saw the team win two National League pennants and one World Series, but his sudden death at the age of 74 came just months before the start of the golden age of Reds baseball.

20 Visit Great American Ball Park

In the 1960s, the trend in ballparks was to create circular, multi-purpose behemoths that were modern looking but lacked much of the character of old-time parks. By the mid-1990s, that trend had shifted all the way back to parks that brought some of the intimacy of baseball back and reminded fans of yesteryear. In both instances, the Cincinnati Reds found themselves following trends, and more than 30 years after moving into Riverfront Stadium, they moved into brand new Great American Ball Park.

GABP was built in a narrow wedge between Riverfront Stadium (then called Cinergy Field) and neighboring US Bank Arena. The location was identified in 1998, the funding was settled in 1999, and the naming rights were sold to Great American Insurance in 2000, but the first game didn't take place in the park until 2003. When the park did open, its seating capacity was a bit more than 42,000, a drop of about 13,000 from Cinergy Field's capacity. What the stadium lost in capacity it made up for in seating quality every seat in the park is pointed at home plate, improving the view even for the outer edges of the park. As they say, there isn't a bad seat in the place.

The seating was not the only upgrade in the park, as the dining options are now varied from typical ballpark fare to fine dining. If the latter is your desire, choices include Riverfront Club, Fox Sports Ohio Champions Club, or even the Diamond Club, which is open to fans who hold tickets for the Diamond Seats, the 310 seats directly behind home plate on the field level. Looking for pub food? The Machine Room Grille has an air-conditioned or a patio option in left field. In 2011, Mr. Red's

Smokehouse opened in the right-field concourse, serving traditional barbecue fare. Mr. Red's Smokehouse resides in the ever-expanding Fan Zone area of the park. The Fan Zone houses a music stage for pregame concerts as well as a picnic area for those looking to sit and eat. For the kids there is a playground area along with the new Reds Heads clubhouse and Wiffle Ball field. Down on the street level, next to the Rose Garden are the only hardball batting cages for fans in the majors.

If you are looking to keep up on all of the action from around the league while you watch the Reds, the left-field wall keeps everyone apprised of the state of each game. Still not enough? There is a bank of high-definition monitors along the left-field concourse showing most of the action from around the league.

In 2009, the Reds installed a $10 million scoreboard that is full-HD and is 138' x 39' in size. The Riverboat Deck in center field harkens back to Cincinnati's history as a bustling river port. Along that theme, the Power Stacks resemble steam stacks from riverboats and house a misting station where fans can cool off on hot summer nights at the park.

Despite being a relatively new park, the franchise's history is prominent throughout. At the main entrance, fans pass through Crosley Terrace, home of four bronze statues featuring Reds greats Frank Robinson, Ted Kluszewski, Ernie Lombardi, and Joe Nuxhall. Murals inside the park pay tribute to the original 1869 Red Stockings and the Big Red Machine. Pennants hang in the outfield to commemorate Reds world championships, and below the press level are markers for all of the franchise's retired numbers.

Ultimately, fans come to the park to watch the game, and with its great views from everywhere in the park, GABP delivers in that aspect. The short history of the park has delivered some

William "Bucky" Walters on September 29, 1939. (AP Photo)

great memories so far, from Adam Dunn's walk-off grand slam versus the Indians to Jay Bruce's division-clinching home run in 2010. And with a bright future in front of the franchise, the list of historic moments at GABP will continue to grow.

21 Bucky Walters

Heading into the 2012 season, the Cincinnati Reds have never had a Cy Young Award–winning pitcher, but that's mainly because from 1938–44, when the Reds had the best pitcher in the National League, the award didn't exist. During those seven seasons, Bucky Walters had 27 more wins than any other pitcher in the NL, threw nearly 200 more innings than any other NL hurler, and had the third lowest ERA and third most strikeouts in the Senior Circuit. Three times he led the league in wins, innings, and complete games. Twice he led in ERA. Not bad for a guy who had never pitched an inning before 1934.

Born William Henry Walters in Mount Airy, Pennsylvania, in 1909, Bucky was always a fantastic athlete, and he was always a third baseman. His professional career began with the Boston Braves organization, and he finally made it to the majors in 1931. Even though he put up some impressive minor league numbers, he was never able to make his career click in the majors. By 1934 Walters was playing for the Philadelphia Phillies—his third organization—and it looked like his major league dream might be coming to a close.

That's when Phillies manager Jimmy Wilson suggested that the rocket-armed Walters give pitching a try. It wasn't an easy decision for Bucky because he still believed he could be an everyday player, but when Wilson reminded Walters that pitching money tended to be higher than what he'd see as a backup infielder, Walters took the mound. There was a considerable learning curve and in 1936, Walters led the NL in losses with 21, though he also paced the circuit with four shutouts.

By 1938 the Phillies were ready to move on from their little experiment and Reds general manager Warren Giles crafted a deal to acquire the right-hander in the days between Johnny Vander Meer's consecutive no-hitters. Now pitching in front of a substantially better defense and for a team with a much more accomplished offense, Walters blossomed as a pitcher. In 1939, he became the only Reds pitcher to ever win the pitching Triple Crown, leading the NL in wins (27), strikeouts (137), and ERA (2.29). He was also tops in innings pitched (319.0) and complete games (31). He easily walked away with the league's MVP Award and carried the Reds to their first NL pennant in 20 years. Walters took two losses in the World Series, though, as the Yankees swept the Reds in four games.

Walters nearly pulled off the Triple Crown again in 1940 as he led the league in wins (22) and ERA (2.48) but finished fifth in strikeouts (115). He finished third in the NL MVP vote behind teammate Frank McCormick and the Cardinals Johnny Mize as the Reds once again captured the National League pennant. This time Walters was a buzzsaw through the Detroit Tigers, winning two games, including an impressive five-hit shutout where he also mashed a home run in Game 6 with the Reds trailing 3–2 in the series. The Reds clinched the Series in seven games, their first title since 1919.

By this point, Bucky had established himself as the preeminent pitcher in the league. *The Sporting News* named him the Leading All-Around Player after the 1939 season, beating out the likes of Joe DiMaggio and Jimmie Foxx. Seymour Siwoff of Elias Sports Bureau called Walters "the money pitcher of his day." Reds GM Warren Giles told Walters in a letter, "When the time comes that you want to sign a contract and you find this one isn't satisfactory, you tell me what figure you want me to put in and it will be put in." It was clear that his peers regarded him as one of the best of his generation. In 1972, President Richard Nixon created an All-Time

All-Stars Team and named Walters as one of the five NL pitchers for the 1925–45 era. Several years after that, Bill James, the father of Sabermetrics, gave Walters three hypothetical Cy Young Awards for his performances in 1939, 1940, and 1944.

Walters made six All-Star appearances in his career, and he even spent a season-and-a-half as player-manager for the Reds in 1948–49. Despite all of his impressive single-season achievements, he never received much consideration for the Hall of Fame. Perhaps the lack of major milestones—198 career wins—and the fact that he didn't start pitching until he was 25 held him back. Nevertheless, he was inducted with the inaugural class into the Reds Hall of Fame in 1958 where he resides as one of the greatest pitchers in Reds history.

22 1976 Playoff Sweep

After the 1975 World Series expunged the demons that would get the team close to but not quite all the way to the promised land, the following season stood as the coronation of the Big Red Machine as one of the great dynasties of all time. And just so there wasn't any doubt, the Machine dominated the playoffs like no team before or since.

With the confidence of a world championship already under its belt, the 1976 squad cruised through the regular season without much of a threat from any of its Western Division competitors. The Reds took over first place for good in early June, and two months later their lead was 10 games with one-third of the season still remaining. All year long the Reds exerted their hegemony over the entire National League. Well, except for one team.

The Philadelphia Phillies were the only team in baseball to post a winning record against the defending world champs in 1976. The Phillies won seven of the teams' 12 meetings, including 4-of-5 games in one week during June. The Phillies also challenged the Reds for the NL's best record, finishing one game shy despite winning 12 of their last 14. The two teams would become the first 100+ win teams in NL history to meet in the League Championship Series.

You wouldn't know that the Phillies had the Reds number from the National League Championship Series result, though. The Phillies managed to lead in every game in the series, but the Reds never let them get too far ahead. The powerful Big Red Machine's offense scored at least six runs in every game against one of the league's best pitching staffs. And this was without a single hit from the NL MVP, Joe Morgan. The offense was led by Pete Rose (.429/.467/.714), Johnny Bench (.333/.385/.667), and Ken Griffey (.385/.467/.538), as well as two home runs from George Foster, the 1976 NL RBI champ.

The most memorable of those blasts came in the bottom of the ninth in Game 3 with the Reds trailing 6–4. Foster and Bench hit back-to-back home runs to tie the game. The Reds followed those homers with a single and two walks to load the bases and clinched the sweep when Griffey, who had narrowly missed winning a batting title on the last day of the season, singled in the winning run.

In the World Series, the Reds faced the New York Yankees, who were in the postseason for the first time in 12 years, the longest drought for the franchise since before Babe Ruth's first year with the team. This would be the third time that the Reds and Yankees met in the Series, with the Yankees having dominated in both 1939 (4–0 sweep) and 1961 (4–1).

The Big Red Machine respected the history of the game, but they had no concern for the past in this Series. They knew their destiny and were determined to capture it. And there wasn't much the Yankees could do about it, either.

Joe Morgan set the tone with a solo home run in the first inning of Game 1, and the Reds hammered out five runs on 10 hits in a brisk 5–1 victory. Game 2 provided a little more excitement as the Reds let slip a 3–0 lead in the seventh inning, but they took advantage of a Fred Stanley error in the ninth as Tony Perez drove in the winning run with two outs to give the Reds a 2–0 lead.

The Series moved on to Yankee Stadium for Game 3 and the Reds, led by Dan Driessen, who went 3-for-3 with a homer and a double, battered the Yanks with 13 hits and six runs in an easy 6–2 victory. In Game 4, the Yankees finally had their first lead of the Series when Chris Chambliss doubled in Thurman Munson in the first. That lead was short-lived as an RBI single from George Foster and a two-run home run from Bench gave the Reds a 3–1 lead. Bench sealed the sweep with a three-run blast in the ninth, the second time in team history that a player had homered twice in a postseason game.

The Reds are the only team since the introduction of divisional play in 1969 to sweep their way through the postseason with a perfect record. Their back-to-back world championships marked the first time that had been done by a National League team since the New York Giants did the trick in 1921–22, and it hasn't been done since by an NL team.

Another oddity of that 1976 World Series was that with the Great Eight plus Driessen in at designated hitter, the Reds used just nine batters in the entire series, the fewest ever used in a World Series. Since the designated hitter was used in both the NL and AL cities, the Reds never had to use another batter once, a feat that is unlikely to be matched with the current rules that determine DH usage based on the league of the home city—just another one of those facts that makes the Big Red Machine so special.

23 1972 Postseason

The 1972 season started out with a black mark on it as a strike during the first two weeks of April—the first player strike in United States professional sports history—delayed the start of the season and cut six-to-eight games per team out of the baseball schedule. The Reds started slow out of the gate and were five games under .500 before catching fire and winning 26-of-32 and moving into first place within a month. Another hot streak a month after that put the Reds up by seven games in the NL West and they never looked back, winning the division by 10½ games over the Houston Astros and Los Angeles Dodgers.

The National League Championship Series brought a matchup against the only team in baseball that had a better record than the Reds' 95–59 mark. The defending world champion Pittsburgh Pirates was a well-balanced team that finished third in the NL in runs scored and easily led the league in run prevention. Their offense was led by future Hall of Famers Willie Stargell and Roberto Clemente, and the pitching was anchored by 19-game winner Steve Blass, who finished second in Cy Young Award voting in 1972.

The series was a back-and-forth affair with the two heavy-weights trading blows throughout. The teams alternated victories through the first four games with the Pirates taking the odd-numbered matches and the Reds covering the even ones. The Reds held a lead in every game, scoring in the first inning in three of the four games. It was the Pirates who got out early in Game 5, scoring two runs on three straight hits off ace Don Gullett to start the second inning. The Reds cut the lead in half in the third only to watch Dave Cash drive in his second run of the game and move the lead back to 3–1, quieting the anxious crowd at Riverfront Stadium.

The crowd erupted in the fifth when right fielder Cesar Geronimo, who had four total home runs during the regular season, sent one over the Riverfront wall to cut the deficit to 3–2. That's where things stood when the bottom of the ninth rolled around and Pirates ace reliever Dave Giusti toed the rubber. Coming to the plate was the presumptive NL MVP, Johnny Bench, whose mother had just yelled a bit of advice to her son as he stood in the on-deck circle. "Hit a home run," she said. They always say to do what your mama tells you. Bench, an extreme pull-hitter, launched a 1–2 pitch into right field that carried over the wall, throwing the crowd into a frenzy. Those in attendance swear that it was the loudest they had ever heard Riverfront Stadium get before or since.

The Reds' comeback wasn't quite complete, however, and back-to-back singles from Tony Perez, who was pinch run for by George Foster, and Dennis Menke led Pirates manager Bill Virdon to call on right-hander Bob Moose to put out the fire. A deep fly ball to right field off the bat of Geronimo put a charge in the crowd, but it was merely deep enough to move Foster to third base as Clemente, who would tragically die in a plane accident that winter, corralled it in. One out later with Hal McRae at the plate, the Reds clinched the series in a most improbable fashion. Reds radio announcer Al Michaels' call said it all, "The stretch and the 1–1 pitch to McRae. In the dirt—it's a wild pitch! Here comes Foster! The Reds win the pennant! Bob Moose throws a wild pitch, and the Reds have won the National League Pennant!"

The Reds then faced the AL champion Oakland A's in one of the tightest World Series on record. Six of the seven games in the Series were decided by one run, and in only one of the games did either team even have a lead of more than two runs. The A's jumped out to a 3–1 lead in the Series in large part due to Gene Tenace, whose two homers in Game 1 were the difference maker.

He also homered early and scored the winning run in the ninth inning of Game 4.

The Big Red Machine didn't go down without a fight, taking Game 5 behind the bat of Pete Rose, who homered to lead off the game and singled in the eventual winning run in the ninth. A fourth-inning home run from Bench and a five-run seventh gave the Reds an easy victory in Game 6, tying the Series and setting up a Game 7 at Riverfront Stadium the next day. Once again it was Tenace doing damage for the A's, driving in two of the three Oakland runs on his way to being named the Series' MVP. The Reds still had a shot to tie it up in the eighth after a Tony Perez sacrifice fly plated Rose, making it a 3–2 game, but with runners at second and third and two outs, Menke lifted a routine fly ball to left field, snuffing out the rally.

The Reds went quietly in the ninth, handing the Athletics the first of three straight world championships and leaving manager Sparky Anderson and many fans wondering if the supposed Big Red Machine had what it took to get over the top and win a championship.

24 Frank Robinson Trade

"Robinson is not a young 30."

It would be hard to find a six-word phrase that motivated a baseball player to greatness more than those six words spoken by Bill DeWitt Sr. about Frank Robinson five months after the Reds' GM dealt the six-time All-Star and former MVP to the Baltimore Orioles. Robinson put up one of the greatest offensive seasons in history after hearing those words from DeWitt, words that angered one of the proudest men in the game. The right fielder led the American League in 1966 in batting average, on-base percentage, slugging, home runs, RBIs, runs scored, and total bases, becoming the first Triple Crown winner in a decade and the first player to win the MVP in both leagues. And with that season, Robinson made it clear to DeWitt that he may have just made one of the worst deals in franchise history.

The deal came about during the winter meetings in December 1965. The Reds came to the meetings ready to deal for some much-needed pitching, and they were willing to part with the 1961 MVP to do it. The Reds' bullpen had let them down on numerous occasions in 1965, and outside of Jim Maloney, the starting rotation left a lot to be desired. Teams were still surprised that DeWitt was willing to deal his superstar. In fact, many teams wondered if Robinson was damaged goods and stayed out of the conversation.

The Houston Astros were rumored to have offered third baseman Bob Aspromonte and pitcher Dick Farrell. It was also rumored that pitchers Larry Dierker and Claude Raymond and outfielder Jimmy Wynn had been discussed, but conversations did not get very far before the Orioles swooped in.

DeWitt had hoped to get outfielder Curt Blefary from the Orioles in a deal, but Baltimore was not interested in letting go of their 1965 Rookie of the Year winner. Instead, the deal, which was announced on December 9, 1965, settled around Milt Pappas, a 26-year-old right-handed pitcher who already had 110 big-league wins under his belt. Pappas had never won less than 10 games in a full season, and he was coming off a 13–9 season with a 2.60 ERA. Also included in the deal were outfielder Dick Simpson and relief pitcher Jack Baldschun—both players had been acquired by the Orioles in separate deals just days earlier.

Robinson's initial reaction to the trade was even-keeled. He knew that it was all just part of the game. Fan reaction was mixed. "I think it stinks," said one man. "At least one of these guys has to come through for the Reds," said another. "Of course they had to make a move some time. Robby was getting old."

It was the belief that Robinson was getting old that put off the slugger. "It seems I suddenly got old last fall between the end of the season and December 9ᵗʰ," Robinson said that following April. "You can tell DeWitt this for me: I'll play more ball games this year for Baltimore than any of the outfielders he's got over there."

He was almost right. In 1966, the 30-year-old played in 155 games. Only his good friend Vada Pinson played in more games (156) in the Reds' outfield. And that was only because manager Hank Bauer rested Robinson for three of the last nine games to get ready for the World Series.

As for Pappas, he was a fine though unimpressive pitcher for the Reds for 2½ years before he was dealt to Atlanta for Clay Carroll, Tony Cloninger, and Woody Woodward. Simpson was traded in 1968 to the Cardinals for Alex Johnson, who was then traded a year later for Pedro Borbon. And ultimately, the Reds' bullpen was improved by the trade of Robinson. It just took another five years to do it.

25 Black Sox Scandal

Virtually any account that one reads of the 1919 World Series lists the Chicago White Sox as heavy favorites over the Cincinnati Reds. Many would even make the case that the outcome was never in doubt once the pairing was determined, that the White Sox were so far superior to the Reds that the Series hardly needed to be played. That's a nice narrative to establish in light of the fraudulence that was revealed a year later, but it's far from clear that the Reds were hopeless going into the series.

Yes, the White Sox were heavy favorites on the early betting lines, a fact that shifted soon after bookies started getting flooded with money on the team from Cincinnati. By the time the Series started, the money was so far in the Reds favor, both legitimately and duplicitously, that the White Sox were slight underdogs. The expectations tilted in the White Sox's favor mainly because of the state of both franchises for the decades prior. The Sox were world champions just two years before and were one of the better teams in the AL for five years running. The Reds on the other hand had been a second-class team in the National League since rejoining the league in 1890. Along with the St. Louis Cardinals, the Reds were one of two NL teams to not have played in a World Series by 1919.

History has little bearing in a short Series, however, and while the White Sox were a formidable foe, the Reds' squad did not deserve the disrespect of being a considerable underdog. The Reds had thoroughly dominated the National League all season, winning the league by nine games over an impressive New York Giants team that went 87–53. At 96–44, the Reds posted a .686 winning percentage that has only been topped once in the NL since. Their 51–19 home record wasn't bested by another Reds team until 1975, which is still the only squad to top it.

Offensively, the team finished second in the league in runs scored and was anchored by batting champion Edd Roush and third baseman Heinie Groh, who led the NL in OPS. The pitching staff was deep, with every pitcher who appeared in at least 15 games posting an ERA better than the league average. The team's defense was tops in the NL, as well, helping the Reds lead the NL in run prevention.

Knowing what we know now, it's hard to say for sure if the Reds would have beaten the White Sox had the Series been played legitimately, but there is no reason to think that they couldn't have done so. The details of the games are so often told from the perspective of the cheaters, and assumptions are made that the Sox only lost when they wanted to lose and always won when they wanted to win. Lacking clear video evidence and precise detailed accounts, it's impossible to know how much of the Reds' success was due strictly to the White Sox's lack of effort.

The Reds were not immune from the lure of gambling conspiracies during that Series. Leading up to Game 8, the league experimented with a nine-game World Series from 1919–21 Roush got wind of gamblers contacting someone on the Reds to fix the game. After sniffing around, he discovered that pitcher Hod Eller had been approached outside his hotel room, but Eller insisted that he had threatened to punch the man in the nose if he did not leave immediately. Manager Pat Moran trusted his pitcher, and Eller responded by carrying his team to victory in the final game.

Despite all of the gambling controversy, the fact remains that the Reds took home the Series title, winning five of the eight games. It's a shame that their championship lacked the legitimacy that it deserved, leaving players like Roush to fight their whole lives to convince people they still would have won had the Series been played straight. It was the franchise's first title, and while it's essentially a footnote in major league history, it's still a point of pride for the Reds franchise.

Bob Howsam

To most people, building one of the greatest baseball dynasties in history would be more than enough to fill one's résumé, but that was simply a bullet point in the impressive life of Robert Lee Howsam. He was also a Navy test pilot, an assistant to a U.S. senator, a founding member of the American Football League, owner of the Denver Broncos, and an integral part in bringing Major League Baseball to the city of Denver. His was quite a life.

Howsam got into baseball in 1947 while working for the Western League, and he eventually bought the Denver Bears with his father and brother. The Bears flourished under Howsam's watchful eye, and he was twice named Outstanding Minor League Executive by *The Sporting News*. His success drew the attention of legendary baseball executive Branch Rickey, who took Howsam under his wing and got him his first major league job as general manager of the St. Louis Cardinals. Howsam served in that role from 1964–66, but he eventually grew tired of answering to too many people there. So when the new ownership took over in Cincinnati and asked Howsam to run the organization, Howsam accepted.

Howsam benefited from a lot of the efforts of Bill DeWitt Sr., the previous owner and general manager of the Reds. Pete Rose, Tony Perez, and Johnny Bench were already part of the organization, and there was a solid nucleus of youngsters ready to blossom. Through trades, Howsam also added key pieces like Clay Carroll, Wayne Granger, Jim Merritt, Jim McGlothlin, and George Foster to the mix, making trades to supplement areas where the burgeoning farm system fell short.

It took Howsam's special brand of management to turn the organization into a first-class franchise. He dramatically increased the size of the scouting department and brought in some top-notch, hard-working men throughout the front office. He cut no corners and expected nothing less from any who worked under him. All employees gave 100 percent toward the final goal of building the best baseball team in the world or they were let go and someone else was hired.

He was always meticulously prepared, even when it appeared to outsiders that a move came out of nowhere. When Howsam hired Sparky Anderson to be the team's field manager before the 1970 season, local headlines asked, "Sparky Who?" But Howsam knew what he was getting in Anderson. Years later, Anderson noticed Howsam watching batting practice. "I thought to myself, *There's the baseball Einstein right there,*" Anderson said. "He knew things about me I didn't even know about myself."

The biggest deal Howsam made as Reds general manager came in 1971 when he dealt All-Stars Lee May and Tommy Helms for Joe Morgan, Jack Billingham, Ed Armbrister, and Cesar Geronimo. He and his staff were taking a large risk with the deal, but they were well prepared and ultimately the deal gave the Reds the final pieces to the Big Red Machine puzzle.

The success the Reds saw under Howsam was unlike any in franchise history as the team won five division titles in seven years and went to four World Series, winning two. After that second championship, Howsam stuck to the principles of his mentor, Branch Rickey, when he traded Tony Perez to the Montreal Expos. He was hoping to deal a player a year too early rather than a year too late—one of Rickey's guiding principles. The truth is, Howsam may have made the deal two years too soon as Perez kept up his level of performance for a couple more years, but even if he had been right, Reds fans felt that the Perez deal was the beginning of the end of the Big Red Machine.

When he turned over the GM position to his second in command, Dick Wagner, more of the Machine was dismantled, and Wagner took the brunt of the criticism though many of the moves were from the same school of thought that Howsam employed. Howsam returned to the role of team president in 1983 after Wagner's firing, and he helped lay the groundwork for returning the Reds to respectability before retiring a year later. In 2004, he was elected to the Reds Hall of Fame, a true celebration of the legacy and greatness of the architect of the Big Red Machine.

27 Tony Perez

He wasn't the first Reds player born in Cuba, far from it, but Tony Perez was arguably the greatest Cuban-born player in Reds history. Signed as a fresh-faced teenager for just enough money to get him from Cuba to the United States, Perez was in for a shock both culturally and climate-wise when he landed in Geneva, New York, in the spring of 1960. As he explained, it was so cold, "I could feel it in my bones, how I missed the heat of my country and the love of my family."

Doggie, as he was affectionately known by his teammates, didn't let those adjustments hold him back. He wanted nothing more than to prove he could play baseball at the highest level, and the Reds gave him that shot in 1965. Perez split time at first base with Gordy Coleman for two seasons before moving to third base in 1967 so that both he and Lee May could get playing time. Perez was selected to his first All-Star Game that same year, and he hit the deciding home run in the 15th inning off future Hall of Famer Catfish Hunter to give the NL a 2–1 victory. It was a sign of things to come for a man who would come to be known as Mr. Clutch.

He was one of the best hitters in the game in the 1969 and 1970 seasons, hitting the third most home runs in the NL and driving in the second most RBIs in those two seasons combined. He finished third in MVP voting in 1970 after batting .317/.401/.589 and hitting 40 home runs with 129 RBIs, leading the budding Big Red Machine to its first of four World Series during the decade.

Tony Perez hits the ball to the outfield, scoring the winning run with two outs in the bottom of the ninth to beat the Yankees 4–3 in the second game of the World Series on October 17, 1976. (AP Photo)

Perez moved back to first base after May was dealt to the Astros following the 1971 season in the deal that brought Joe Morgan aboard. Perez and Morgan, along with Johnny Bench and Pete Rose, were the big dogs in the Big Red Machine clubhouse, setting the tone for success on the field and off it. Perez was the jokester of the group, always ready with a wisecrack to lift up a slumping player or to knock down someone whose head was getting too big. "Tony cast a net over the entire team with his attitude," Bench explains. "He was always up, always had a sense of humor."

It was that always-positive attitude that made Perez a fan favorite and earned him the nickname, "The Mayor of Riverfront." Perez always played with a smile, and his relaxed demeanor helped him when the game was at its tightest. Former manager Sparky Anderson called Perez the greatest clutch hitter he'd ever seen. His biggest hit came in Game 7 of the 1975 World Series when Doggie launched a Bill Lee "blooper" pitch to deep center field, igniting a Reds comeback to clinch their first World Series title in 35 years.

Fourteen months after that home run, Perez was dealt to the Montreal Expos as part of a cost-cutting measure and to get more playing time for Dan Driessen. Offensively, the Reds didn't see much drop-off without Perez, but the clubhouse sorely missed his attitude and leadership. The Big Red Machine would have come apart eventually, but the trade of its leader seemed to hasten that deterioration.

Perez came back to the Reds in 1984 and played three seasons as a reserve, banging out his 379th career home run in his second-to-last career game to tie Orlando Cepeda for the most homers by a Latin player. (That mark has since been passed by several players.) In 1993, he managed the Reds to a 20–24 record before he was unceremoniously let go by general manager Jim Bowden. That moment hurt Perez, but somehow he did not let it take his smile.

He was inducted into the Reds Hall of Fame in 1998 and into the National Baseball Hall of Fame two years later. The Reds retired his No. 24 that season, joining former teammates Frank Robinson, Joe Morgan, and Johnny Bench who had all received the honor.

Jose Rijo

Jose Rijo put together one of the greatest postseason performances by a pitcher in Reds history in 1990. Facing two dominant offensive teams in the Pittsburgh Pirates and the vaunted Oakland Athletics, Rijo went 3–0 with a 2.28 ERA in four starts, including a masterful 8⅓ inning gem in Game 4 of the World Series where he retired 20 straight A's hitters en route to capturing the Series' MVP Award.

It's amazing to think that Rijo almost wasn't given the chance to pitch in those games. In late August 1990, manager Lou Piniella was tinkering with the idea of going to a four-man rotation. Rijo loved the idea until he learned that he might be the one moved to the bullpen. The 25-year-old Dominican had yet to establish himself as the dominant starter of our memories, posting a career 47–50 record up to that point in a mix of starting and relieving. His inconsistency frustrated Piniella, but the threat of demotion to the bullpen lit a fire under Rijo. He went 6–2 with a 1.27 ERA for his last nine starts of that year, averaging nearly eight innings a start. And from that point forward, Jose Rijo was one of the most dominant right-handed pitchers in the game.

From 1991–93, he had the lowest ERA in the National League for any pitcher with at least 400 innings pitched. He was third in strikeouts and winning percentage and fourth in total wins. Somehow, Rijo never finished higher than fourth in the

Greatest Playoff Pitching Performances

Jose Rijo's performance in the 1990 World Series earned him the Series' MVP honors, but was it the top postseason pitching performance in Reds history? Not quite.

5. Ross Grimsley—1972 NLCS, Game 4
(9 IP, 2 H, 1 R, 1 ER, 0 BB, 5 K)
Facing elimination at the hands of the Pirates, the 22-year-old extended the series that the Reds eventually won in five games.

4. Paul Derringer—1940 World Series, Game 7
(9 IP, 7 H, 1 R, 0 ER, 3 BB, 1 K)
The only Reds pitcher to throw a complete game in a sudden-death postseason match, Derringer was still on the mound when the Reds clinched the Series at home.

3. Jose Rijo—1990 World Series, Game 4
(8.1 IP, 2 H, 1 R, 1 ER, 3 BB, 9 K)
Rijo stumbled through the first two innings and then put down 20 straight Oakland hitters before turning it over to Randy Myers to close out the Series sweep.

2. Hod Eller—1919 World Series, Game 5
(9 IP, 3 H, 0 R, 0 ER, 1 BB, 9 K)
Eller retired 26 of the last 28 hitters he faced, but the cloud of suspicion on every game in the Series leads one to wonder how much the White Sox helped him with that.

1. Bucky Walters—1940 World Series, Game 6
(9 IP, 5 H, 0 R, 0 ER, 2 BB, 2 K)
The 1939 NL MVP also homered in a must-win game for the Redlegs, carrying the team on his back before turning over the ball to Derringer for Game 7.

Source: Baseball-Reference.com

Cy Young Award voting, and he didn't make an All-Star Game in any of those three seasons. The league knew what kind of a pitcher Rijo was—and fans in Cincinnati knew it, as well—but somehow he still failed to get the national attention a pitcher of his caliber deserved.

Rijo finally made his first All-Star Game in 1994, but he didn't pitch. The strike that year kept him from his fifth straight season of double-digit victories, but injuries the following year brought Rijo's career to a grinding halt. Rijo had thrown more than 1,000 innings in the five seasons prior to 1995. That's 1,000 innings of a mid-90s fastball and a devastating slider. Eventually that catches up to some guys, and for Rijo, it led to five surgeries during the next three years and countless hours of rehabilitation. Every year, Rijo attempted to rejoin the Reds, and every year the pain returned.

Finally, by 1998 he was left to rehabilitate on his own. And for two years, that's what he did. While he did that, he also started a baseball academy in his native Dominican Republic, establishing a possible future as a valuable member of some team's front office. But for Rijo, that was a distant future. For now, he still planned to pitch in the big leagues again.

Amazingly, his desires were realized almost exactly six years and one month after he last pitched in the majors. On August 17, 2001, Rijo pitched two innings of relief for the Reds, striking out two and walking two, to the amazement of fans and medical staff alike.

"We're not really sure how much of Jose's ligament is there," team doctor Timothy Kremchek said. "But he has enough arthritis in his elbow, scar tissue, changes, bone spurs that have stabilized his elbow, plus his knowledge of pitching, to make him effective. We kept telling him, 'Jose, you can't pitch without a ligament.' Well, he's proven everybody wrong."

The 36-year-old Rijo pitched 92 more innings in the big leagues during the 2001 and 2002 seasons, including nine starts, before finally calling it a career. After retirement, Rijo joined GM Jim Bowden in the Washington Nationals front office where he worked until 2009 before being implicated in an alleged conspiracy involving the falsification of information about prospect Carlos

Jose Rijo pitches in the early innings of a World Series game in Oakland on Saturday, October 20, 1990, against the Athletics. (AP Photo/Rusty Kennedy)

Alvarez (aka "Esmailyn Gonzalez"). In 2012, a warrant for Rijo's arrest was put out in the Dominican Republic, accusing the former pitcher of laundering money for a drug trafficker.

Still possibly the greatest Reds pitcher since Mario Soto, Rijo's legacy with the Reds is one of dominance and perseverance. He ranks fourth in franchise history in strikeouts and ERA, and in 2005 he was inducted into the Reds Hall of Fame.

29 Attend Redsfest

Being a diehard Reds fan isn't a six-month proposition. You scour newspapers in the off-season, looking for any little nugget of information, a possible transaction, maybe an autograph session in town, or a newsbite about that up-and-coming short-stop playing in the Dominican Winter League. True fans are fans all year long.

At some point, that excitement and energy about the Reds needs a release, and that's where Redsfest comes in. Every year, usually early in December, the Reds put together a convention of Reds fandom at the Duke Energy Center in downtown Cincinnati. Redsfest is a two-day event that focuses on giving fans of all levels a memorable wintertime experience. It's an event that is considered by many around the league to be the best of its kind in baseball.

Typically there are more than 50 current and former players in attendance, serving a variety of functions. A lot of the weekend is focused on celebrating the success of the prior year's team and building anticipation for the upcoming season. Throughout the weekend there are interview sessions on the main stage, often with questions asked directly from the audience. The players are also available during the weekend for autograph sessions—one of the biggest draws for many fans. Occasionally, some of the players and coaches have photo sessions, letting fans capture some memories with their favorite players.

Kids are a big focus of the event, as well. The main stage usually features a couple of different Q&A sessions for the kids, letting young Reds fans interview some of their favorite current players.

There are separate autograph sessions just for kids, giving them a chance to meet their heroes face to face without having to battle the massive lines of the other sessions. The Reds Heads Kids Club has a booth with program information and also a bounce house for the little ones who need to burn off some energy. There are live batting cages, a speed pitch, and a 90' run for the kids who want to test out all of their baseball skills.

An indoor Wiffle Ball field sits in the back of the convention center. Fans can gather to watch a celebrity home run contest, head-to-head matches between teams, or even take a few swings themselves. When you need a break, there's a full sports bar set up with televisions tuned to the top NCAA football and basketball games of the day.

Redsfest has something for collectors, as well. Local traders bring their memorabilia from a variety of sports to sell or trade with other fans. Reds Authentics has regular auctions during the weekend, selling everything from player jerseys to game-used bases from Great American Ball Park. Redsfest is a good place to find an unexpected gem to add to any collection.

The event also has some off-the-beaten-path components. An annual talent show gives fans the opportunity to put themselves in the spotlight, highlighting everything from musical to magical talents. The event wraps up every year with a celebrity poker tournament to benefit the Reds Community Fund. Current and former Reds players along with local celebrities sit at tables with fans, all competing for a large jackpot if they can survive the grueling competition. It's a lively and spirited end to an exciting weekend of Reds festivities.

30 Jim Maloney

There is a saying in the pitcher's union that sometimes you just pitch on the wrong day—meaning that no matter how well you pitch, your offense just can't get the runs you need to win. For Jim Maloney, he didn't just pitch on the wrong day, he pitched in the wrong decade.

Maloney was scouted by several teams out of high school in San Jose, but he turned down all offers on the advice of his father, who felt that the dollar amounts were never enough. Maloney gave college a try, but that did not work out so well for him academically and he eventually signed with the Reds on April Fool's Day 1959, still at the ripe age of 18.

He wasn't a big man, standing 6'2" and weighing much less than the 190 lbs. that he'd be listed at later in his career. But boy oh boy could he throw. The right-hander put the fire in fireballer and was once clocked as high as 99.5 mph with his fastball. And when it was on, he was devastating.

It took a few years before his fastball was on, though. He made his big-league debut while still only 20 years old, going 2–6 with a 4.66 ERA in 11 games in 1960. He pitched mostly out of the bullpen with a few spot starts for the 1961 pennant winners. He spent a little more time on the farm in 1962 before finally putting it all together in 1963. That year he went 23–7 with a 2.77 ERA, striking out 265 batters, and obliterating the previous franchise record of 239 set by Noodles Hahn in 1901.

The growth for Maloney came when he decided to, in his words, "stop babying my arm." By mixing in pitches other than the fastball, Maloney learned to be a better pitcher, but he also developed shoulder soreness that would plague him off and on for the rest of his career. That didn't stop him from averaging 16 wins and 213 innings during the six seasons from 1964–69.

The elegance of Jim Maloney didn't lie in his season numbers. He was one of those rare pitchers that fans wanted to watch pitch because he could throw a no-hitter on any given night. By the time June 14, 1965, rolled around, Maloney had already taken three no-hitters into the seventh inning, so it was no surprise when he finally took one to the ninth. What was surprising was when he took one into the 10th after the Reds failed to scratch across even one run for their ace. By the end of 10 innings, Maloney had broken the Reds' single-game record for strikeouts by a pitcher with 17, and he still hadn't allowed a hit, but his teammates were unable to dent the plate. That's when Johnny Lewis led off the top of the 11th inning with a home run on a 2–1 pitch, breaking up Maloney's no-hitter, his shutout, and eventually hanging the snake-bitten starter with the loss as the lone run was enough to give the visiting Mets the victory.

Maloney would get another shot at immortality a mere two months later when he once again threw nine no-hit innings, this time against the Cubs, only to have to face a 10th inning when his teammates were unable to dent the plate through nine. This time, however, Maloney held on to his no-hitter long enough for the Reds to plate a run as Leo Cardenas smacked a long ball off the left-field foul pole to give the Reds a 1–0 victory and Maloney his first official no-hitter. As of 2012, he is still the only pitcher since 1917 to throw a complete game no-hitter of more than nine innings.

The fireballer would throw another no-hitter on April 30, 1969, vs. the Astros—this time getting a little room for comfort as his teammates staked him out to an 8–0 lead by the fourth inning. Maloney cruised the rest of the way, striking out 13 as the Reds ultimately won 10–0. This made Maloney the second Reds pitcher to ever throw two no-hitters with the team.

His career came to a screeching halt less than a year later. On April 16, 1970, Maloney was batting in the bottom of the third. He had been dealing with a sore ankle for more than a year at that point, but he didn't realize that the injury was weakening his Achilles tendon.

"I hit a ball to deep short against Los Angeles," he recalled. "I took three steps out of the batter's box and bang, it was over. The tendon rolled up like a window shade."

Maloney didn't pitch again until September, but he wasn't effective and he was not put on the postseason roster. That winter he was traded to the Angels, but he was never able to regain what he once had. He tried to latch on with the Cardinals and Giants in 1972, but the writing was on the wall and by June of that year he retired mere days after his 32nd birthday.

It's hard to say what Maloney's career track would have been like had he not been injured so severely. Since 1918, only Nolan Ryan and Bob Feller have more complete games where they have allowed one or fewer hits. No pitcher in Reds history has more strikeouts than Maloney's 1,592.

And who knows how he would have been remembered if he had the chance to be the ace of the Big Red Machine in the 1970s? Could he have ended up in Cooperstown? He will always be one of the great what-ifs in Reds history.

 **Marge Schott**

It would be hard to find a more controversial character in Reds history than Marge Schott, the team's majority owner from 1984–99. Schott was a rarity in big-time sports, a female owner who was also the chief executive officer. Breaking into the boys club of sports ownership is not easy, and holding that spot can prove to be even more difficult.

Schott was born Marge Unnewehr in Cincinnati on August 18, 1928, one of five daughters for lumber baron Edward Unnewehr and his wife, Charlotte. Her father taught her much about business, lessons that would serve her well after her husband, Charles Schott, died suddenly of a heart attack in 1968. Marge, who was a widow at the age of 39, took control of her husband's businesses, including a car dealership and a brick factory. She had to fight to keep control of those ventures, often butting heads with the men who were running the businesses.

Partly because of those battles, Marge developed some rough edges to her personality, which, when coupled with her deep raspy voice from years of smoking, hid a sweeter, more loving facet of her identity. It was that loving side that drove her to buy into the Cincinnati Reds franchise, first a small minority chunk and then a majority ownership in 1984. Schott loved the city of Cincinnati, and her passion for the city drove her to try to put the best shine on the city's jewel, the baseball team. She was instrumental in bringing native son Pete Rose back to town to break the hits record, and she worked hard to keep the stadium as fan-friendly as possible, famously demanding that hot dog prices never exceed $1.

But she was also a notoriously cheap owner. She once suggested firing all of the scouts because as far as she could tell, all they did was watch baseball games. She refused to pay for an out-of-town scoreboard so that fans could see scores from other MLB games, believing it wasn't worth the money since fans should be watching the Reds play anyway. But while corners were frequently cut, she did open her checkbook to pay her players. Under Schott, the Reds were usually in the top 10 in player salary, something that hasn't been true much since she left.

Those player payments paid off as the franchise had nine winning seasons under Schott, making the playoffs twice and winning the World Series in 1990. However, after that Series win, Schott was heavily criticized for her refusal to pay for a private jet to get outfielder Eric Davis, who had lacerated his kidney in Game 4 of the sweep, back to Cincinnati. From that point forward, even when the Reds had on-field success, it seemed like the story of Marge Schott was more about controversy than anything.

In 1991, she was sued by a former employee for her alleged refusal to hire black people. During that trial, it came out that Schott referred to Davis and Dave Parker has her "million-dollar n--gers," which understandably angered both men. A couple of years after that she told the *Cincinnati Enquirer* that she wouldn't allow her players to wear earrings "because only fruits wear earrings." When home plate umpire John McSherry died of a massive heart attack during Opening Day in 1996, Schott insensitively responded with, "I feel cheated. This isn't supposed to happen to us, not in Cincinnati." It was reported that she later sent flowers to the umpire's room, but the flowers were allegedly some that had been sent to her earlier that day.

The list of Schott's flubs carries on—praise of Adolf Hitler, racially insensitive language in meetings, mocking caricatures, and so forth. It's hard to argue that Schott was not insensitive, but the devil that really drove her was alcohol. A fan of cheap vodka, Schott's drinking was her ultimate downfall, first forcing Major League Baseball to push her to sell her team, and then destroying her health. Schott sold her shares of the team to local businessman Carl Lindner in 1999. She continued to do charitable work around Cincinnati for the next few years, but ultimately her demons beat her and she died in March 2004 at the age of 75.

32 Eric Davis

There's a saying that you might find on a cheap sign hanging in a knick-knack store or souvenir shop: "The Worst Curse in Life is Unlimited Potential." It's not something that most of us have to worry about. Our limitations are often as plain as the noses on our faces. But every now and then, a player comes along with that limitless potential, and far too often we learn that clichés often have a basis in truth.

When Eric Davis arrived on the scene in Cincinnati in 1984, he came with the label of unlimited potential. As so often occurred in that era, that label frequently came with the moniker of "the next Willie Mays" since the Hall of Famer was the standard bearer for players who could do it all on the baseball field. And Davis, a legitimate five-tool player if there ever was one, could indeed do it all.

His greatness was quickly recognized by teammate Dave Parker, who said, "Eric is blessed with world-class speed, great leaping ability, the body to play until he's 42, tremendous bat speed and power, and a throwing arm you wouldn't believe. There's an aura to everything he does. I tell you frankly that I'd pay to see him if I had to."

It wasn't long before Davis was no longer referred to as "the next Willie Mays" and was now being called "the first Eric Davis." His amazing combination of power and speed led to 27 home runs and 80 stolen bases in 1986, levels that have only been reached by one other player, Rickey Henderson, in the same season. The following year, Davis walloped 37 long balls and stole 50 bases, the first player ever to reach those two marks in the same year. He also won the first of three straight Gold Gloves in 1987 while finishing

Eric Davis lets loose with one of the three home runs he hit on July 10, 1989, during a home run contest in Anaheim, California. The event was part of the All-Star Game festivities, and the National League won the contest. (AP Photo/ Eric Risberg)

ninth in the MVP vote. Overall, from 1986–89, he averaged 39 home runs and 58 stolen bases per 162 games played, garnering MVP votes in each season. It was an astounding offensive pace that hadn't been seen before in baseball.

The problem was that despite averaging those numbers per 162 games, he never came close to playing that many games in a season. Every season was marked with an injury of one sort or another, and Davis never played more than 135 games in a single year once in his 17-year career—a fact that makes his outrageous season numbers even more remarkable. Limitless potential, indeed.

Davis only reached the playoffs once in his career with the Reds, and that came in 1990. While he struggled during the NLCS, he hit one of the most important home runs in Reds postseason history in the first inning of Game 1 of the World Series versus Dave Stewart and the Oakland A's. Davis, the emotional leader of that team, single-handedly set the tone of the Series for his teammates, putting the baseball world on notice that the Reds were not intimidated by the defending world champs.

Sadly, Davis did not get to pop champagne with his teammates at the end of that Series as a lacerated kidney, suffered while diving for a ball in the first inning of Game 4, forced Davis into the intensive care unit at a local hospital in Oakland. Once again, injuries that so often robbed Davis of his potential glory, robbed him of that one moment on the field for which he so desperately longed. It would be more than a week before Davis was able to get back to Cincinnati—a sequence of events that led to bitterness from Davis toward Marge Schott and the Reds' organization—and more importantly, it would be two years before Davis would even feel normal again health-wise.

By that point, he had been dealt from Cincinnati to Los Angeles to play for his hometown Dodgers. Two years after that, Davis decided to retire after struggling with the Detroit Tigers. The time off did him some good, and in 1996 he returned to baseball and Cincinnati, posting a 26 HR, 23 SB season as a 34 year old. It was his sixth 20/20 season with the Reds, the most in franchise history. The outstanding season garnered a Comeback Player of the Year Award for Davis.

Even with that successful year at the plate, a year when he finally started to feel the love of Cincinnati fans, he was unable to settle on a contract with the Reds and left to play for the Baltimore Orioles. While in Baltimore, Davis was diagnosed with colon cancer, robbing him of most of the 1997 season. He won the battle with cancer and with that victory also was awarded the Hutch Award, the Roberto Clemente Award, and the Tony Conigliaro Award, all celebrating Davis' positive outlook while faced with adversity. He also took home a second Comeback Player of the Year Award in 1998 when he hit a career-high .327 with 28 home runs for the Orioles.

The outfielder played three more seasons before hanging up the cleats in 2001. In 2005, he was inducted into the Reds Hall of Fame. Eventually, he would come back to the Reds once again, this time as a special assistant to the general manager and roving minor league instructor.

33 Pete Rose Banned

Posted in every major league clubhouse is Rule 21(d):

BETTING ON BALL GAMES. Any player, umpire, or club official or employee, who shall bet any sum whatsoever upon any baseball game in connection with which the bettor has no duty to perform shall be declared ineligible for one year.

Any player, umpire, or club or league official or employee, who shall bet any sum whatsoever upon any baseball game in connection with which the bettor has a duty to perform shall be declared permanently ineligible.

In many ways, it is considered baseball's most sacred rule. Before this rule, baseball was frequently marred with gambling scandals of varying degrees. It was before this rule that one of baseball's darkest events occurred—the intentional loss of the 1919 World Series by the Chicago White Sox. It was events like the Black Sox scandal that forced the league to implement this rule to prove to its fans that the competition on the field was legitimate and not being manipulated by bookies and gamblers.

This rule has kept Pete Rose out of the game of baseball since August 24, 1989.

The formal investigation into Pete Rose was revealed on March 20, 1989, when the commissioner's office announced that it was investigating "serious gambling allegations against Rose." Within two weeks the IRS had seized betting slips with Rose's handwriting and fingerprints. Just more than a month after that, commissioner Bart Giamatti received a 225-page report from investigator John Dowd that contained documents, depositions, and other materials that demonstrated that Pete Rose gambled on baseball, including bets on his own team.

At a press conference in New York on August 24, Giamatti stood at the podium and announced, "One of the game's greatest players has engaged in a variety of acts which have stained the game, and he must now live with the consequences of those acts."

Giamatti went on to say, "In absence of evidence to the contrary…yes, I have concluded that he bet on baseball." He even agreed that he believed that Rose bet on his own team.

Rose had signed a document the previous evening stating that he accepted a lifetime ban from baseball with the ability to request reinstatement a year later. The document was neither an admission nor denial of guilt, though Rose publicly denied betting on baseball during his own press conference.

"Despite what the commissioner said today, I didn't bet on baseball," he explained, though he did admit that he bet on other sports. "I made some mistakes, and I'm being punished for my mistakes."

A year-and-a-half after the banishment, Rose was also banned from the Hall of Fame ballot by the Hall of Fame board of directors. Despite that banishment, Rose was written in on 41 ballots during the next election.

Rose continued to deny that he bet on baseball for 15 years. However, in his 2004 autobiography, *My Prison Without Bars*, he admitted that he did actually bet on the game. Three years later, Rose told ESPN, "I bet on my team every night. I didn't bet on my team four nights a week. I was wrong."

Rose's admissions were portrayed as attempts at reconciliation, but whether or not he was truly contrite does not seem to matter to the baseball commissioner's office. There has been little progress in the discussions of Rose's re-instatement, and outside of a couple promotional events here and there, Rose has been invisible in any official baseball capacity. Based on the current state of his relationship with the commissioner's office, there is little reason to believe that will change.

34 The 1940 World Championship

In a summer when Adolf Hitler rampaged through Europe, the Cincinnati Reds put together the finest season in the franchise's history to that point. Led by the greatest pitching tandem in Reds history and a solid defense, the team reached the 100-win mark for the first time ever and left the rest of the NL in the dust. This was achieved despite experiencing one of the greatest in-season tragedies in major league history and having to deal with injuries to a former MVP. It was quite a year, indeed.

The 1940 Reds were the defending National League champs, and despite falling in four straight games to the powerhouse New York Yankees the year before, the team had high expectations. It came out firing on all cylinders when the season started, winning 28 of its first 39 games and scoring more than five runs a game while holding its opponents to merely 3½ runs per game. Led by reigning NL MVP Bucky Walters, who was 9–0 with a 1.62 ERA with nine complete games in his first 10 starts, the Reds had a three-game lead over the Brooklyn Dodgers at the beginning of June.

The Reds stumbled a little through June and lost their lead to the Dodgers, but after the nation celebrated its 164th birthday, the Redlegs were nearly unbeatable. From July 4–26, the Reds went an amazing 18–2, outscoring their opponents by 50 runs in those 20 games. Both Walters and his partner in crime, Paul Derringer, went 5–0 in five starts each, and eventual MVP Frank McCormick mashed out a .342/.409/.570 line during the stretch. The team built a nine-game lead that they would never relinquish, though it's fair to say they still had some bumps ahead.

The first bump came when backup catcher Willard Hershberger took his own life in his hotel room while the team played a double-header in Boston against the Bees. Hershberger was well-liked among both his teammates and the fans—he'd been named the second most popular player in a fan poll just a few weeks earlier—but the demons he battled on and off the field were too much to handle. His death shocked and saddened his teammates immensely. As one might expect, playing baseball was difficult over the next few weeks and the team struggled, losing 12 of the next 21 games.

The Suicide of Willard Hershberger

For some major league ballplayers, the stress of the day-to-day grind of a season can really take its toll. The ups and downs players feel from one day to the next often lead to an emotional rollercoaster that can be daunting to overcome. Now imagine also trying to deal with the fact that you discovered your father dead a little over a decade prior after a self-inflicted gunshot to the chest. The world can be damn near unbearable at that point.

That's what Willard Hershberger was up against in 1940. The 30-year-old back-up catcher had some talent and was having a good season filling in for the frequently injured Ernie Lombardi behind the plate. But he could not handle the emotional struggle that is a baseball season. Several times during the season he went into deep depressions, blaming himself for losses even when the Reds had a comfortable lead in the standings.

By August it had gotten to be too much. Hershberger blamed himself after the team blew a lead late in the game to the Boston Bees two days after blowing a similar lead late to the New York Giants, both mediocre teams that the Reds should have beaten. His teammates, unable to understand what "Hershey" was going through, told him to let it go and that he was making too much out of it. But Willard couldn't let it go.

After the Reds loss on August 2, he went to his manager, Bill McKechnie, to talk about what he was going through, how he felt like he was letting his teammates down, how he'd never really gotten over his father's suicide, and how he had been considering suicide himself. The two talked at length that evening, and Hershberger told his manager that the talk helped.

The next day, Hershberger relayed a message to the team that he was not up to playing. McKechnie encouraged his catcher to come watch from the stands anyway, and Hershey said he would. But when McKechnie did not see him in the stands by the seventh inning of the first game that day, he dispatched Dan Cohen, a Cincinnati shoe store owner traveling with the team, to check on Hershberger. By the time Cohen found Hershberger in his room in the Copley Plaza, he was already dead. He had sliced his own neck with a razor blade and bled out in the bathtub.

The demons that haunted Willard Hershberger were more than he could handle. He remains the only big-league player to have committed suicide during the regular season.

The team's lead slipped to as low as four games late in August before it put together another impressive run to lock up the NL pennant. The squad went on a 24–4 run through most of September and were once again led by Walters and Derringer, who both posted 4–0 records with ERAs less than 2.20. The offense was powered by third baseman Billy Werber (.330/.407/.431) and newly acquired Jimmy Ripple (.324/.425/.541).

The Reds were on fire as they cruised to their second straight NL pennant, but two key injuries left some doubts about how the team could handle the AL champion Detroit Tigers. Catcher Ernie Lombardi severely sprained his ankle and left the team scrambling to find a catcher, eventually pulling 40-year-old coach Jimmy Wilson out of retirement for the Series. The team also lost second baseman Lonny Frey five days before the Series when a metal cover from the dugout water cooler fell on his foot, leaving a large gash and a broken toe. Backup shortstop Eddie Joost filled in for Frey during the Series, but he made little contribution offensively.

The World Series itself was an exciting back-and-forth contest between the Reds and Tigers. Detroit won the first game handily, but the Reds came back in Game 2 behind the pitching of Walters and the bat of Ripple, who hit the first World Series home run in franchise history. The teams split the next two games in Detroit, and an 8–0 shellacking in Game 5 left the Reds on the brink of elimination as the series moved back to Cincinnati.

The Reds got to Tigers starter Schoolboy Rowe early in the first inning for two runs, and that would be more than enough for Bucky Walters who shut out the Tigers on five hits and even added a home run of his own as the home team won 4–0. That set the stage for Paul Derringer in Game 7.

Derringer had been hit hard in the Series opener, but he bounced back with a solid performance in the Reds 5–2 win in Game 4. In Game 7, he'd put together an impressive outing that demonstrated why he was a top 10 finisher in MVP voting for three straight seasons. The Reds fell behind in the third inning when Charlie Gehringer drove in an unearned run on a single with a throwing error by Werber. A little luck in the fourth kept the score right there as the Tigers' two-out rally fizzled when a batted ball hit Pinky Higgins. After that, the Tigers never again put together much of a threat with only one base runner passing second base the rest of the way.

The Reds finally dented the plate when Ripple, who hit .333/.440/.571 during the Fall Classic, drove in his team-leading sixth run of the Series with a double and then later scored on Billy Myers' sacrifice fly to give the Reds a 2–1 lead, which would be the final score as the Reds clinched their second World Series title in franchise history. It is still the only time in team history that the team has clinched a title at home. Derringer became just the third pitcher in big-league history to win a sudden-death game with a complete-game performance. The Reds and the St. Louis Cardinals were the only NL teams to win a World Series title between 1935 and 1953.

Frank McCormick led the NL in hits for the third straight season—a record—and took home his first career MVP after finishing in the top five in voting the two prior seasons. The 1939 MVP, Bucky Walters, was once again the Senior Circuit's top pitcher, leading the league in wins, ERA, complete games, and innings pitched. Manager Bill McKechnie became the first manager to win a World Series title with two different franchises, having won a title in 1925 with the Pittsburgh Pirates.

35 Edd Roush

Hall of Famers are rare enough that when one is traded, it's note-worthy in a team's history. It's nearly unheard of to deal three of them in the same transaction. Of course in 1916, the National Baseball Hall of Fame was still 20 years off, so you'll have to forgive the people of the day if they didn't shut down their workday when the Reds announced they had acquired Christy Mathewson, Bill McKechnie, and Edd Roush for Buck Herzog and Red Killefer. Mathewson, brought in to be the player-manager, was at the end of his career and would only pitch one game with the Reds. McKechnie wasn't much of a player and would actually go into the Hall of Fame as a manager after winning world titles with the Pirates and Reds.

But Roush would become something special for the Reds. Just 23 years old when he was acquired, the outfielder from Oakland City, Indiana, had played part of the previous three seasons in the American and Federal Leagues. Manager Mathewson put Roush in center field at the advice of his former manager John McGraw. The fleet-footed Roush flourished in that position, and he was considered by many to be the finest defensive center fielder of his day. *Baseball Magazine* once declared, "In ground covering, he has no superiors and few approximate equals."

It was with the bat that Roush made a name for himself. Lugging a thick-handled 48-ounce bat to the plate, the left-hander would often just flip his bat at the ball with a half-swing, reposi-tioning his feet to adjust the direction of the swat. From there, his bat would do the rest of the work, often placing the ball safely between the outfield and infield. It was that style that captured two

Cincinnati Reds in the Hall of Fame

As of the summer of 2013, there are 35 players who played at least one game for the Reds and made it into the National Baseball Hall of Fame, some as managers or executives. The players listed below are listed with their primary position with the Reds and how many games they played with the team.

Jake Beckley (1B)—880 games
Johnny Bench* (C)—2,158 games
Jim Bottomley (1B)—394 games
Mordecai Brown (P)—39 games
Charlie Comiskey# (1B)—268 games
Sam Crawford (RF)—403 games
Kiki Cuyler (CF)—323 games
Leo Durocher# (SS)—399 games
Buck Ewing (1B)—175 games
Clark Griffith (P)—2 games
Chick Hafey (OF)—471 games
Jesse Haines (P)—1 game
Harry Heilmann (RF)—157 games
Miller Huggins# (2B)—783 games
Joe Kelley (LF)—487 games
George Kelly (1B)—375 games

batting titles in three years for Roush. He batted .339 during his first 10 full seasons with the Reds, second in the National League only to the great Rogers Hornsby. Roush even led the league in slugging percentage in 1918 despite only hitting five home runs. Then again, Babe Ruth changed everything a year later when he belted 29 long balls.

Roush was notorious for finding ways to get out of spring training, but it never seemed to affect his game that he did not have that extra prep time. As Pat Moran, his manager from 1919–23, said, "All that fellow has to do is wash his hands, adjust his cap, and he's in shape to hit. He's the great individualist in the game."

Barry Larkin* (SS)—2,180 games
Ernie Lombardi* (C)—1,203 games
Rube Marquard (P)—39 games
Christy Mathewson (P)—1 game
Bill McKechnie*# (IF)—85 games
Bid McPhee* (2B)—2,138 games
Joe Morgan* (2B)—1,154 games
Tony Perez* (1B)—1,948 games
Old Hoss Radbourn (P)—29 games
Eppa Rixey* (P)—440 games
Frank Robinson (OF)—1,502 games
Edd Roush* (CF)—1,399 games
Amos Rusie (P)—3 games
Tom Seaver (P)—160 games
Al Simmons (OF)—9 games
Joe Tinker (SS)—110 games
Dazzy Vance (P)—6 games
Lloyd Waner (OF)—55 games
Deacon White (c)—174 games

*Inducted as a Red
#Inducted as a manager or executive
Source: Baseball-Reference.com

He only played in one postseason, the infamous 1919 World Series versus the Chicago White Sox. Roush struggled in the Series, hitting a paltry .214, but he did whack a two-run triple in Game 5 that gave the Reds a 3–0 lead in a game they eventually won 5–0. The Reds won the Series in eight games and it was later determined that eight players on the White Sox had conspired to throw the World Series in return for payment from gamblers. As the years went by, the legend became that the White Sox were a far superior team, something that angered Roush greatly. Until his dying day, Roush argued vehemently that the Reds not only were the better team but that they would have won the Series even if the Sox hadn't been on the take.

Roush finished with 12 seasons as a member of the Reds, posting a .331 average with the team, the franchise high for any player with at least 2,500 plate appearances. In 1960, he was elected to the Reds Hall of Fame, and two years later he became the first player to go into the National Baseball Hall of Fame as a Cincinnati Red. Also inducted on that day was his lifelong friend, Bill McKechnie. As part of a 100-year anniversary celebration of the Reds franchise in 1969, Roush was named the center fielder of the all-time team and was declared the greatest player of the team's first century. In 1988, while attending a spring training game at McKechnie Field in Bradenton, something he loathed to do as a player but did frequently after retirement, Roush died of a massive heart attack at the age of 94. He was one of the lucky gentlemen who died doing what he loved.

36 Major League Baseball's First Night Game

For more than 50 years National League baseball was played in the sun. It took two cutting-edge minds and a little bit of desperation to see that if God wanted baseball to be played only during the day, he wouldn't have allowed for the invention of artificial illumination capable of lighting a whole baseball diamond.

In 1934, new Reds owner Powell Crosley and team vice president and general manager Larry MacPhail were looking down every avenue for ways to increase team revenue. Attendance was in a nosedive, and the 206,773 fans who visited Crosley Field that season became the lowest total number in more than 15 seasons. The team was in the dumps financially and needed a new way to draw fans to the park.

That's why the two men petitioned the National League to allow them to host night games at the park for the 1935 season. The idea, which had been done in Negro League and minor league parks for a couple of years, met some resistance among the owners of the other seven NL teams. However, according to *Spalding's Official Baseball Guide of 1935*, they relented, "more to see if it could help its less fortunate neighbor than because of any desire to be a part of the innovation."

In fact, many owners felt the Reds' problems were more about their fourth straight last-place finish and the failure to finish in the upper half of the league in nearly a decade. The common sentiment was that if the Reds could simply field a winning team, they wouldn't need the spectacle of night baseball to draw fans.

Nevertheless, the league went forward with the plan to let the team host seven night games during the 1935 season. The innovation was in no way considered to be a permanent plan, and even with the option being offered to every team, the Reds were the only team to move forward with it.

Crosley installed $50,000 worth of the finest lighting equipment available on eight towers around the park, four banks on the grandstand and four in the outfield. The first night game was scheduled for May 23, 1935, versus the Philadelphia Phillies, but rain postponed the event, leaving some people to believe it was divine intervention. The event was rescheduled for the following evening, and just after dusk on the May 24, President Franklin D. Roosevelt gave the signal from Washington, D.C., to flip the switch to turn night into day at Crosley Field. The event was so sudden and dramatic that the 20,422 fans in attendance erupted in applause at the success of the illumination. The game finally got under way at 9:00 PM, and Paul Derringer outdueled Joe Bowman to give the Reds a 2–1 victory.

Night baseball would be quite a boon for the Redlegs as they averaged more than 14,000 more fans a game in their seven night games that season than they averaged in the 69 day games. Even with that draw, other owners saw night baseball more as a carnival sideshow than something worthy of America's grand game. In fact, it would be three years before another team installed lights in its home park. That team was the Brooklyn Dodgers and their general manager was Larry MacPhail, the same man who brought night baseball to the Queen City.

Teams gradually realized the benefits of night baseball, and by 1940 half of the teams in the league scheduled home night games. Eventually, the league upped the number of home night games to 14 per year. A decade later the majority of the Reds' home games were played at night. It wouldn't be long before night games were the norm, and even small-market teams were drawing more than 1 million fans a year.

37 Visit Reds Hall of Fame and Museum

Baseball, more than any other professional sport, celebrates its history nearly as much as it celebrates its present. Cincinnati, with a professional baseball history dating back to 1869, has as much history to celebrate as any major league city, and thankfully it has a place like the Cincinnati Reds Hall of Fame and Museum where all of that history is on display. Founded in 1958 and located next to Great American Ball Park, the Hall of Fame and Museum is a must-see for every Reds fan.

The Reds were the second big-league team to have a Hall of Fame, following the lead of the Cleveland Indians in 1951. The Indians' Hall soon went under, though, making the Reds' Hall the longest-running Hall of Fame in baseball. The Reds' Hall was the brainchild of the Sports Committee of the Cincinnati Chamber of Commerce, which ran the Hall until the Reds took it over in the 1980s. Hall of Fame classes were selected by a fan vote, with ballots printed in local newspapers. The first class elected was a set of teammates from the 1939 and 1940 World Series teams, consisting of Ernie Lombardi, Frank McCormick, Bucky Walters, Johnny Vander Meer, and Paul Derringer. Fans held the vote until 1988 when the Hall went dormant for 10 years. Elections resumed in 1998, but voting was done by the Cincinnati chapter of the Baseball Writers Association. Finally in 2005, voting was returned to the fans.

As of 2012, the Reds Hall of Fame has 81 inductees that include 74 players, four managers, and three executives. Each inductee is awarded a plaque similar in style to the one received by Hall of Fame inductees in Cooperstown. While the team was in Crosley Field, those plaques resided around the park for perusal by the fans. When the team moved into Riverfront Stadium, the plaques were treated like mom's fine china and put in storage, only to be brought out for special occasions. In 2004, the plaques were put on permanent display at the Hall of Fame Museum.

The Reds first opened the doors of their newly built Museum in 2004, which is set just outside of Great American Ball Park near the Fan Zone area in right field. Open year-round, the museum has 16,000 sq. ft. of exhibit space taking up two floors of the building. Aside from the plaques, other permanent displays include statues of the Great Eight celebrating a walk-off victory, award trophies and plaques from the numerous individual awards received by players, World Series trophies from the Big Red Machine and Wire-to-Wire teams, and informational and educational displays about some of the great teams and players in the franchise's history. For the more interactive fan, there is a speed pitch booth as well as a chance to sit down at a microphone and call the play-by-play for a famous moment in Reds history.

The museum keeps fans coming back every year with spectacular annual exhibits celebrating the best of the best in Reds history. Past exhibits have given fans insight into players like Edd Roush, Joe Nuxhall, Johnny Bench, Pete Rose, and Barry Larkin. Great teams like the 1919 world champions, the 1990 Wire-to-Wire squad, and of course the Big Red Machine have been featured. The artifacts from the careers and lives of these players and teams whisk fans back to the days when these players roamed the friendly confines of Crosley Field and Riverfront Stadium. For fans who lived through these times, the memories will come rushing back. For those who did not, there is no better way to capture the feelings of the times than looking at old uniforms and photos and listening to historic radio calls. Each exhibit is well executed, rivaling anything that baseball fans would see in Cooperstown. Fans are fortunate to have such a great location to celebrate the team's storied history.

38 The Nasty Boys

Having a shutdown closer can ease the mind of any manager. Having three of them in the same bullpen is better than any antidepressant on the market. In 1990, Lou Piniella managed a lot of six-inning games and then turned it over to the Nasty Boys—Norm Charlton, Rob Dibble, and Randy Myers—to seal up the victory.

The three men created one of the most dominant bullpens in baseball history. Each one quirkier than the next, they intimidated opponents into submission and forced teams to try to scrape for runs early, knowing they wouldn't have much chance if they trailed late. Dibble was boisterous, a hothead who could snap at any moment. Myers, who frequently dressed in military fatigues, once left a dormant hand grenade in a teammate's locker as a prank. And Charlton—he was the quiet one who fostered the kind of fear that builds in a horror flick where you just can't figure out what the villain is up to.

It certainly wasn't fair to opponents.

"First they get Charlton," pitching coach Stan Williams said. "He throws 93, 94 miles per hour and has a great assortment of breaking stuff. Then you get to Myers. He throws 95, 96. Then you get Dibble. He throws 97, 98. In spring training we'd kind of laugh about bringing those guys in one after another because, when you think about it, it was kind of a dirty trick."

The name Nasty Boys came from a conversation Randy Myers had with a reporter after the Houston Astros' Glenn Davis was unhappy about being hit by a pitch three times.

"Well, I've got the radar readings right here, and it says the last three of us all hit at least 95 on the gun," Myers replied. "So if it comes down to [a retaliation war], just let 'em know."

"That's pretty nasty," the reporter said.

"Well, we're pretty nasty guys," Myers said.

The nickname stuck—and once you have a good nickname, the marketing engine isn't far behind. T-shirts, bumper stickers, and even license plates started showing up with the Nasty Boys name on them. As the Reds continued piling up victories, the Nasty Boys' popularity continued to grow. Both Myers and Dibble were named to the All-Star team in July. At the same time, Charlton was moved to the starting rotation, where he filled in admirably for a struggling staff.

By the playoffs, however, the trio was back together again and the bullpen dominated in the postseason, pitching 31 innings and allowing only one earned run (0.29 ERA) while striking out 33 batters. Myers and Dibble were named co-MVPs of the NLCS and, despite being the only reliever to give up a run, Charlton performed well over five innings.

Like all brilliant flames do, the Nasty Boys burned out quickly. Dibble was never happy in the setup role and eventually talked his way into the closer spot. With the team in desperate need of starting pitching, both Charlton and Myers spent time in the rotation in 1991. Myers was eventually dealt to the Padres that off-season for Bip Roberts. Charlton and Dibble split the closer role in 1992, each saving at least 25 games. Charlton was traded to Seattle for Kevin Mitchell after that season, leaving Dibble as the last Nasty Boy. Injuries and ineffectiveness plagued his 1993 season, and he missed all of 1994 after surgery. He spent 1995 in the AL with Chicago and Milwaukee before leaving the game for a broadcasting career.

They weren't around long, but much like the Big Red Machine in the seventies, the Nasty Boys set a new standard by which all future bullpens are compared. That's quite a legacy right there.

39 Visit Reds Spring Training

When the Cincinnati Reds decided to move their spring training facilities from Sarasota, Florida, to Goodyear, Arizona, starting in 2010, it was not an easy decision. Except for three years during World War II, the Reds had trained in Florida since 1923. The considerable change in distance from Cincinnati was a concern not only for fans but for the team, as well. However, the opportunity to build a brand new training facility customized to exact specifications was too good to pass up, and so after more than 80 years in Florida, the team headed out west.

Located about 20 minutes outside the heart of downtown Phoenix, Goodyear Ballpark rises out of the beautiful scenery of the desert plains. Dusty mountains set the backdrop for the picturesque oasis of the Goodyear training complex. The complex houses both the Cincinnati Reds and the Cleveland Indians—both teams work out in separate, state-of-the-art training facilities. Mornings at the practice facility are a great time for fans to watch the players get loose, run drills, and take batting practice. Early morning practice time is a good bet for obtaining autographs. Gates usually open at the training facility at 9:00 AM.

While still in the same relative area, the Reds training facility is actually located about three-quarters of a mile away from Goodyear Ballpark where both the Reds and Indians play their spring training games. The park seats more than 10,000, including six suites and a party deck that can seat up to 500 guests. For a more comfortable experience, try the club seating where wider, padded seats are covered in shade. If you are looking for more of a picnic-type atmosphere, there are also 1,500 berm seats available. For children, there is an interactive kid's zone with inflatable bounce houses and a kid-sized Wiffle Ball field.

The smaller crowds and relaxed atmosphere of spring training make it a great opportunity for autographs or to simply interact with the players while they get loose. If autographs are your thing, the gates usually open 90 minutes before game time, and many players will sign right up until the National Anthem.

One of the advantages of spring training in Arizona is that all of the teams' facilities are in close proximity to each other. In Florida, teams are spread throughout the state, creating travel times of up to 2½ hours to reach a game. All of the Cactus League teams are spread around the Greater Phoenix area, meaning the longest drive from one facility to another is usually no more than 30 minutes. Because of this, fans don't have to be confined to watching just one team during their stay, and in fact, it's possible to watch multiple games in different parks during the same day. In terms of the experience for fans who want to watch baseball, Cactus League teams have a big advantage over their brethren in the Grapefruit League.

Another big advantage of the Cactus League is the variety of teams in Arizona that fans of the Reds may not see all that often during the season. All of the West Coast teams, who typically only come to Cincinnati once a season and whose games are often on late on the East Coast, train in Arizona. The Cactus League gives fans a chance to see a variety of players in person that they may never get the chance to see in Cincinnati. Arizona may not be an ideal travel distance for fans from Ohio, but the beauty of the Arizona desert coupled with the unique experiences of the Cactus League make a visit to Goodyear a must.

40 Bob Castellini

Bob Castellini isn't the first Reds owner to be passionate about his team, but he may be the first to recognize the value of the team as a catalyst for change within the community. When Castellini said, "At my core, I am a fan," he could just as easily be talking about the city of Cincinnati as he is about the Reds. Both the city and the team mean so much to the Cincinnati native that it's natural for him to work to augment both, realizing that without one, the other just isn't the same.

When Castellini headed up a group of owners looking to purchase the Reds from Carl Lindner in 2006, he did it because he had become saddened by the state of affairs within the Reds organization. The team had just finished its fifth straight losing season, the longest such streak by the franchise in 50 years. Castellini, who at one time had held a minority stake in the Reds before selling it off in 1984, had been involved with the ownership of three other franchises prior to coming back to Cincinnati. Moving from the

Texas Rangers to the Baltimore Orioles to the St. Louis Cardinals, Castellini saw how baseball teams were intertwined with the fabric of their communities. He believed that rebuilding the Reds into a successful franchise would return the storied organization to a point of pride for the local citizens.

For Castellini, stepping into a larger role made sense for him in Cincinnati. "I would not be the lead person in ownership outside of Cincinnati," he said. "I just would not have had that passion to do that."

Shortly after buying the team, Castellini hired Wayne Krivsky to be general manager. At the press conference, he made it clear that the Reds were not going to wait around to be winners again and that winning was the only goal. The team threatened a quick turnaround in 2006 as it surprised everyone and nearly won a weak National League Central Division, but a stumble in September kept it from a winning season and left the team in third place. It would be four more years before the Reds threatened success again.

During that time, Castellini, who uses the word "empowerment" to describe his management style and trusted his people to start laying the groundwork for success. The Reds spent money and developed ideas throughout the organization, ramping up programs in marketing, baseball operations, ballpark development, and community outreach. The Reds Community Fund has taken on a much larger role for the team and as such, its budget has nearly tripled since Castellini's group took over. All of these changes have been done with the mindset that money spent early will lead to even larger returns down the road, both financially and with regards to building a sustainable fan base for years to come.

When the Reds finally had success again on the field, Castellini opened his wallet to reward and keep those players who were keys to that success. Since 2010, the Reds have given large multi-year contracts to Joey Votto, Jay Bruce, Brandon Phillips, Johnny Cueto, Bronson Arroyo, Aroldis Chapman, and Sean

Marshall. The wisdom of any of those deals might be questionable, but what can't be questioned is Castellini's willingness to spend money to build a core group of players that the fans will cheer for—an essential step in rebuilding a fan base. It may not work out for the Reds in the long run, but as a fan, you can't help but appreciate the owner's commitment to building a winner. Then again, would you expect anything less from a fan who happens to own the team?

 **Mario Soto**

When Mario Soto made his first big-league start, he was barely 21 years old and the defending world champion Reds were mired in an eight-game losing streak, the longest for the franchise in 11 years. Those facts didn't faze the young Dominican as he struck out nine Cubs and allowed two runs in a complete-game victory. It's rare that such a young player shows up as the stopper for a big-league team—let alone the world champs—but Soto was a rare pitcher, both for his time and in Reds history.

When Soto was signed by the Reds in 1973, he was 17 years old and working as a laborer on housing projects in his native Dominican Republic. The $1,000 signing bonus he received seemed like a fortune to Soto, who had lived in poverty his whole life. A decade later that amount seemed like a pittance when Soto signed the largest contract ever given out by the Reds to that point.

Soto had to earn his way into the rotation. That was no easy task for the youngster who didn't land a permanent spot in the Reds rotation until 1981, four years after his impressive debut as a starter. When he finally did find a spot in the rotation, Soto quickly put himself on the map as one of the best starting pitchers in baseball. He went 12–9 with a 3.29 ERA in the strike-shortened 1981 season, finishing third in the NL in strikeouts with 151. In 1982, he was brilliant on one of the worst teams in Reds history, posting a 2.79 ERA in 257.2 innings while striking out a franchise-record 274 batters. Pitching for the league's most anemic offense, however, left Soto with just a 14–13 record as the team lost seven starts where he pitched at least six innings and gave up two or fewer runs—second only to teammate Bruce Berenyi who had nine such starts.

His won-lost record did not hamper the recognition he received around the league as he was regularly listed among the best pitchers in the NL in player polls, and his devastating changeup was considered one of the best pitches in baseball. That changeup, paired with a mid-90s fastball, is what helped Soto earn an All-Star Game start in 1983. He was the first Reds pitcher in 20 years to receive the honor. He only went two innings that day and allowed two runs with two walks and two strikeouts, and was hung with loss as the American League trounced the National League 13–3, breaking an 11-game win streak for the Senior Circuit.

He finished that season, another dismal one for the Redlegs, with a 17–13 record and a 2.70 ERA, his second consecutive top-five finish in ERA. His 242 strikeouts once again placed him second in the NL behind Steve Carlton, but his 18 complete games set the standard in 1983. He finished second in Cy Young Award voting that year, and the Reds rewarded him with a five-year $6 million contract despite having another year before free agency.

The following year he posted an impressive 18–7 record for a 92-loss team and made his third consecutive All-Star team, but the season was scarred by two on-field incidents that led to two separate suspensions for the right-hander. The first came in May when Soto

Johnny Vander Meer Award Winners

Every year the local chapter of the Baseball Writers Association vote for the Outstanding Pitcher of the Reds for that season. This award was named in honor of Johnny Vander Meer, one of the greatest pitchers in team history. Here are the winners of the award for the Reds since it was first given out in 1970. (Note: The award was not given out in 1976 or 1977.)

1970 Jim Merritt	1993 Jose Rijo
1971 Don Gullett	1994 Jeff Brantley
1972 Clay Carroll	1995 Pete Schourek
1973 Jack Billingham	1996 Jeff Brantley
1974 Don Gullett	1997 Jeff Shaw
1975 Don Gullett	1998 Pete Harnisch
1978 Doug Bair	1999 Pete Harnisch
1979 Tom Hume	2000 Danny Graves
1980 Mario Soto	2001 Scott Sullivan
1981 Tom Seaver	2002 Jimmy Haynes
1982 Mario Soto	2003 Chris Reitsma
1983 Mario Soto	2004 Paul Wilson
1984 Mario Soto	2005 Aaron Harang
1985 Tom Browning	2006 Bronson Arroyo
1986 John Franco	2007 Aaron Harang
1987 John Franco	2008 Edinson Volquez
1988 Danny Jackson	2009 Bronson Arroyo
1989 Tom Browning	2010 Bronson Arroyo
1990 Jose Rijo	2011 Johnny Cueto
1991 Jose Rijo	2012 Johnny Cueto
1992 Jose Rijo	Source: Reds.com

bumped an umpire while arguing a fair call on a home run that he thought was clearly foul. The second suspension was handed down after a June fight with the Braves' Claudell Washington, an incident where Soto threw a baseball at Washington while he was being held on the ground. Both suspensions were five-games long and the fines totaled $6,000, which was a hefty amount for a fine at that time. Perhaps more importantly, Soto was labeled as a Dominican hothead, a reputation he would have a hard time shaking for the rest of his career.

When 1985 rolled around, Soto had a new manager in Pete Rose, and Rose was adamant about going from a five-man to a four-man rotation. Soto was vocal in his disapproval of the plan, but he honored his manager's wishes and pitched every fourth day. At first it looked like everything was going to work out great as Soto started the season 5–2 with a 2.10 ERA in his first eight starts. But that's about when the shoulder pain started and after much deliberation, Rose went back to a five-man rotation for most of the remainder of the season.

The change may have come too late, though, as Soto struggled off and on throughout the 1985 season. The pain continued into 1986 before Soto finally had arthroscopic surgery on the shoulder late that year. He only made six starts in 1987, missing the Opening Day start for the first time in six years. There was hope for a healthy return in 1988 as once again Soto got the ball on Opening Day, but by that point he no longer had the 90+ mph fastball and his killer changeup lost effectiveness. By mid-June he was 3–7 with a 4.66 ERA when the team released him.

Soto finished his career 100–92 with a 3.47 ERA, pitching in 12 seasons, all for the Reds. When he retired, his 1,449 career strikeouts were the second most in franchise history behind only Jim Maloney. And much like Maloney, Soto spent his career pitching for the Reds at the wrong time, joining the team at the tail end of the Big Red Machine and leaving just before the Wire-to-Wire squad won it all in 1990. He's still part of the franchise today, working as a roving pitching instructor and teaching young pitchers how to throw one of the best changeups ever.

42 Lou Piniella

Lou Piniella wasn't Marge Schott's first choice for Reds manager heading into the 1990 season. She wanted Dallas Green. In fact, in the words of her general manager, Bob Quinn, "She didn't know Lou Piniella from a Puerto Rican rum drink." But when a deal couldn't be worked out between Green and the Reds, Quinn knew the man he wanted was Piniella. And Sweet Lou rewarded his confidence with one of the most memorable seasons in Reds history.

Piniella had managed the New York Yankees for 2½ seasons in the mid-eighties, but he was never able to meet owner George Steinbrenner's lofty expectations and so, like so many before and after him, he was given the axe by The Boss. When Piniella came to Cincinnati, it was a chance for a fresh start, not just for him, but for the team, as well. The Reds had just suffered through one of the most tumultuous seasons in franchise history. The club was riddled with injuries, and the dark cloud of Pete Rose's gambling investigation hung over the team wherever it went. Bringing in Piniella from outside the organization allowed everyone to move on.

And Lou got them moving right away. The fiery manager instilled a new attitude in the talented team. They were too good to fail. He wouldn't stand for it. His players bought into his energy completely. They won their first nine games and 33 of their first 45. The team played with a fire and attitude that had been lacking in 1989, and that attitude could be traced directly back to its manager. Piniella was ejected from a game five different times in 1990, including a spectacular scene in August when he threw first base not once but twice into right field. Whenever the team started to look a little flat, Lou could be counted on for a dramatic gesture to re-ignite that fire.

Manager Lou Piniella tosses first base into right field during a game with the Chicago Cubs at Riverfront Stadium in Cincinnati on August 21, 1990. Piniella threw the base after being ejected from the game for arguing a call at first base. (AP Photo/David Kohl)

Piniella dramatics weren't all an act, however. He knew what he had in that team, and he wasn't going to let them rest until they had achieved the ultimate goal, a world championship. It was a goal he was supremely confident they could achieve. After the Reds beat the Pirates 4–2 in the playoffs, Lou told his coaches that the Reds would "beat the A's asses." Sure enough, they did, sweeping the vaunted Athletics in four games.

Lou also knew that the Reds couldn't rest on their laurels in 1991. He petitioned his owner to keep building on the success they'd had, but Schott was never one to spend unnecessary money and the Reds stood pat. Injuries and ineffectiveness led to a disappointing 74–88 fifth-place record.

The Reds did spend some money and made some moves before the 1992 season and it paid off when they won 90 games, just one fewer than the 1990 season. However, the Atlanta Braves were in the early stages of their long dynastic run, and the Reds were out of the race by mid-August.

By that point, Piniella felt underappreciated in his role. He didn't like that the Reds had not offered him a new contract by the end of the season when his original three-year deal ended. He also didn't like that the owner was taking potshots at him in the media. Concerned about where the organization was going, Piniella left the Reds to take the job in Seattle where he would manage for 10 years.

With only three seasons at the Reds' helm, Piniella ranks just 14th on the all-time managerial wins list. However, he is just the fourth manager in team history to win a World Series title, something that hasn't been done by any of the nine managers since.

43 Ted Kluszewski

Ted Kluszewski is one of those rare baseball players whose legend casts a shadow over his real life accomplishments. Standing at 6'2" and weighing 225 lbs., Big Klu was a large man with unusually large arms for his day. Legend has it that the former Indiana University tight end was unable to comfortably fit his massive biceps into the sleeves of the standard major league uniform and so he was forced to cut off the sleeves. That led to Klu's signature sleeveless look with his arms bulging out of the holes as he effortlessly swung two baseball bats with one hand in the on-deck circle. Few images are more iconic in Reds history than Klu's monolithic arms squeezing through those cut-off sleeve holes.

It's a shame that Kluszewski is known mainly for his size because in some ways it distracts from what a great hitter he was. Oh sure, he had unparalleled power for his day. He drew interest from the Reds in college when they saw him hitting balls over an embankment at the Indiana University field that wasn't even being reached by the major leaguers practicing there that day. From 1953–56, he led all of baseball with 171 total home runs. Before Klu, only Ralph Kiner ever had more home runs in a four-year stretch in the NL. Big Klu's arms weren't just weapons of intimidation, they were weapons of destruction.

But Kluszewski wasn't a slugger in the same sense that we've come to know sluggers over the years. He didn't stand in the box and swing from his heels, hoping just to make enough contact to put the ball in the seats. He batted better than .300 in seven of his first eight full seasons with the Reds, and only twice in his 15-year career did he play at least 100 games and have more strikeouts than walks. He's the only player in big-league history to have three seasons of 40 or more home runs in which he also had more home runs than strikeouts, a feat that's only been accomplished once since Kluszewski retired.

His four years from 1953–56 might be the greatest offensive quartet of years in Reds history. During that span, Kluszewski averaged a .315/.383/.585 batting line along with 43 home runs and 116 RBIs. Besides Kluszewski, there have only been three seasons of .300+ average, 40+ HR, and 100+ RBIs in Reds history, and Big Klu averaged better than that during those four years.

Amazingly, Kluszewski never finished higher than second in the National League MVP voting. That second-place finish came in 1954 when he led the league with 49 home runs and 141 RBIs, but he finished fifth with a .326 batting average. Willie Mays won the batting title that year with a .345 average, walloping 41 homers and driving in 110 RBIs while playing sparkling defense in center field. He won the MVP Award easily over Klu, who finished seventh in 1953 and sixth in 1955.

Big Klu was on a Hall of Fame path until a back injury suffered during a clubhouse fight in 1956 sapped much of his power and derailed his future. He only played in parts of the next five years, leaving the Reds in a trade after the 1957 season. Only once would he hit more than six home runs in a season, and that was a meager 15 in his final year in the big leagues. The giant man of muscle that Pete Rose once said could hit a ball out of Yellowstone Park was no longer a power threat, and he left the game quietly after the 1961 season.

Kluszewski eventually came back to the Reds as the hitting coach for the Big Red Machine, a job that he handled with great aplomb. A lot of great hitters aren't able to translate that success as a coach, but Kluszewski knew that hitting wasn't easy. "How hard is hitting?" he said. "You ever walk into a pitch-black room full of furniture that you've never been in before and try to walk through it without bumping into anything? Well, it's harder than that."

Kluszewski worked with the team until his death in 1988 at the age of 63. He was inducted into the Reds Hall of Fame in 1962, but the team added other honors to the slugger's resume after his death. In 1998, the team retired his No. 18 jersey. Five years later, when Great American Ball Park opened, Big Klu was honored with a statue in Crosley Terrace where he stands in the on-deck circle with his arms bulging out of his cut-off sleeves—just like he'll always be remembered.

# Brandon Phillips

After the Reds traded for Brandon Phillips in 2006, they didn't know for sure what they were going to get. Would he be the talented youngster who was picked by *Baseball America* to be the seventh-best prospect in all of baseball prior to the 2003 season? Or would he be the cocky kid who called himself "The Franchise," hit .206/.246/.310 as a big leaguer, and spent most of the last two seasons in Triple A? General manager Wayne Krivsky felt like the talent was too great to pass up. So on April 7, the Reds dealt a player to be named later (minor league pitcher Jeff Stevens) to the Indians for Phillips, pulling off one of the biggest trade coups in team history.

Phillips, who mostly played shortstop in the minors, made his first start for the Reds on April 13 at second base, and three days later he made the position his for good. He impressed everybody with his play on the field, hitting better than .300 for a large

Shortstop Brandon Phillips throws to first after fielding a ground ball against the Chicago Cubs during a game on Friday, September 22, 2006, in Cincinnati. (AP Photo/Al Behrman)

portion of the season and showing a nice mix of power and speed. Although he was 25, he was still maturing and fans could see his game developing. Most of all, they could see how special he was on defense. Still possessing a shortstop's arm and incredible range, Phillips was already dazzling fans with his glove work. Little did they know that he was just getting started.

In 2007, Phillips hit .288/.331/.485 while leading the team in runs, hits, triples, and stolen bases. He also joined Alfonso Soriano as the only second basemen in history to hit 30 home runs and steal 30 bases in the same season. He was the third Reds player to accomplish the feat, joining Eric Davis and his idol, Barry Larkin. "It amazes me," he said. "It's a good feeling to be in the category, especially with my favorite player growing up. It's a blessing."

The next year brought the achievement of another personal goal for Phillips when he won his first Gold Glove. It was an award that Phillips felt he deserved the year before, but he used that shun as motivation. He considers himself a defense first player, so when he was finally recognized with the award, it drove Phillips to say, "I really think it was the best thing that ever happened to me. I really take pride in my defense. It's my passion, and I love doing it."

He has since won two more Gold Glove awards and is consistently recognized as among the best defensive players in the game. That recognition does not come without hard work. "In all my years of baseball, I've been around a lot of good players and great players," manager Dusty Baker said. "None work any harder or exert more energy and effort than Brandon Phillips. He comes to play every day. You can count on him. He hustles and tries hard during the game."

The Reds rewarded that hard work with a six-year contract until 2017, which should keep Phillips in a Reds uniform until he is 36 years old. It was a special moment for Phillips, who had been vilified in Cleveland for arrogance and perceived laziness. Many fans in Cincinnati have grown to love Phillips' infectious smile, his friendly, outgoing demeanor, and his openness to interacting with them. Popular on Twitter, @DatDudeBP (his Twitter handle) has been known to show up at a fan's baseball game just because he was invited or to fly fans to whatever city the team is in as part of a contest. He also won the hearts of one passionate fan base (and the hate of another) when he openly expressed his dislike of the St. Louis Cardinals during the 2010 season. In an era when many players are afraid to speak in anything more than clichés, Phillips' willingness to put himself out there is a breath of fresh air for many and a big reason why he is one of the most popular players on the team today.

45 Crosley Field

For the 86 years from 1884 until 1970, the home of Reds baseball sat at the corner of Findlay and Western in the West End of Cincinnati. First it was League Park, and then the Palace of the Fans, but for the majority of those 86 years, the park was Redland/ Crosley Field. Opened in 1912, the ballpark featured a terrace in left field that was one of the stadium's defining characteristics. The location was originally a brickyard that was set below street level. The terrace, a gradual hill up to the street, was left in play and gave Crosley Field a unique feature not seen in other parks. Originally the terrace was only in left field, but in 1936 the decision was made to extend it all the way around to right field, which in turn made Crosley Field the only park without the need for a warning track. The terrace incline served as enough of a warning of the approaching wall.

Through the years, Crosley Field became known as a homer-friendly park, but initially that wasn't the case. The distance to the wall down each line was 360' and 420' to center field. It wasn't until nine years after it opened that Pat Duncan hit the first ball over the wall in a big-league game at Redland Field. A few years later, home plate was moved forward to allow for the addition of more seating and in turn shortening the distance to the fences.

Redland Field was renamed Crosley Field after Powel Crosley Jr. purchased the team and made many renovations to the stadium. In 1937, the city of Cincinnati suffered a great flood, and Crosley Field was not spared. More than 21' of water settled upon Crosley, covering the field and into the grandstands. It was not the first time the field had flooded, but it was the worst and it did a large amount of damage to the grandstands.

Another iconic image of Crosley Field was the massive 58' scoreboard in center field, which was added to the park in 1957. The scoreboard had space for both lineups, all of the league scores, and advertisements, but the thing most people remember is the Longines clock at the top—right smack in the middle. Fans of the Reds during the 1960s almost always mention that scoreboard as one of the clearest images they have of Crosley Field.

The memories aren't limited to the structure, however. Crosley Field hosted four World Series (1919, 1939, 1940, and 1961) and two All-Star Games (1938 and 1953). Joe Nuxhall made his major league debut on the mound at Crosley Field at the ripe age of 15 in 1944. Ernie Lombardi, Bucky Walters, Frank McCormick, and Frank Robinson all won MVPs, and Johnny Bench played half of his first MVP season in 1970 in Crosley's friendly confines. Lombardi hit the fabled "longest home run ever" when a shot off his bat landed in the back of a pickup truck driving by the park, unbeknownst to the driver who didn't discover the ball until much later in his trip.

Construction of the new highway system spelled the beginning of the end for Crosley Field. The newly constructed Millcreek Expressway, which later became I–75, ran right next to Crosley Field's center-field wall and required the demolition of much of the neighborhood around the park. The West End was also becoming more industrialized and less residential, leading to the deterioration of the surrounding area. Around that time, a new wave of ballparks was being built throughout the league, and many within the Reds' organization wanted to get in on the action. The city also wanted to bring more commerce downtown, and so it was decided that Riverfront Stadium would be built along the banks of the Ohio, and for the first time in team history, Reds baseball was played somewhere other than on the west side of the city. The final game was played at Crosley Field on June 24, 1970, and home plate was dug up and transported to Riverfront Stadium immediately afterward. Two years later, Crosley Field was demolished.

Today, fans can still check out some landmarks around the site at the corner of Findlay and Western. From time to time, the Reds Hall of Fame will host formal tours of the site, giving old fans the chance to relive memories and new fans an opportunity to learn some of the team's great history.

46 Ken Griffey Jr.

"Well, I'm finally home."

It was a phrase saturated in hope. The Kid, a son of Cincinnati, was returning to the place where he grew up and developed the talents that would make him the only active player on the All-Century Team. The numbers were staggering—398 home runs, 10 Gold Gloves, an MVP Award, and four straight years of at least 48 home runs and 134 RBIs. And he had just turned 30 years old. When the Reds traded for Ken Griffey Jr. on February 10, 2000, he was still in his prime and arguably the greatest player in the game. And he was being added to a team that had just won 96 games the season before. A revitalization of the Big Red Machine, a team Griffey's father had been an integral part of, seemed inevitable.

Hope can be cruel, though. It can often leave you wondering what happened, what could have been, or just asking, "Why?" Junior's tenure in Cincinnati started out slowly. His first Opening Day at home ended in a sixth-inning rain-out and a 3–3 tie. Through the team's first 28 games in 2000, he was batting .198 with seven home runs. They were a game under .500, and fans were getting impatient to see The Kid do his thing. Right about then is when Griffey got hot and hit 25 home runs over the next 78 games. His teammates followed suit, cutting the first-place Cardinals' lead to four games by the end of July. That was as close as they came, however, as the team sputtered through August and finished 10 games back.

On September 11, 2000, Griffey and the Reds experienced what would become an all-too-common occurrence as the superstar suffered a partial tear of his hamstring while trying to score on a Dmitri Young base hit. Griffey didn't start another game that season, though he did manage to pinch hit three times, homering in one of those at-bats. It was his 40th home run of the season, making him the fourth player ever to hit 40 in a season in five straight years. The others were Babe Ruth, who did it in seven straight seasons and Ralph Kiner and Duke Snider five straight seasons.

Griffey, who was never much of a workout freak, injured the hamstring again during the following spring training. The injury relegated him to a pinch-hit role for the month of April, though he wouldn't manage to actually get a hit before the Reds finally put him on the disabled list on April 29. He missed 41 games before making his first start of the year on June 15, but by that point the Reds were 14 games under .500 and 13½ games out of first place. He came back strong, hitting 22 home runs in the 95 games he played, but the season was lost before it started.

Junior made it six games into the 2002 season before he partially tore the patella tendon and partially dislocated his right kneecap. He missed 41 games again. Later that year he injured his right hamstring, forcing him to miss 25 more games. By this point, injuries, not home runs, were becoming the main storyline for Ken Griffey Jr. Five games into 2003 he dislocated his shoulder while diving for a ball in center field—a play where he was famously booed by disgruntled fans as he was helped off the field. The honeymoon of hope was over. In July he shredded a tendon in his ankle while running out a double, ending his season with merely 53 games played.

In 2004 it was the right hamstring again that limited Junior to 83 games. In 2005 he managed to stay healthy for most of the year and he put together his last great season, hitting .301/.369/.576 with 35 HR and 92 RBIs. His season ended prematurely once again as he injured his foot after awkwardly stepping on second base, and he missed the last 25 games of the season.

By this point the smiling kid with his hat on backward was rarely seen. The frustration of injuries coupled with the angry jeers he often received from hometown fans had jaded Junior, reminding everyone of the cliché, "You can't go home again." He did manage to take the field for 144 games in 2007, and his gorgeous swing, one that writer Joe Posnanski said "should be set to music" still carried him to a 30 HR, 93 RBIs season. However, his diminishing defensive range had forced him to move to right field. By the trade deadline the following year, he was dealt to the Chicago White Sox for Nick Masset and Danny Richar, closing out one of the saddest chapters of Reds baseball in franchise history.

Ken Griffey Jr. hits a three-run homer in the first inning against Pittsburgh Pirates pitcher Ian Snell at Pittsburgh on Wednesday, August 29, 2007.
(AP Photo/Gene J. Puskar)

It was a chapter that started with such optimism, and even after the 85-win season of 2000, there were still much reason for hope. But all fans are left with now are visions of what could have been. Griffey still finished with an incredible career. His 630 home runs were the fifth most all-time when he retired, and his 1,836 RBIs ranked 12th. He's a sure-fire first-ballot Hall of Famer, but even with that, it's hard not to feel like there could have been so much more. Sometimes going home isn't all it's cracked up to be.

47 Ernie Lombardi

Born in Oakland in 1908, Ernie Lombardi attended McClymonds High School, the school that eventually produced Reds greats Frank Robinson and Vada Pinson as well as basketball great Bill Russell. Lombardi started his professional baseball career with the Oakland Oaks but was quickly noticed by the Brooklyn Robins (soon to be the Dodgers), who acquired him in 1931. He played a season in Brooklyn, but they couldn't figure out what exactly to do with him since they already had a young catcher in Al Lopez. A year after acquiring Lombardi, they dealt him to the Cincinnati Reds and the rest, as they say, is history.

Lombardi was an affable man who was a fan favorite for most of his career in the Queen City. It didn't hurt that he was a hell of a hitter, too. He batted .311 in 10 seasons with the Redlegs, including a four-year stretch where he never hit less than .333. He wasn't much of a bopper, though he did hit 20 home runs in 1939, and he only drove in more than 75 runs twice in his career. But you couldn't ask for much more at the plate from a catcher than what "The Schnozz," as he was affectionately known, could give you.

In 1938, he put together one of the best batting seasons by a National League catcher to that point. Lombardi batted .342/.391/.524, mashing 19 home runs and driving in 95 RBIs. The .342 average gave the Reds their first National League batting champion since Bubbles Hargrave a dozen years earlier. With the stellar batting line at a difficult defensive position, Lombardi easily won the National League MVP Award, the first player to take home the award in franchise history.

His numbers dipped a little in 1939, but he was still a cornerstone to the Reds National League championship team. Again in 1940, the Schnozz was back up over .300, this time hitting .319 as the Reds won 100 games for the first time in team history. A late-season ankle sprain kept Lombardi from contributing much to the team's seven-game series win over the Tigers since he only had four plate appearances in the series. A little more than a year later, Lombardi was purchased from the Reds by the Boston Braves, unceremoniously ending his tenure with the team. He won another batting title with the Braves in 1942 before finishing his career with five decent seasons for the New York Giants.

That Lombardi was such a good hitter was a testament to the amazing bat control the right-hander displayed. Listed at 6'3" and 230 lbs.—though some reports say he reached close to 300 lbs. in his career—Lombardi was not what you'd consider fleet of foot. In fact, he was believed to be one of the slowest men to play the game, which meant that to be successful, he needed to put the ball in play with authority. And that he did. Wielding a 42-oz. bat, one of the heaviest in the game, he was able to make contact at a prodigious rate. In 1935, he struck out just six times in 351 plate appearances, a ratio that is usually reserved for flea-like slap-hitters, not a relative giant like Lombardi. He attributed his superior bat control to the interlocking grip that he used on the bat, similar to what a golfer would use. The grip wasn't a strategic move by Lombardi; rather he simply did it because, "No one ever told me to take a regular grip on a bat."

Life after baseball wasn't easy for Lombardi as he battled a depression that took him to some dark places. Lombardi, known as "Big Slug," was the starting catcher in 1940 when his backup Willard Hershberger ("Little Slug") committed suicide. It's

Ernie Lombardi Award Winners

Every year the local chapter of the Baseball Writers Association votes for the Most Valuable Player of the Reds for that season. This award was named in honor of Ernie Lombardi, one of the most popular players ever to put on a Reds uniform and also the first player from the franchise to win a National League MVP award. Here are the winners of the award for the Reds since it was first given out in 1955:

1955 Wally Post, OF
1956 Roy McMillan, SS
1957 Don Hoak, 3B
1958 Johnny Temple, 2B
1959 Frank Robinson, 1B
1960 Eddie Kasko, 3B
1961 Frank Robinson, 1B
1962 Frank Robinson, 1B
1963 Jim Maloney, P
1964 Frank Robinson, 1B
1965 Deron Johnson, 3B
1966 Pete Rose, 2B
1967 Tony Perez, 3B
1968 Pete Rose, OF
1969 Pete Rose, OF
1970 Johnny Bench, C
1971 Lee May, 1B
1972 Johnny Bench, C
1973 Pete Rose, OF
1974 Joe Morgan, 2B
1975 Joe Morgan, 2B
1976 Joe Morgan, 2B
1977 George Foster, OF
1978 Pete Rose, 3B
1979 Ray Knight, 3B
1980 Ken Griffey, OF
1981 Dave Concepcion, SS
1982 Mario Soto, P
1983 Mario Soto, P
1984 Dave Parker, OF

1985 Dave Parker, OF
1986 Dave Parker, OF
1987 Eric Davis, OF
1988 Danny Jackson, P
1989 Eric Davis, OF
1990 Barry Larkin, SS
1991 Barry Larkin, SS
1992 Bip Roberts, INF
1993 Joe Oliver, C
1994 Hal Morris, 1B
1995 Barry Larkin, SS
1996 Barry Larkin, SS
1997 Willie Greene, 3B
1998 Bret Boone, 2B
1999 Greg Vaughn, OF
2000 Danny Graves, P
2001 Dmitri Young, OF
2002 Aaron Boone, 3B
2003 Jose Guillen, OF
2004 Sean Casey, 1B
2005 Ken Griffey Jr., CF
2006 Rich Aurilia, INF
2007 Brandon Phillips, 2B
2008 Joey Votto, 1B
2009 Brandon Phillips, 2B
2010 Joey Votto, 1B
2011 Joey Votto, 1B
2012 Brandon Phillips, 2B

Source: Reds.com

unknown how much that event stuck with Lombardi, but in 1953 the Italian attempted suicide at the home of his friend in much the same manner as Hershberger. Doctors were able to save him despite his protestations, and Lombardi went on to live another 24 years before passing away in 1977 at the age of 69 in Santa Cruz, California.

Lombardi's death came nine years before the big catcher finally received the honor of a plaque in Cooperstown next to some of the greatest players of all time. The Schnozz never received much support from the baseball writers, topping out at 16 percent of the vote in 1964, but the Veterans Committee selected him for induction in 1986, a worthy choice for a man who was one of the greatest catchers of his era. He was so well-liked in Cincinnati that the award given to the Reds' Most Valuable Player each year is named in his honor. The franchise also honored him as one of four players to receive a statue outside Great American Ball Park when it opened in 2003. He'll be out in Crosley Terrace forever—down in his squat and ready to receive a pitch as one of the greatest catchers in Reds history.

48 Harry and George Wright

Born in Sheffield, England, the son of a prominent cricket player, Harry Wright came to Cincinnati to play cricket years after his family had immigrated to New York. He and his brother, George, 12 years his junior, had been brought up around sports and had played a fair share of baseball growing up. Harry had been a member of the famous New York Knickerbocker club but had returned to cricket when he came to Cincinnati where he was offered a salary to play for the Union Cricket Club. A year later, in 1866, he joined up with the Cincinnati Base Ball Club as the team captain (aka "manager").

Already 31 years old, Harry was still an athletic performer, serving as the squad's primary pitcher for three seasons. Wright played a role similar to today's general managers, seeking out new talent to add to the team and ensuring a quality nine took the field. He had recruited three players to the 1868 squad, all of whom were salaried players. The success of that team, which was a mix of paid and amateur players, convinced the Cincinnati club to announce that the following year's squad would feature all salaried players.

By that point, 21-year-old George Wright had established himself as one of the best baseball players in the country. Brought up on cricket like his brother, George took to baseball like a duck to water. In 1868 he was awarded the prestigious Clipper Medal as the best shortstop in the game. That winter, Harry contacted him with a chance to come and play for the Cincinnati Red Stockings as one of the salaried nine. George accepted the offer and the $1,800 contract that came with it.

Harry also recruited five other new players, giving the Reds not only the best player in the land but the best overall roster. Harry moved himself into center field, though his greatest contribution came as the team's manager. He was considered good-natured but firm in his management style. Author Harry Ellard wrote of Harry, "In correcting any mistake of his men, he never did it in an offensive or arbitrary manner. His favorite expression, 'You need a little more ginger,' acted as effectively as stronger language to infuse an extra amount of vim and action in his players. He was considered the best captain in the world."

George was the clear star of the team, a fan favorite with both the men and the women. He led the Red Stockings in just about every conceivable offensive category, and typically the next closest player was a considerable distance behind. The Wrights carried the

Red Stockings to an undefeated 57–0 record that year, drawing numerous fans to games wherever they traveled.

George suffered a serious knee injury in 1870, leading to some mild struggles by the Cincinnati nine. Despite those struggles, the squad still went 67–6–1 for the year, but by that point the club was losing money and the team management voted to return to amateur status in 1871.

Harry and George left Cincinnati that year to form the Boston Red Stockings, a team that would eventually become the Boston Braves, who are now housed in Atlanta. George became the first-ever batter in the newly formed National League in 1876, a special honor for the game's greatest star. In 1937, George was inducted into the National Baseball Hall of Fame. Sixteen years later, Harry, who had been given the unofficial title of "The Father of Professional Baseball," joined him. Both men were inducted into the Reds Hall of Fame in 2005 for their contribution toward making Cincinnati the birthplace of professional baseball.

49 Attend Reds Fantasy Camp

Imagine yourself waking up to a fresh, crisp morning. You drive to the ballpark, but you're not going there to watch. No, you walk in the back entrance and head to the clubhouse. Inside there are rows of lockers, each filled with a full set of uniforms. One of them has your name on it. You pinch yourself. It has to be a dream. But it's not—it's a fantasy.

Every year in Goodyear, Arizona, just before the big-league players come to town, the Reds host approximately 100 men and women for a week-long baseball experience unlike any other. Reds

Fantasy Camp is an opportunity for grown-up Reds fans to live the dreams of their youth and don a real big-league uniform to play the greatest game ever invented. That's just the tip of the iceberg, though. Fantasy Camp is so much more than just playing baseball.

For many of the attendees, the highlight of the week is the former big-league players who come to the camp as coaches. Players like Jim Maloney, Lee May, Jack Billingham, Tom Browning, and Billy Hatcher change the week from just a bunch of games to an unforgettable experience. They may give you a hint or two about how to improve your game, but the real reason they are there is to tell stories, and the first thing you learn at this camp is that big leaguers have some Doozies.

The camp is not all fun and games. There is some serious baseball to be played. Campers are drafted into teams by the coaches on the first day. A schedule is laid out with each team playing two games a day, one in the morning and one in the afternoon. While the games are competitive, there are plenty of at-bats to go around and every player is given a chance to play whatever position they'd like. So if you've ever dreamed of donning the tools of ignorance and setting up behind home plate, the opportunity is there.

The level of skill varies from former high school and college players to people who haven't played the game since they were kids. A couple of days into the week, however, the playing field is much more level as everyone's body starts to remind them of their age. This is why there are full-time Reds trainers on site to help with all the aches and pains one develops during the week. There is a price to pay to live that dream of being a big leaguer.

The fun doesn't end with the games. A couple of times during the week the coaches hold a Kangaroo Court where anything can and will happen. Teams typically take their coaches out to dinner one night and get to know the person, not just the player. Friendships build throughout the week, and some of the campers become so close that they hang out even after camp is over.

The final highlight of the week is when the campers take on the big leaguers for three innings each. Each team gets the chance to bat at least once against a big-league pitcher, which is a major thrill even if a Brad Lesley curveball is the most terrifying thing you've seen in the batter's box. The games are rarely close—they are major leaguers after all—but the excitement of playing against a boyhood idol can't be topped.

The excitement doesn't end once the camp is over as the Reds invite all the campers to Great American Ball Park during the summer to be introduced before a real Reds game. The following morning, campers get together for a friendly game on the field at GABP complete with a live scoreboard and PA announcer. From start to finish, Reds Fantasy Camp is a one-of-a-kind experience.

50 Bill McKechnie

In the history of the Reds during the World Series era, only one former Reds player has ever gone on to lead the team to the postseason. That man was Bill McKechnie. His playing days with the Reds were not particularly memorable. He spent a little more than a year with the team and only played 85 games as a backup infielder. The most memorable thing about his time as a player with the Reds is that he came to the team with two other future Hall of Famers, Christy Mathewson, who was finishing up his Hall of Fame career, and Edd Roush, who was just getting started on his. McKechnie would join the duo in the Hall of Fame, but for his work in the dugout, not on the field.

McKechnie's first managerial job was in Pittsburgh where he pushed a burgeoning team over the top and into the World

Reds Managers in the Hall of Fame

The Cincinnati Reds have been managed by 14 members of the National Baseball Hall of Fame, but only three of the managers made it into the Hall for their accomplishments as a manager. The Chicago Cubs, with 15, are the only team with more managers in the Hall. Here are each of the 14 Reds managers with their records and how they entered the Hall:

Manager	Years	W	L	PCT	HOF Reason
Charlie Comiskey	1892–94	202	206	.495	Pioneer/Exec
Buck Ewing	1895–99	394	297	.570	Player
Bid McPhee	1901–02	79	124	.389	Player
Joe Kelley	1902–05	275	230	.545	Player
Ned Hanlon	1906–07	130	174	.428	Manager
Clark Griffith	1909–11	222	238	.483	Player
Hank O'Day	1912	75	78	.490	Umpire
Joe Tinker	1913	64	89	.418	Player
Christy Mathewson	1916–18	164	176	.482	Player
Bobby Wallace	1937	5	20	.200	Player
Bill McKechnie	1938–46	744	631	.541	Manager
Rogers Hornsby	1952–53	91	106	.462	Player
Sparky Anderson	1970–78	863	586	.596	Manager
Tony Perez	1993	20	24	.455	Player

Series three years after grabbing the reins. Under McKechnie, the franchise won its second world championship, but a year later the manager was fired after a third-place finish. Hall of Famer Paul Waner, who played for McKechnie during his rookie season in 1926, had nothing but respect for his manager. "He knew baseball—the complete book," Waner said. "He knew the percentages, and he applied them to the ability of his players with amazing accuracy. I played for other good men, but McKechnie was in a class by himself."

That would be a common refrain for McKechnie as he moved on to St. Louis and took the Cardinals to the World Series in his only full season as manager. Next he managed for eight seasons in

Boston, toiling with the lowly Braves who had a small budget and little talent. He still managed to extract three winning seasons out of the squad, gaining the respect of many around baseball. When his contract was up after the 1937 season, his services were in high demand. Reds general manager Warren Giles outbid three other teams with a $25,000 contract, making McKechnie the third-highest-paid manager in the game. The hiring produced immediate results for the Reds.

In his first season with the team, McKechnie, who had earned the nickname "Deacon" for his quiet, clean living, turned a last-place team into a respectable winner. They only made it to fourth place, but an 82–68 record was the team's best record in a dozen years. The following year, McKechnie had fully implemented his pitching and defense mentality, and the Reds won their first NL Pennant in 20 years. A quick sweep at the hands of a powerful New York Yankees squad did not deter the Redlegs, and they came back in 1940 even more powerful.

That 1940 squad was the first Reds team to win 100 games in a season, and it was due in large part to a pitching staff that allowed half-a-run per game fewer than the rest of the league. McKechnie had a knack for getting the most out of his pitchers. It was said that, "If a pitcher can't win for McKechnie, he can't win for anyone." Both Bucky Walters and Paul Derringer thrived with McKechnie as their manager, in large part because the Deacon also knew the value of a great defensive unit. The Reds were in the top three in the NL in defensive efficiency every year that McKechnie was manager, and not coincidentally, they finished last the first year after he was gone.

McKechnie managed his squad through lots of hardship in that 1940 season, including the shocking suicide of backup catcher Willard Hershberger. All the while, he managed to keep an even keel in the clubhouse, garnering the respect of each of his players.

Third baseman Billy Werber described his manager as "the type of man who inspired players, won their confidence and affection, and built high team morale." The team responded with the franchise's second championship, McKechnie's second, as well.

The Reds remained on the winning side of the ledger for the next four seasons before stumbling back into futility in 1945. McKechnie stayed as manager until September of the following season before resigning his post. He never managed again in the big leagues, though he was a coach for Cleveland for three years and the Red Sox for two. He was inducted into the Hall of Fame in 1962, and he passed away from pneumonia three years after that. In 1967, he was inducted into the Reds Hall of Fame as the winningest manager into team history, although he has since been passed by Sparky Anderson.

51 Hometown Reds

Cincinnati has been known as a great baseball town for decades, but that reputation did not come about simply because of the Reds. Cincinnati's amateur talent pool rivals any metropolitan area, and the history of great players who have come out of the greater Cincinnati area is long and storied. It's even more special when those great players play for the hometown Reds, something that has happened frequently throughout the years.

Local stars making it big with the hometown club has been part of the Cincinnati history going all the way back to the 1869 Red Stockings. Charlie Gould played first base for those Red Stockings, socking 21 home runs and batting .457, which actually was the lowest average on the team. He returned to the Reds when they joined the National League in 1876 in its inaugural season, but still wasn't much of a hitter.

Hall of Famer Buck Ewing, born in nearby Hoagland, Ohio, finished his playing career in Cincinnati. He managed the Reds for five seasons with an impressive 394–297 record but the team never finished higher than third place. In 1939, he was the first person from the Cincinnati area to be elected to the National Baseball Hall of Fame. He was joined 25 years later by Miller Huggins, a Cincinnati native and University of Cincinnati grad who spent six seasons as the Reds' second baseman near the turn of the century. He is more famously known as Babe Ruth's first manager with the Yankees who led that team to six pennants and three World Series titles.

The years of World War II forced the Reds to look everywhere they could for talent. That's why in 1944 they brought in 15-year-old Joe Nuxhall from Hamilton High School. Nuxhall only made one appearance for the Reds that year, but he returned in 1952 as a 23-year-old and spent 14 of the next 15 years with the franchise, winning 130 games before calling it quits on the field and moving to the broadcast booth for nearly 40 years.

The story of Western Hills High product Herm Wehmeier is less happy. He joined the Reds for two games as an 18-year-old in 1945, but he didn't stick with the team until 1948. Over the next 6½ seasons he struggled to find control of his pitches or success, and fans booed him relentlessly because of it. "He was one of the greatest natural athletes we ever had in Cincinnati," Reds general manager Gabe Paul told *The Sporting News*. "But never in my long baseball experience have I heard a man booed as bitterly as was Wehmeier. Nothing he could do was right. Even when he won, they booed him." Eventually he was dealt to Philadelphia, and once away from the pressure of pitching at home, Wehmeier had some mild success with the Phillies and Cardinals.

Another Western Hills product who had no such trouble playing at home was Pete Rose. Cincinnati's favorite son spent 22 years with the franchise as a player and manager and still today gets a standing ovation whenever he's at the ballpark. Rose had the honor of playing with five other Cincinnati natives on the 1986 squad that he managed. Buddy Bell and Barry Larkin both graduated from Moeller High School, while pitcher Chris Welsh attended rival St. Xavier High School. Withrow's Ron Oester manned second base for 11 seasons in Cincinnati, and right fielder Dave Parker attended Courter Tech High School, even though he was born in Mississippi. Larkin went on to the Hall of Fame, Rose should be there, and both Parker and Bell had solid arguments for their candidacy. Not a bad group to come from one city.

A common theme for many of the Cincinnati natives who play for the Reds is a chance to come back home. Bill Doran and Todd Benzinger returned home to play for the world champion 1990 squad. Ken Griffey Jr., who also attended Moeller, famously said, "I'm finally home," before putting on a Reds hat the first time. Elder High's Jim Brosnan came home midway through his career and eventually turned that story into two successful books.

There is something special about baseball in Cincinnati that makes it a dream of local amateurs to play for the big-league squad here. This was merely a sampling of the number of players who have done so, with nearly 80 players born in or growing up in the Greater Cincinnati area playing at least one game with the team. And there is no reason to think that list won't continue to grow well into the future.

52 Join a Reds Fan Group

Rooter groups have been part of Reds baseball nearly since the start of Reds baseball. Fans used to organize themselves into cheering sections for the games, and during the Opening Day Parade, they would often march as a unit. Those types of groups still exist today, though they come in different shapes and sizes now.

One of the largest Reds rooter groups is Rosie Reds, a collection of about 2,000 fans whose membership earns them discounts on tickets and merchandise, entrance to special events, and, of course, the chance to march in the Opening Day Parade. The group, whose name is actually an acronym for Rooters Organized to Stimulate Interest and Enthusiasm in the Cincinnati Reds, was started in 1964 when then owner Bill DeWitt considered moving the Reds to another city because of a lack of attendance at the ballpark. Founded by Margaret Zimmer and Jeanette Heinze, the group was initially meant for women, but their success led to such high demand that they eventually allowed men to join, as well. At its peak, the group had more than 3,000 members with a waiting list of up to five years. Today, they have expanded to philanthropic work, as well, supporting the local Kid Glove program as well as contributing to scholarship funds.

Little Reds fans have a group of their own to join. The Reds Heads Kids Club is the official fan club for Cincinnati Reds fans ages 14 and younger. The club is organized by the Reds, and every year one of the players is chosen to be the "captain" of the Club. Kids who join the club get ticket vouchers, access to special autograph sessions, free admission to the Reds Hall of Fame and Museum, and a chance to run the bases or walk around the park in a pregame parade. Membership also comes with some quality prizes such as a hat, sunglasses, and a backpack that kids received with a 2012 membership. It's a good way to get a budding young fan more interested in the Reds.

For the fans who aren't satisfied to just watch the games at home, Provident Travel has annual Reds Rooters tours to enemy ballparks to catch the Redlegs in action. For more than 50 years, Reds Rooters have been going on road trips around the country to support the Reds. If you are looking for a short Reds-related vacation, Reds Rooters tours might be the thing for you.

However, if staying inside is more your thing, the Internet provides a bounty of fan sites to get involved in. Blogs such as RedReporter.com, RedlegNation.com, and BlogRedMachine.com, as well as message boards like RedsZone.com, give fans a sense of community as they discuss the latest goings on with the team. Twitter and Facebook also provide outlets for Reds fans to share their fandom with people from around the country. The Reds are one of the biggest embracers of social media in the majors, and they regularly hold events like tweet ups to bring fans together using social media as another way to connect with fans.

Rooting for the Reds isn't something you have to do all alone. There are lots of opportunities out there for socialization if you just know where to look.

Vada Pinson

In the 1960s, one Reds hitter had four separate 200-hit seasons by the age of 26 and it wasn't Pete Rose. Only four players (Ty Cobb, Mel Ott, Rogers Hornsby, and Hank Aaron) had more hits by their 29th birthday than the 1,691 hits this man had when he turned 29. And yet, many fans are unfamiliar with the accomplishments of Vada Pinson, perhaps the greatest center fielder in franchise history.

Pinson spent most of his career in the shadow of other great players. He grew up in West Oakland and attended the famous McClymonds High School that had produced Ernie Lombardi, Frank Robinson, Curt Flood, and NBA great Bill Russell. Pinson's first love wasn't baseball, but music. During high school, his intention had been to take on the trumpet as a career, but legendary Coach George Powles convinced Pinson that he had the athleticism to make a career out of baseball. And two years after graduating, Pinson was playing in the big leagues.

He made the Reds team out of spring training in 1958 at the age of 19. In his seventh big-league plate appearance, he launched a grand slam off Ron Kline, leading the Reds to a 4–1 victory, but as Pinson said, the home run may have set him back a bit.

"Probably the worst thing that happened to me was hitting that homer against Pittsburgh," Pinson said one year later. "It won the game but didn't do me any good. I started thinking of myself as a slugger."

He struggled over the team's next 18 games, and by mid-May he found himself back in the minors. By September he was recalled and he never played in the minor leagues again.

Pinson had an incredible season in 1959, doing things that very few 20-year-olds had ever done. His 47 doubles were the most ever by someone his age, and he joined Mickey Mantle and Willie Mays as the only 20-year-old center fielders to hit 20 or more home runs. He also joined teammate Frank Robinson as the only 20-year-olds to lead their league in runs scored. (Robinson led the NL in 1956 at age 20.)

Success at a young age was not the only thing Pinson and Robinson had in common as their friendship blossomed right

Outfielder Vada Pinson poses in Tampa, Florida, on March 4, 1968, during spring training. (AP Photo)

away. As Robinson recounted in his biography, "We were always together, Vada and I. We roomed together, lockered and dressed side by side.... We usually ate breakfast and dinner together. I had never been very close to anyone before, and it felt good."

The two players supported each other throughout their careers, and they were the Reds' top two hitters for the first half of the 1960s, especially in 1961 when Robinson won the MVP award with Pinson finishing third. Pinson would go on to lead the NL in hits, doubles, and triples twice each. He's still the only Reds player since 1940 to hit 12 or more triples in a season, something he did three times.

By the end of the 1968 season, the 30-year-old had amassed more hits as a Reds player than anyone other than Bid McPhee, but the team felt like his skills were diminishing and they shipped him off to St. Louis for Bobby Tolan and Wayne Granger. Pinson played another seven years in the big leagues, but he was never able to get back to the brightness of his early peak years and he retired in 1976 at the age of 37.

Pinson went on to be a big-league coach for several organizations, including the Detroit Tigers where he worked under Sparky Anderson, who had this to say after Pinson's death in 1995 from a stroke, "Vada never got the recognition, he never got any recognition at all. But not one time did I ever hear Vada bad-mouth anybody about it. He never said a bad word about it.... He would spit-shine those shoes of his every day. And he was one of the nicest men I've ever known."

Sparky was not alone in his praise of Pinson, not just as a player, but as a man. Former teammate Jerry Lynch called Pinson "a fine gentleman and the neatest person I have ever known." He also wondered, "How could a guy have over 2,700 hits and not be in the Hall of Fame?"

Lynch may have a point. Of players who are eligible for the Hall as of 2012, only Rafael Palmeiro (3,020) and Harold Baines

(2,860) have more career hits than Pinson's 2,757 and are not in the Hall—and both of those players have major question marks in their careers. As a Gold Glove–caliber center fielder with great speed and pretty good power, Pinson put together an impressive career, but he only made two All-Star Games and was rarely considered one of the superstars of the league. And ultimately that may be what keeps him out of the Hall.

54 George Foster

Great teams aren't just made up of stars. To be a truly great team, you need complementary players who fill in key roles as needed. When one of those complementary players becomes a star in his own right, then you know you've got something very special.

When the Reds traded with the San Francisco Giants for George Foster in May 1971, they were actually looking at a different outfield prospect at first. Bernie Williams was a promising 22-year-old prospect who had torn up Triple A in back-to-back years, but he had yet to translate that success to the big leagues. Either he or Foster would be the heir to center field once Willie Mays decided to hang up his cleats. At least that was the plan. General manager Bob Howsam and his crew had been working on a deal for Williams when the Giants suddenly decided they wanted to keep him, choosing to deal Foster instead. This was just fine for Howsam since he believed Foster, who had shown more pop up to that point, had a brighter future. So on May 29, 1971, the Reds dealt Frank Duffy and Vern Geishert for Foster. And then they waited patiently.

The quietly shy Tuscaloosa, Alabama, native was still a very raw prospect when the Reds acquired him. He made 98 starts in center after the trade but only hit .234/.289/.386 with 10 home runs and 50 RBIs. His playing time was greatly reduced the following year, starting just 31 of the 59 games he played that season. Foster did score the NLCS clinching run in Game 5 versus the Pirates on a Bob Moose wild pitch, his only appearance in the series, but otherwise the Reds demonstrated that they did not feel the thin right-hander was ready for regular playing time.

That fact was driven home even more when the 24-year-old was sent to Triple A Indianapolis at the start of the 1973 season. Foster was crestfallen, believing this was likely the end of his time with the Reds. However, the work that he put in at Indianapolis as well as in the Dominican Winter League impressed the Reds' brass and made them believe their patience was about to pay off. He saw more playing time in 1974, though he was still just a part-time player. Then the 1975 season came, and the 26-year-old started to put it all together.

That May, Sparky Anderson famously went to Pete Rose and asked him to play third base in order for the manager to get more offense into the sputtering Big Red Machine lineup. To that point, George Foster had been an occasional pinch hitter and right fielder, but Anderson knew that needed to change. With the move, Foster finally had a regular starting job in the big leagues, and after a slow start the first couple of weeks, he erupted. From the end of May until season's end, Foster hit .311/.373/.519 with 16 HR and 64 RBIs in 98 games. It's no coincidence that the Reds romped to the best record in baseball after the lineup change. He completed the year with a .300 average, finishing second on the team with 23 home runs and fourth with 78 RBIs.

The following year was even more impressive as Foster hit .306 and led the team in home runs with 29. He also led the National League with 121 RBIs, finishing second in the MVP voting to teammate Joe Morgan. He followed that season with the greatest power performance in Reds history. In his 1977 MVP season, he

George Foster follows through and watches the flight of his RBI-producing hit in a game with the Atlanta Braves in Cincinnati on October 2, 1977. Foster set a new club mark for RBIs with 149, but he failed in his bid to top Hack Wilson's National League home run mark. The Reds batter checked out with 52 homers, a club mark, and he ended the season with a .320 average to lead the club.
(AP Photo)

set franchise records in home runs (52) and RBIs (149) that still stand today. His .631 slugging percentage was only topped by Ted Kluszewski's .642 in 1954. Foster also led the league in runs with 124, and he led his team with a .320 batting average, finishing second on the team with a career-high 197 hits. His MVP was the third straight for the Reds and the sixth in eight seasons. Foster had become a star in the league, but unfortunately for him, his star was at its brightest during a period when the Big Red Machine was being disassembled.

Despite Foster's incredible year, the 1977 Reds finished well out of the race in second place with an 88–74 record. The 1978 team won 92 games but was again unable to topple the Los Angeles Dodgers, even with another league-leading performance from Foster who paced the NL with 40 home runs and 120 RBIs. With that 1978 season, Foster became the first player to lead the National League in RBIs for three consecutive seasons since Joe "Ducky" Medwick did it for the St. Louis Cardinals 40 years earlier.

Foster posted three more quality seasons with the Reds before he was dealt to the New York Mets prior to the start of the 1982 season. His career fizzled in the Big Apple, and what looked like a surefire Hall of Fame career wound up on the outside looking in. He joined his Big Red Machine teammates in the Reds Hall of Fame in 2003, and he can be seen at numerous fan events throughout the year.

55 Three Consecutive MVPs

Of the eight franchises that started the twentieth century in the National League, the Cincinnati Reds were the last team to have a league Most Valuable Player Award winner. Some of that is due to bad timing as the award was not doled out regularly in the NL until 1924, five years after the Reds' lone pennant win of the century's first three decades.

The franchise made up for lost time quickly in 1938 when Ernie Lombardi did something that only one catcher had ever done to that point—he led the National League in batting average. The

Schnozz hit a robust .342, knocking 30 doubles and 19 home runs while driving in 95 for the season. His .915 OPS was the second highest ever by an NL catcher.

Lombardi faced stiff competition for the award, especially from Cubs pitcher Bill Lee (22–9, 2.66 ERA), Pirates shortstop Arky Vaughan (.322/.433/.444), and Giants outfielder Mel Ott, who led the Senior Circuit in home runs, runs, and on-base percentage, and was second in RBIs and slugging percentage. Many voters were still drawn to Lombardi as he received 10-of-15 first-place votes and finished a safe distance in front of Lee, who came in second.

One of the most important factors in Lombardi's candidacy was the fact that the Reds were no longer the dregs of the National League. After a decade of futility, the team was on the way up, and a pennant win in 1939 placed them as the premier team in the National League.

The success helped catapult pitcher Bucky Walters to the 1939 MVP Award, just the fifth National League pitcher to win the award. The 30-year-old Walters went 27–11 with a 2.29 ERA and delivered one of the most dominating seasons ever assembled by a Reds pitcher, leading the NL in wins, innings, ERA, strikeouts, and complete games. His 31 complete games was the most by a Reds pitcher in 14 years, and only three big-league pitchers have topped that total since. But Walters wasn't just a force on the mound. The former third baseman hit an impressive .325 with eight doubles, a triple, and a home run in 131 trips to the plate.

Perhaps the most amazing thing about Walters' selection for the award was that his biggest competitors were his own team-mates. Fellow starting pitcher Paul Derringer (25–7, 2.93 ERA) finished third in the voting behind Johnny Mize (.349, 28 HR, 108 RBIs) of the Cardinals. First baseman Frank "Buck" McCormick (.332, 18 HR, 128 RBIs), who finished fifth in 1938, finished fourth in what turned out to be a tight three-way race for second place. Walters received 18-of-24 first-place votes and won the award handily.

McCormick's day arrived the following year as he became the Reds' third straight MVP winner in 1940. His win made the Reds the first major league team to have three different players win the award in three consecutive years, a feat that was matched by the 1942–44 St Louis Cardinals but hasn't been matched since in the National League.

Standing at 6'4", McCormick was the tallest everyday player in the majors in 1940, and the giant right-hander was an intimidating force at the plate. From 1938–40, Buck led the NL in hits, doubles, and RBIs, and he was fourth in average. The 1940 season might have been his worst of the three, but the voters had a hard time overlooking his 127 RBIs—53 more than any teammate—on a pennant-winning team. He also led the league in hits and doubles, making him a solid MVP, even if it was a down year for him.

For the second straight year, the Reds finished with three of the top four vote-getters for the NL MVP. Johnny Mize (.314, 43 HR, 137 RBIs), who was likely feeling cursed at this point, finished second again despite nearly winning the Triple Crown. Walters (22–10, 2.48 ERA) and Derringer (20–12, 3.06 ERA) joined McCormick in the top four, making the Reds the only team in NL history to have three of the top four vote-getters in the MVP race in back-to-back years.

The franchise would go on to win nine more MVPs in the next 70 years, including six in eight seasons during the 1970s, which is more than any other team besides the Cardinals. It may have taken the Reds a while to put themselves on the map come awards season, but they've been well represented ever since.

56 Don Gullett

By the time Don Gullett was drafted by the Cincinnati Reds in June 1969, he was already somewhat of a legend. At McKell High School in South Shore, Kentucky, Gullett was a multi-sport star who was worlds better than the competition. In one football game, Gullett scored six touchdowns and kicked six extra points. In a seven-inning baseball game with dozens of scouts on hand, Gullett struck out 20 batters and retired the other on a weak grounder back to the mound. Coming from a small town in Kentucky, one would suspect that there were legends of Gullett killing a bear with a toothpick, but legends aren't necessary when the real thing is so impressive.

The Reds knew when they drafted Gullett that he wouldn't spend much time in the minor leagues. He dominated at Sioux Falls after the draft, going 7–2 with a 1.96 ERA. His performance earned him an invite to spring training the following year, and that's where Gullett set about making jaws drop. The 19-year-old fireballer impressed everyone in camp and even a few opponents. Future Hall of Famer Willie Stargell put it succinctly, "Man, that kid throws nothing but wall-to-wall heat!"

Gullett made the team out of camp and pitched out of the bullpen during the 1970 season. He posted a 2.43 ERA while striking out nearly a batter an inning, but his control was a little shaky. Manager Sparky Anderson had great confidence in the lefty, though, making him the youngest NL hurler ever to pitch in the postseason. The fearless youngster handled the opportunity with great skill, allowing one earned run in 10⅓ innings in the NLCS and World Series. "I wasn't nervous a bit going in there," Gullett said. "Talking to all these reporters is a lot tougher than facing Willie Stargell or Roberto Clemente."

The Reds moved him into the rotation in 1971 and set about turning the lefty into a legitimate ace. That season, at the age of 20, Gullett went 16–6 with a 2.65 ERA, but the Reds stumbled to a fourth place finish. The following year, he contracted hepatitis early in the season and struggled with low energy. Anderson moved him back into the bullpen to help him get some rest. He returned to the rotation in August and went 5–3 with a 2.67 ERA over nine starts to close out the year. The Reds returned to the postseason, making it to the World Series despite two rocky starts from Gullett versus the Pirates, but they fell short of the championship, losing to the A's in seven games.

Gullett flirted with 20 wins in each of the next two seasons, winning 18 in 1973 and 17 in 1974, but that would be the closest the lefty would get. There was little doubt that he was one of the two or three best left-handed pitchers in the league, but injuries plagued the second half of Gullett's career. In 1975, he was 9–3 with a 2.09 ERA and was one out away from his fourth straight complete game when a line drive from Larvell Banks caromed off his pitching hand and broke his thumb. He returned two months later and won six of his eight remaining starts, finishing 15–4 with a 2.42 ERA. One can only imagine what could have been had Gullett remained healthy. Maybe he would have won the first Cy Young Award ever for the Reds.

It was shoulder and neck pain that got in the way of the 1976 season, causing Gullett to miss a month midway through the season. He still managed to go 11–3 with a 3.00 ERA, and his mid-90s fastball and tough forkball allowed him to continue to dominate hitters. He was the unquestioned ace of the Big Red Machine, starting Game 1 in each of the team's World Series championships.

Still only 25 when the Reds clinched their second straight title, Gullett had already amassed a 91–44 record with a 3.03 ERA. It was also the start of free agency, and general manager Bob Howsam had no interest in getting into a bidding war for Gullett's services. The New York Yankees swooped in and made Gullett their first ever free-agent signing, giving the young man a six-year deal worth nearly $2 million. Little did they know that less than two years later, a shoulder injury would force Gullett to retire long before his 30th birthday.

Perhaps if he had pitched in a later era with better medical technology, Gullett might have been able to continue what was surely a Hall of Fame career. It's a question we'll never be able to answer. However, for seven years Gullett put up impressive numbers with the Reds. His .674 winning percentage is easily the highest in franchise history for pitchers with at least 50 decisions. He returned to the Reds in 1993 as the team's pitching coach, a position he held until 2005. During that time, he helped several pitchers return to success after injury, something he was never able to do.

57 The 1970 NL Pennant Winners

By the time the 1960s ended, the Reds' offense had already been dubbed the Big Red Machine, but their pitching made them one of the more disappointing teams in baseball. In back-to-back seasons to closeout the '60s, the Reds led the National League in runs, but their run prevention was at the bottom of the barrel, leaving the team with a fourth- and third-place finish in consecutive seasons. Recognizing that changes needed to be made, general manager Bob Howsam made one small change and one big one with hopes of igniting his team. He traded Alex Johnson and Chico Ruiz to the Angels for Pedro Borbon and Jim McGlothlin. Borbon solidified the bullpen, and McGlothlin gave the Reds some much-needed starting pitching depth.

The big change came when Howsam fired manager Dave Bristol and replaced him with an unknown minor league manager named Sparky Anderson. Despite the coif of prematurely graying hair, Anderson was only 36 years old, which was not an issue since the Reds were the youngest team in the league. An early injury to ace Jim Maloney meant that 26-year-olds McGlothlin and Jim Merritt were the veterans on the staff. Twenty-nine-year-old Pete Rose was the team's elder statesman. Anderson had his hands full with the young but supremely talented team.

The Reds once again had a high-powered offense finishing third in the NL in runs scored. They were led by league MVP Johnny Bench, who swatted 45 home runs and drove in 148 runs, which was a team record at the time. Third baseman Tony Perez added 40 homers and 129 RBIs of his own. Bobby Tolan led the NL with 57 stolen bases, and Perez, Tolan, and Pete Rose all finished in the top 10 in batting average. The much-improved pitching staff featured excellent performances from youngsters Wayne Simpson (14–3, 3.02 ERA) and Gary Nolan (18–7, 3.27), while Merritt went 20–12 and McGlothlin added a 14–10, 3.59 ERA performance. The trio of Wayne Granger, Clay Carroll, and 19-year-old Don Gullett was nearly unhittable, giving the Reds one of the league's top bullpens. The combination of excellent hitting and improved pitching led to a 102–60 record, the franchise's second 100-win season, and a 14½-game lead in the NL West at season's end.

The Reds swept through the playoffs, scoring only three runs in each game but stifling the Pittsburgh Pirates' offense in the first of four postseason meetings between the two teams during the 1970s. The offense was led by Perez and Tolan, but it was the pitching staff that deserved most of the credit as only two of the seven pitchers used surrendered a run. With the sweep, the Reds headed to their first World Series in nine years to take on the powerhouse Baltimore Orioles squad that had won 108 games—it was their second straight season with at least that many victories.

The Big Red Machine made their presence known early, taking a 3–0 lead in Game 1, but the Orioles battled back and then third baseman Brooks Robinson took over. First, to lead off the bottom of the sixth inning, Robinson made a dazzling play in the field, ranging well to his right, snagging a ground ball, and throwing blindly to first base to nab Lee May. Then with one out in the top of the seventh, Robinson hit a go-ahead home run that would seal the 4–3 victory for the Orioles.

From that point forward, Robinson had one of the greatest individual World Series performances in history. Defensively, he made one sparkling play after another, robbing hits from May, Perez, and Bench like clockwork. At the plate, he was unstoppable, batting .429 and slugging .810 with two home runs and six RBIs in the series. He was undoubtedly the Series MVP as the Orioles topped the Reds 4–1. All manager Sparky Anderson could do after the Series was tip his cap to the Orioles third baseman and hope that he'd never see him again in future World Series games.

58 Gary Nolan

The history of Reds pitching is replete with hurlers with great stuff whose careers were cut short by injury. Jim Maloney, Don Gullett, Mario Soto, and Jose Rijo are just some of the many pitchers who have had great but short-lived success in a Reds uniform. Of them all, the brightest star to be snuffed out by injury may have been right-hander Gary Nolan.

Nolan was a first-round pick of the Reds in June 1966 out of Oroville, California. A dominating performance in Sioux Falls that summer earned Nolan an invite to spring training where he wowed everyone from his teammates to the umpires with a blazing fastball and an impressive curveball. "He's the best-looking pitcher I've seen this spring—and I mean the best," umpire Augie Donatelli exclaimed after watching Nolan shut down the Red Sox for three innings. Nolan's performance earned him a spot in the Reds' rotation even though he was still only 18 years old.

When Nolan made his big-league debut on April 15, he was the first 18-year-old pitcher to start for the Reds since Herm Wehmeier did it 22 years prior. The difference is that while Wehmeier helped fill a roster depleted by the war, Nolan was legitimately ready to pitch in the big leagues. He struck out eight Cubs in 7⅓ innings in his first start, capturing his first win. His second start was a nine-inning gem where he struck out a dozen Dodgers while only allowing one run, but the Reds' failure to score more than one run until extra innings kept Nolan from back-to-back victories.

He cruised through his rookie season with a 14–8 record and a 2.58 ERA. His 206 strikeouts were the second most all time by a teenager behind only Bob Feller (since passed by Dwight Gooden). Nolan led all rookie pitchers in strikeouts and ERA, but somehow he only managed a third-place finish in Rookie of the Year voting behind pitchers Tom Seaver and Dick Hughes.

It was the following spring training when the pain in Nolan's shoulder started to make itself known. He missed the first two months of the season but pitched well when he returned, going 9–4 with a 2.40 ERA in 22 starts. He hit the disabled list once again in 1969, missing most of the middle of the season and only making 15 starts for the year. He came back healthy in 1970 and made 37 starts, going 18–7 for the pennant-winning Reds. He started Game 1 in both the NLCS and World Series, but it wasn't long before a bitterness developed between Nolan and his manager.

Nolan looked like he could be on his way to a Cy Young Award midway through the 1972 season when he started the year 13–2 with a 1.71 ERA. However, during an awkward throw on a defensive play, Nolan heard something pop, and he was in great pain. The Reds' medical staff was unable to find any structural damage and even sent Nolan to the dentist to have an abscessed molar removed, thinking that might be the cause of the pain. When that didn't relieve the issue, manager Sparky Anderson was convinced that Nolan's problem was mental. Nolan was hurt that the Reds didn't believe him, but he tried to pitch through the pain. Eventually, it became too much, and the doctors were forced to try multiple surgeries to remove bone spurs from his shoulder.

The Reds' ace missed most of the next two seasons, and when he finally did return for the 1975 season, he had remade himself from a power pitcher into a control artist. Nolan went 15–9 for each of the Big Red Machine's championship teams, throwing more than 200 innings each season and leading the NL in fewest walks per nine innings both years. Injuries crept up again in 1977 and by then the Reds were ready to move on, dealing Nolan to the California Angels for a minor leaguer. He made five disastrous starts for the Angels that year before he was released. He tried to catch on with the Milwaukee Brewers in 1978, but the writing was on the wall and Nolan's career was done before his 30th birthday.

As with many Reds pitchers of the 1960s and '70s, it's hard not to think about what Nolan's career would have been like with more advanced medical care. He was inducted into the Reds Hall of Fame in 1983 where he resides as one of the greatest pitchers in team history, even if he was never able to reach his full potential.

59 Paul Derringer

Born Samuel Paul Derringer in Springfield, Kentucky, in 1906, the man they nicknamed "Oom Paul" was both short-tempered and highly competitive. Derringer toiled in futility with the bad Reds teams of the 1930s before joining forces with Bucky Walters to create the greatest pitching tandem in team history.

Derringer's career with the Reds got off to an inauspicious start. After he was acquired from the Cardinals in a deal for Leo Durocher, he went 7–25 with the Reds in 33 games despite a solid 3.23 ERA. Having made three starts previously for St. Louis that year, he finished the year with 27 losses, the only pitcher since 1910 to reach that mark. Even with the terrible record in his first season, the Reds never gave up on the hard-throwing right-hander, but it was not because they didn't want to.

After a 10–14 season where he posted a below-average 4.04 ERA in 1937, new Reds general manager Warren Giles sent a message to incoming manager Bill McKechnie saying, "Derringer lacks guts, should try to trade him." McKechnie was familiar with Derringer from his days in St. Louis, and he convinced Giles to hold on to the pitcher. Good thing he did because under McKechnie, Derringer shined. In 1938, as the Reds started to right the ship after years of mediocrity, Oom Paul led the National League in complete games and innings pitched, posting the lowest ERA of his career at 2.93 and winning 20 games for the second time as a Red.

He was even better the following year when he finished third in the MVP race behind teammate Bucky Walters. Derringer made himself into a control artist, and he led the league with 1.0 walks per nine innings pitched, compiling a 25–7 record and once again posting a 2.93 ERA. With those 25 wins, Derringer joined Walter

Johnson as the only pitchers of the modern era to lose 25+ games in a season and then win 25+ games in a later season. Walters and Derringer carried the Reds to their first pennant in 20 seasons, but they fell to the powerful Yankees in four games.

Derringer led the league in walk rate the following season, as well. According to Lonnie Wheeler and John Baskin from their book, *The Cincinnati Game*, Derringer's "control was so good that he once stood on the mound blindfolded and threw six of 10 pitches over the plate for strikes." He went 20–12 with a 3.06 ERA that season, joining Noodles Hahn as the only Reds pitchers to win 20 games in three straight seasons. He finished fourth in the MVP voting and once again led the Reds to the postseason. This time they faced the Detroit Tigers. Derringer made three starts, winning two of them, including a Game 7 complete game to clinch the title for the Reds.

For all of his success, Derringer was also known as a hothead, frequently ending up in fights with teammates, opponents, and even a politician. In 1936, Reds general manager Larry MacPhail fined Derringer for not sliding into second base during a game. Furious, Derringer flung an inkwell at MacPhail, just missing him. Startled, MacPhail screamed, "You might have killed me," to which Derringer replied, "That's what I was meaning to do." MacPhail reportedly wrote a check for a $750 bonus to Derringer, saying, "That's a bonus for missing me."

Derringer stayed with the Reds until 1942 when he was sold to the Cubs. He made it to the World Series one more time with the Cubs in 1945 before hanging up his spikes. He was inducted into the Reds Hall of Fame as part of the initial class in 1958. His 161 career wins as a Red ranks third in team history and hasn't been topped by any pitcher since he retired.

60 David Concepcion

David Concepcion's father had high hopes for his son to one day become a doctor or lawyer, but that wasn't in the stars for the young Venezuelan. His father would just have to settle for him being one of the best shortstops to ever play baseball.

When Concepcion joined the Reds' big-league squad in 1970, he was so thin that he was practically translucent. Teammate Pete Rose kidded that the young shortstop was unlikely to ever pull a muscle since he didn't appear to have any. Concepcion's rail-like figure disguised some burgeoning talent that not everyone saw coming, but manager Sparky Anderson did.

Despite being fairly raw at 21 years old, Anderson started Concepcion at shortstop in 38 of the team's first 43 games of the 1970 season. The youngster held his own at the plate, batting around .260 for most of the season, but he was prone to many mental mistakes at the plate and in the field, forcing Anderson to cut back on his playing time.

The mental mistakes would keep Concepcion in a part-time role for the next two seasons, as well, but the support of his teammates eventually helped him to blossom into an All-Star at the shortstop position. Tony Perez became his roommate early in his career and taught him several things about hitting, but mostly helped Davey learn to let go of the bad days and keep a positive attitude. Teammate Joe Morgan taught Concepcion how to be a better base runner and constantly reminded him not to take plays off while in the field. And Rose was always there to keep his shortstop loose with a quick barb now and then.

The excitable youngster wasn't one to miss out on the fun, though. One time in Chicago while mired in a long slump,

Retired Numbers

Any Reds player would be honored to one day get a plaque in the Reds Hall of Fame, but the ultimate honor that the franchise could give to a player, the one that makes them the elite of the elite in franchise history, is to retire his number permanently. Only 10 numbers in Reds history have been officially put on the permanently unavailable list (let's be honest, no one is ever getting No. 14 again while there is a Stowe running the clubhouse). Those men include two managers, four Big Red Machiners, two other Hall of Famers, and an iconic slugger and coach. There is also the No. 42 belonging to Jackie Robinson, which has been retired by every team in baseball.

Here are the numbers retired by the Cincinnati Reds and when they were retired.

No. 1 Fred Hutchinson—1965
No. 5 Johnny Bench—1984
No. 8 Joe Morgan—1998
No. 10 Sparky Anderson—2005
No. 11 Barry Larkin—2012
No. 13 Dave Concepcion—2007
No. 18 Ted Kluszewski—1998
No. 20 Frank Robinson—1998
No. 24 Tony Perez—2000
No. 42 Jackie Robinson—1997

NOTE: The Reds have also retired the microphones of legendary broadcasters Waite Hoyt, Joe Nuxhall, and Marty Brennaman.

Source: Reds.com

Concepcion jokingly got into an industrial clothes dryer, claiming he was going to "warm up." Pat Zachry closed the door on Davey, which automatically started the machine. Startled, Zachry jerked open the door quickly, and Concepcion tumbled out with a few singed hairs. The move seemed to work as Davey had three hits that day and hit better than .340 for the next two months.

Concepcion eventually managed to put together some solid offensive seasons, especially when you consider the level of offense that was typically expected of shortstops in his day. For his peak years from 1973–82, Concepcion batted .282 with a .723 OPS. Only Garry Templeton topped those two numbers for NL shortstops, and he had some two-thousand fewer plate appearances during that span.

However, it wasn't Concepcion's bat that put him on the field. It was his glove. He was a genius at the shortstop position, and his manager knew it. "He was an Einstein out there," Anderson said.

Morgan, who played second base next to him for eight seasons, called him "the best shortstop I ever played with and the best shortstop I ever saw." Even his opponents had incredible respect for his abilities with the glove. "I would have been a .300 lifetime hitter if it wasn't for him," former Cardinal Joe Torre once said. "He made shortstop look so easy."

Concepcion would win five Gold Gloves at shortstop, more than any National Leaguer besides Ozzie Smith. He is also credited with inventing the intentional one-hop, quick-release throw from the hole at shortstop, which allowed him to play much deeper at shortstop and get to more balls than the average player.

When Concepcion retired after the 1988 season, he had spent more consecutive years with the Reds than any player in history and his 2,488 games with the franchise are the second most all time behind only Rose. In 2007, the team gave him its highest honor by retiring his number 13. At the time of the retirement, Reds owner Bob Castellini noted his defensive prowess, saying, "Davey made the No. 13 bad luck to any player to hit the ball to the left side."

Despite all of the honors and accolades within the organization, Concepcion still remains on the outside looking in at Cooperstown. There are certainly arguments to be made that Concepcion is better than several of the shortstops already in the Hall, but a lack of defining landmarks—he did not reach 2,500 hits, 400 doubles, or 1,000 runs or RBIs—as well as having been overshadowed by so many great teammates, will make it difficult for Davey to ever join his teammates in Cooperstown. He is no longer on the writers' ballot, and while the Veteran's committee has elected similar players like Phil Rizzuto and Pee Wee Reese in the past, Concepcion has not come close to induction at this point.

Perhaps one day Davey will be recognized as not only the best shortstop of his era but as one of the greatest of all time. Until then, he will always be remembered by Reds fans as the defensive glue of the Big Red Machine and one of the greatest Reds of all time.

61 The Ragamuffin Reds

The build up of the Cold War at the end of World War II coincided with one of the coldest periods in franchise history for the Reds, er, Redlegs. From 1945–60, the franchise averaged a 71–83 record, a record that only topped the Cubs and Pirates in the National League. In those 16 seasons, the Reds finished fifth or worse in the NL 13 times, never better than third place, and every other NL team played in the World Series at least once. But not the Reds. Not even a name change to the more politically correct "Redlegs"—lest the franchise be mistaken as communist sympathizers—could shake the decade-and-a-half-long doldrums.

Hope began to stir in the mid-fifties though with the emergence of one of the game's great young players, Frank Robinson. A couple of years later, another 20-year-old and a former high school mate of Robinson's named Vada Pinson joined the fray, and the Reds found themselves with one of the best young outfield tandems in baseball. All that was needed now was some pitching to give the offense some support.

On December 15, 1960, the Reds made a three-way deal involving the Milwaukee Braves and the Chicago White Sox. In the deal, the team parted with long-time shortstop Roy McMillan and pitcher Cal McLish. In return they received third baseman Gene Freese from the White Sox and a 25-year-old starting pitcher named Joey Jay from the Braves. Jay had been a "bonus baby" who was never able to reach the potential that the Braves saw when they signed him in 1953. By most accounts, Freese was the more important player acquired in the deal. He had averaged 20 HR and 74 RBIs during the previous two seasons. Both players would play key roles in the success of the 1961 Reds.

Tragedy affected the team early on. During spring training, team owner Powel Crosley Jr. died of a heart attack. He had owned the team for 27 years, and ownership was transferred to a trust run by some of his family members. The season started on a bit of a down note, and despite winning its first three games and five of its first seven, an eight-game losing streak had the team at 5–10 and already four games out of first place. Coming off a dark decade, there was little reason to believe that this season would be the one to turn it around.

But things did turn around, and quickly. The Reds followed their eight-game losing streak with a nine-game winning streak, tallying up 13 wins in 15 games overall. By the end of May they were 26–16 and tied for first place with the San Francisco Giants. By the middle of July they were 25 games over .500 and had a six-game lead on the second-place Los Angeles Dodgers.

A major agent for the Redlegs rally was Joey Jay, who was outstanding during the first half of the season, posting a 12–4 record and 2.65 ERA at the All-Star break. He paced the NL in wins and ERA at the break, making his only All-Star team that year. An 8–10 stretch out of the break coupled with a white-hot 12–1 streak from the Dodgers dropped the Reds back into second place, and the teams bounced back and forth in the standings for the next two weeks. The Reds took over first place during a series sweep in Los Angeles in mid-August, and they never looked back.

The season featured many great individual performances. Robinson set a career high in extra-base hits and led the league in slugging, OPS, and intentional walks on his way to being named the Reds first league MVP since 1940. Pinson finished second in the NL with a .343 batting average, the highest average by a Reds player in 23 years. His 208 hits paced the National League. Jerry Lynch set the franchise's single-season pinch-hit home run record with five such bombs. The pitching staff was led by Jay (21–10, 3.53 ERA), Jim O'Toole (19–9, 3.10), and Bob Purkey (16–12, 3.73), the first time in 20 years the team had three pitchers win 16+ games.

After unexpectedly winning 93 games—including seven different win streaks of five or more games—the World Series was a letdown as the Reds ran into the buzz saw New York Yankees who were in the middle of another one of their dynasties. The Yankees won the series 4–1, taking the last two games in Cincinnati in convincing 7–0 and 13–5 fashion.

Despite the sour ending, the season marked the beginning of a new era for Reds baseball. During the 21-year span from 1961–81, they were the only NL team to average more than 90 wins a year. The chilly 1940s and '50s quickly melted into the golden age of Reds baseball, all starting with the excitement of 1961.

62 Catch the Reds Caravan

Winter can be a cruel time of year for baseball fans. Thankfully Reds fans have Redsfest every year to help get them through the coldest months of the year. While Redsfest is a great event, what are fans supposed to do in the two months between Redsfest and spring training? If you live in the area known as Reds Country, just wait until January and the Reds will come to you.

The Reds Winter Caravan is an annual event spanning four states and more than 2,600 miles of travel. Each year, three buses carrying current, former, and future Reds players, front office members, broadcasters, and mascots set out from Cincinnati to a variety of stops around Reds Country to meet fans, sign autographs, and tell stories. Each bus tours a different region, with the North Tour making stops in places ranging from Dayton, Ohio, to Parkersburg, West Virginia. The Southern Tour covers towns from Charleston, West Virginia, to Bowling Green, Kentucky, and the Western Tour goes from Muncie, Indiana, to Louisville, Kentucky. All three tours make multiple stops along the way, with the 2012 tour featuring 15 stops altogether.

Each event is free and open to the public, though seating can be limited by the space of the hosting facility. Events typically last about two hours and feature a panel discussion by the players and management, a question-and-answer session involving the fans, and time for autographs and pictures. It's a one-of-a-kind opportunity for fans who do not often get a chance to see players up close to meet some current and future stars of the team.

Fans unable to make it out to the tour stops will still have ample opportunity to hear from the players and management since the majority of local Reds affiliates often interview the tour members during their stops. Since it's the off-season, these interviews tend to be more open and irreverent, giving fans insights into the player's personality that they normally wouldn't see. The highlight of the tours is storytelling and humorous banter among the former and current players and broadcasters, and this usually comes through in the interviews, as well.

While the Winter Caravan is mainly a pep rally to drum up interest for the upcoming season, there are also some sales aspects to the trip. Fans can buy a limited number of tickets at some of the events, and those fans with kids have the opportunity to register their kids for the Reds Heads Kids Club. There is also a select-a-seat event for prospective season-ticket holders held every year at the Great American Ball Park stop.

The thing that sticks out more than anything at these stops is the camaraderie among the members of the organization. One of the tours, always fronted by Marty Brennaman, calls themselves the Rock Star tour in a flourish of self-promotion. It's all done in fun, but the competition of who is the best group on the tour drives each group to make each stop the best one yet. As Brennaman said, "We simply work harder to put a smile on every face at each stop along the way." There's not a lot more to ask for when you are just trying to make it through a long winter slog and get back to baseball.

63 Dolf Luque

When it comes to playing in the Major Leagues, Dolf Luque was lucky. He wasn't lucky in the sense that his statistics were much better than his performance. In fact, it was quite the opposite. In the 12 years that he pitched for the Reds, he posted an ERA that was about 20 percent better than the league average, one of the top 20 in the game during that span, yet all he had to show for it was a 154–152 record. He was one of the true hard-luck pitchers of his era.

Luque was lucky because he happened to be fair-skinned and blue-eyed. During a time when the integration of the game was still 30 years off, the Cuban-born Adolfo Domingo de Guzman Luque never would have gotten a shot in the big leagues had his skin been darker. That didn't protect him from the racism that was common in the game at the time, but at least he got to be on the field, which is more than a lot of talented players could say.

Luque was very talented, too. The game's first Latin star, he twice led the National League in ERA, and in 1923 he put together arguably the best pitching season in Reds history. That year he went 27–8 with a 1.93 ERA, leading the NL in wins, ERA, winning percentage, and shutouts. His 27 victories are the most by any Reds pitcher in the modern era, and his 1.93 ERA has not been matched by any qualifying Reds pitcher since. More impressively, his 27-win season came on the heels of a year when Luque went 13–23, leading the NL in losses. He was the first NL pitcher in more than 40 years to lead the league in losses one season and in wins the next.

The Cuban was one of three 20-game winners for the Reds in 1923, but a powerful New York Giants team dominated the NL that season and trapped the Reds in second place. They would finish second three times during Luque's tenure with the team, though they did win the World Series in 1919, his second season with the organization. Luque was mainly used as a reliever that season but he was effective, going 10–3 with a 2.63 ERA in 106 innings.

While possibly just part of the stereotyping that was common of early Latin players, Luque is often remembered as having one of the hottest tempers of his time. In what may be an apocryphal incident, Luque was said to have been pushed over the edge one day by Giants center fielder Casey Stengel. Stengel was supposedly slinging racial slurs at Luque from the dugout, though one version of the story says it was outfielder Bill Cunningham, not Stengel. Luque, having reached his boiling point, laid down the ball and his glove on the mound and charged into the Giants dugout throwing haymakers, one of which landed on Stengel's jaw, ending Luque's day on the mound and leaving Stengel in a great deal of pain.

Whether that specific story is true or not, there are many like it that describe Luque's temper, including another where he brandished a weapon in the clubhouse while managing in Cuba as a means to convince his pitcher to take the mound that day. It was that fire that made him one of the more memorable Reds pitchers in history. His 154 victories as a Red ranks fifth all time, garnering the right-hander election to the Reds Hall of Fame in 1967. If only he could have been a little more lucky on the mound, perhaps that would not be the only Hall of Fame to induct him.

64 Clinchmas 2010

The 2000s weren't the worst decade of baseball in team history, but given the level of expectation that fans had going into the decade, it may have been the most disappointing. The century started with the acquisition of Ken Griffey Jr. and a respectable 85-win season. But the next nine years would see five general managers, five managers, and not a single winning season on the ledger.

There was hope but very little expectation for the team when the 2010 season started. After years of neglecting the farm system, the team had finally built up a bevy of young talent to hopefully carry them back to glory. But there were still questions about the readiness of that talent.

Two days into May, the team was already five games out of first place after having allowed the third-most runs in the National League. Whatever expectations fans may have developed were mostly trashed at that point. Things turned around quickly though as the team won 9-of-10 and moved into first place by themselves after May 1 for the first time since 2006. The next two months would see the Reds and St. Louis Cardinals trade blows, both figuratively and literally, swapping first and second between them several times during the summer.

Finally on August 15, just five days after an ugly brawl that was part of a three-game sweep by the Cardinals in Great American Ball Park, the Reds took over first place for good. Their lead eventually got up to eight games as the team went 14–4 while the Cardinals went into a tailspin.

Despite the large lead, it would still be nearly a month before the Reds could pop the champagne, but when they finally did, it would come on one of the most memorable nights in Reds history.

The Reds returned home on September 28 from a nine-game road trip needing one win to clinch their first playoff birth in 15 years. They faced the third-place Astros, who had been one of the NL's better teams since the end of July. The Reds got a quick run in the bottom of the first inning, but a two-spot from the Astros in the top of the second meant the Reds would have to re-earn the nickname fans had given them during the year, "The Comeback Kids."

The Reds led the league in come-from-behind victories in 2010 with 45, showing the resilience of a team that was hungry for its first taste of the postseason. Led by league MVP Joey Votto, the team outpaced the NL in runs scored with 790 and boasted one of the game's best defenses with Gold Glove–caliber play at just about every position. Both of those facets of the team would be factors on this night.

In the third inning with a man on first base, Astros slugger Carlos Lee launched a ball deep to center field that looked destined for the grassy plot in front of the black batter's eye. Center fielder Drew Stubbs glided back to the wall, tracking the ball's path the whole way, and then he leapt just as he reached the wall to snatch it from its intended destination and saved two runs for the Redlegs.

The Reds strung together some hits three innings later to tie the game on Brandon Phillips' bases-loaded single, and the 30,000+

home fans salivated at what looked like a big inning. However, Jay Bruce hit into an inning-ending double play and the fans were left unsatiated.

Bruce would get a chance to redeem himself, but it wouldn't come until the bottom of the ninth inning. The Reds left-hander led off that inning with the score still tied and left-hander Tim Byrdak on the mound. Bruce blasted the first pitch delivered to him deep off the center field batter's eye and ebulliently floated around the bases with his fist thrust into the air. He had not only delivered the sockdolager to the Astros, but to the Cardinals and the rest of the NL Central, as well. The Reds were playoff-bound for the first time in a decade-and-a-half.

With his blast, Bruce joined Bobby Thomson, Hank Aaron, Alfonso Soriano, and Steve Finley as the only walk-off home runs to clinch a postseason berth for their team. Tampa Bay Rays third baseman Evan Longoria would join the group in 2011.

The Reds went on to get swept in the Division Series by the Philadelphia Phillies, but that did not take the shine off the team's return to national prominence and the memory of one of the most exciting home runs in franchise history.

The Lost Seasons of 1981 and 1994

Labor disputes have been part of the game for more than 40 years now, but outside of shortening the schedule of a couple of seasons, the postseason has only been directly affected by labor strife twice. And the Reds were victims in both cases.

In 1981, players went on strike on June 12 over a dispute about the nature of free-agent compensation. At the time of the strike, the Reds were 35–21, a half-game behind the Los Angeles Dodgers in the NL West. When the dispute was finally settled on July 31, teams had lost between 52 and 60 games on their schedule. Since there wasn't time to make up those games, Major League Baseball looked for other possible solutions. Inexplicably they settled on a split-season format with a first-half division winner and a second-half division. Why they couldn't just pick up where they left off is anyone's guess.

The main issues with the split-season is that it left little incentive for the first-half winner to be competitive in the second-half since they had already captured a playoff spot. Not surprisingly, the four first-half winners—the Dodgers, Philadelphia Phillies, New York Yankees, and Oakland A's—finished the second half a combined 104–101 after being 54 games over .500 as a group in the first half.

The Reds had just missed out on a first-half title by a half-game and finished in second in the NL West in the second half, just a game-and-a-half behind the Houston Astros. What was bigger news, from the Reds perspective, was that when you combine the records from both halves of the season, the Reds finished with a 66–42 record, the best in all of baseball. Rather than splitting the season into two halves, if the league had chosen to pick up where it left off, the Reds would have won the NL West by four games over the Los Angeles Dodgers. Similarly, in the NL East the St. Louis Cardinals finished in second place in both halves of the season, leaving them with the division's best record but on the outside of the playoffs.

It was a last gasp of success for what was left of the Big Red Machine as the Reds followed up a disappointing year of success with one smothered in futility.

Thirteen years after a work stoppage ruined the Reds' chance at a postseason berth, another labor dispute threatened to ruin the season of possibly the best Reds team assembled since the Big Red

Machine. Managed by Davey Johnson, the 1994 Reds were an offensive dynamo in a league built on offense. Carried by former NL MVP Kevin Mitchell, the team scored runs at will, leading the NL in runs per game and threatening the modern franchise record of 857 runs scored set by the 1976 squad. The pitching staff was headed up by Jose Rijo and John Smiley, and games were closed out by Jeff Brantley. It wasn't an unstoppable staff like they had in Atlanta, but it was still one of the best in the league.

As labor negotiations heated up throughout the summer, it became more and more apparent that a work stoppage was imminent. When the day finally came—August 12 to be precise—there was still hope among all parties that the season would be resumed in time for the playoffs. At the time, the Reds were in first place, a half-game up on the Houston Astros. A month later, little progress had been made and acting commissioner Bud Selig was forced to cancel the remainder of the season and the playoffs. A postseason berth was far from guaranteed, but the disruption of a possible playoff run once again left a bitter taste in the mouths of Reds fans.

No fan likes a labor dispute to get in the way of enjoying baseball, but you'll have to excuse Reds fans if they are particularly turned off by it. Getting burned twice in 13 years will do that.

66 Support the Reds Community Fund

With their high profile in the Cincinnati area, the Reds organization knows that they have a unique ability to affect change within the surrounding community. This is why, in 2001, the team created the Reds Community Fund, a non-profit arm of the organization that connects at-risk children with baseball and develops fundraising programs that connect baseball with the community. The primary goal of the Reds Community Fund is to use baseball as a conduit to improve the lives of less fortunate children in the Cincinnati area.

The RCF works with organizations like Reviving Baseball in the Innercity (RBI) to give kids in urban settings a place to learn and play baseball. The Reds take it one step further and rebuild fields throughout Reds Country to improve those opportunities for as many communities as possible. Since 2006, the RCF has worked with local communities and governments to renovate more than 275 baseball fields, making baseball and softball more accessible to youth and coaches.

The Reds also run an Urban Youth Academy in Winton Place through the Reds Community Fund that provides free year-round baseball and softball instruction to youth ages 8–18. The facility is open year-round and offers training clinics for players and coaches as well as full indoor facilities for teams to utilize during the winter months. The RCF also supports programs such as Reds Rookie Success League, Knothole Baseball, and Miracle League fields.

Recently, the Reds Community Fund has put on summer baseball camps around the tri-state area. Boys and girls ages 6–14 have a chance through these camps to train with and learn from real big leaguers. Camps take place from Indianapolis to Columbus to Lexington and Louisville, but every camp member will get a chance for a VIP trip and a behind-the-scenes look at Great American Ball Park. It's a one-of-a-kind experience that would not be available without the support of the Reds Community Fund.

While the RCF is a traditional charity that takes regular donations, it also has several entertaining fundraisers throughout the year. At every home game, fans have the opportunity to buy a Split-the-Pot ticket, earning a chance to split up to $10,000 with the RCF. Every June, the Redlegs Run features a 10K, 5K, one-mile family run, and a kids' fun run to benefit the Reds Community Fund. The 5K and 10K start at Great American Ball Park and loop around downtown, ending on the field inside of GABP.

If running is not your thing, the Family Catch lets fathers and sons, mothers and daughters, have a day on the field at GABP to toss the ball around together. If you've still got that competitive fire burning inside of you, the Summer Wiffle® Classic is held every year for both youth and adults. Teams of four face off in a Wiffle Ball tournament with the champions getting a special opportunity to play on the indoor Wiffle Ball field during Redsfest.

Speaking of Redsfest, the Reds wintertime celebration is closed out every year by a competitive poker tournament to benefit the Reds Community Fund. Fans sit at tables with players in a grueling match to see who is the top Texas Hold 'Em player, with the competition usually lasting until the wee hours of the morning before a champion is crowned.

For baseball fans who want to give back to the community, participating in one of the many Reds Community Fund events during the year can be both fun and rewarding. Who knows—maybe the work done by the Reds Community Fund might lead to the next great Reds star.

67 Riverfront Stadium

By the late 1960s, it was clear that Crosley Field was outdated. The park, built in 1912, had been through many renovations, but it was not able to keep up with the times, and the neighborhood around the park was run down. Around the league, cities were building new-age cookie-cutter parks that featured the latest in innovations such as luxury boxes, giant scoreboards, and multi-purpose Astroturf. These massive parks typically sat more than 50,000 fans and were commonly used to support multiple sports franchises as well as concerts and tractor pulls. Owner Bill DeWitt wanted one of these stadiums built, possibly even a dome, but he wanted it in Blue Ash. The city had no interest in that location, hoping to get a stadium built along the river in order to build up the city's downtown area. After threatening to move the team to San Diego, DeWitt relented and sold the team to local investors, and plans to build a new 55,000-seat, multi-purpose stadium along the Ohio River were put in place.

Riverfront Stadium (renamed Cinergy Field in 1996) looked a lot like other parks built during that era. In fact, the stadium was often confused with Three Rivers Stadium in Pittsburgh because of its similar style, waterfront location, and name. The Reds' new park had four levels of seating signified by the color of the seats in that level. The field-level seats were blue, followed by green, yellow, and red seats in the upper deck. The red seats became associated with a "red-seat home run," identifying a blast that landed in the upper deck. Tony Perez hit the first red-seat home run on August 11, 1970, less than two months after the park opened. Twenty-eight years later, his son, Eduardo, would also launch a homer into the red seats, the only father-son duo to accomplish the feat.

What the park lacked in character it made up for in memories. Opened in June 1970, Riverfront Stadium hosted an All-Star Game and a World Series in its first year of existence. The All-Star Game will forever be remembered by Reds fans as the day Pete Rose scored the winning run by barreling over catcher Ray Fosse. Sadly, that World Series is mostly remembered for incredible plays by Brooks Robinson.

The stadium would host 30 postseason games in its 33 years of existence, and it would be the home to three different world champion teams, though none of those teams clinched the title at home.

Red Seat Home Runs

In the 33 seasons played at Riverfront Stadium/Cinergy Field, Reds players hit 21 home runs into the upper deck red seats. Nobody did it more often than George Foster, who had six red-seat shots in his career. Reds opponents hit 14 upper deck home runs. St. Louis Cardinals Ray Lankford is the only player to hit multiple red-seat bombs in the same game, when he did the deed twice off Brett Tomko on July 15, 1997. Greg Vaughn, who smashed one into the upper deck in 1998 for the Padres, is the only player to do it as both a Red and as an opponent. On September 26, 1999, Mark McGwire and Eddie Taubensee both launched a ball to the red seats, marking the only time both teams had a red-seat shot in the same game. Lankford and McGwire are the only opponents to reach the red seats twice. McGwire's second bomb traveled an estimated 473', the longest recorded home run in the stadium's history.

Reds players who reached the red seats at Riverfront Stadium:

Player	Date
Tony Perez*	8/11/1970
Tony Perez	7/7/1975
George Foster	6/14/1976
George Foster	8/3/1977
George Foster	9/7/1977
George Foster	7/29/1978
Champ Summers	9/12/1978
Dave Concepcion	6/9/1979
George Foster	9/6/1979
George Foster	8/14/1981
Kevin Mitchell	5/13/1993
Reggie Sanders	7/15/1994
Reggie Sanders	6/18/1995
Eric Anthony	6/25/1995
Eric Anthony	5/7/1996
Eduardo Perez	7/19/1998
Greg Vaughn	6/12/1999
Greg Vaughn	6/18/1999
Eddie Taubensee	9/26/1999
Dmitri Young*	8/21/2000
Russell Branyan	9/12/2002

*Grand Slam
Source: 2003 Reds media guide

Four no-hitters were thrown on Riverfront's turf, including Tom Seaver's lone career no-no and the perfect game by Tom Browning. Hank Aaron hit home run number 714 over Riverfront's left field wall to tie Babe Ruth's all-time record in 1974. Roberto Clemente's last hit and last home run both came at Riverfront Stadium during the 1972 NLCS.

The stadium saw 32 Opening Days and far more elephant and dog poop than any ballfield should ever see. Lou Piniella threw a base there and Eric Davis launched a Game 1 home run off Dave Stewart in 1990 World Series. Johnny Bench hit 161 home runs at Riverfront Stadium, more than any other player, but none was bigger than his ninth-inning blast off Dave Giusti to tie Game 5 of the 1972 NLCS. Dave Concepcion had the most hits in Riverfront with 1,139, but nobody had a more electrifying hit than Pete Rose on September 11, 1985, when he broke Ty Cobb's all-time hit record.

Memories are all that we have left of Riverfront Stadium now. The park was demolished in December 2002 to make room for Great American Ball Park, which opened that following spring. The lifespan of the space-age ballpark ended up being fairly short, but for Reds fans, Riverfront Stadium hosted the golden age of Reds baseball, and for that, it will never be forgotten.

Noodles Hahn

Frank Hahn's manager, Buck Ewing, didn't want to bring the 19-year-old rookie back to Cincinnati to start the season after spring training in 1899. Even though Hahn impressed many during the camp, *The Sporting News* reported that Hahn had "terrific speed, good curves, and the best control ever displayed by a green southpaw," Ewing felt like the young left-hander was not ready for the big leagues. Fortunately for Ewing, he was overruled by owner John Brush, and the boy everyone called "Noodles" made his debut on April 18, 1899.

The youngster dazzled the league in his first season, posting a 23–8 record with a 2.68 ERA as he paced the National League with 145 strikeouts in 309 innings pitched. Hahn credited his success to the fact that he gave up alcohol. "This year shows me what I can do when I am not drinking," he told the *Cincinnati Enquirer*. "I'll never again indulge in any kind of strong drink."

He led the league in strikeouts again the following season, but his 16–20 record and 3.27 ERA were a letdown over the previous year's work. On July 12 of that year, Hahn threw the season's only no-hitter and the first of the new century, shutting down a powerful Philadelphia Phillies lineup. It was the highlight of a dismal year for the Reds, whose 62–77 record left them in seventh place in the National League.

The Reds wouldn't be much better in 1901, but Hahn put up the finest season of his career. His 22 wins represented 42 percent of the team's wins that season, a percentage that has only been topped by Steve Carlton, who had 46 percent of the Phillies' wins in 1972. Hahn threw 41 complete games and 375⅓ innings that season, both league-leading totals. He also led the NL in strikeouts for a third straight season, this time with a career-high 239 whiffs. On top of the strikeouts, he demonstrated excellent control, which is why national publications started calling him the best left-hander in the National League.

Still only 22 years old, Hahn was unusually astute for his age. In a time long before pitch counts and innings limits, Noodles knew that the 375⅓ innings he threw in 1901 took a toll on his body. He told *The Sporting News* after the season, "I am wise enough to know that I cannot last forever and that I am greatly shortening my career by pitching as I did last season." Helped by competing offers from the nascent American League, Hahn negotiated a $4,200 salary with the Reds for the 1902 season, making him the highest paid Reds player of the time. Even with that salary though, he started to take steps to prepare for his career after baseball, enrolling in veterinary school.

The move proved to be prescient, for while Hahn was still one of the top pitchers in baseball for the next three seasons, an arm injury in 1905 labeled Hahn with the dreaded "dead arm" and earned his release from the Reds. He signed on with the New York Highlanders in the AL the next season, but it was clear that he had nothing left in his toolbox. He was released later that season and was done with pro baseball at the age of 27, falling back on the veterinary career he had been planning. He occasionally returned to Crosley Field during the next 40 years, frequently suiting up in a uniform and throwing batting practice. In 1963, three years after he died at the age of 80, the Reds inducted him into the team Hall of Fame. His 127 wins and 900 strikeouts are still in the top 15 all time in franchise history.

69 Fifty Years and Four Shortstops

You'll have to forgive Reds fans if they are a little anxious to crown someone the starting shortstop for the next decade. For more than half a century, they were spoiled rotten by a string of four great shortstops who held down the hardest position on the field with great aplomb. Having yearly turnover at the position just doesn't feel right.

It all started in 1952 when a skinny 22-year-old from Bonham, Texas, who had played just one game of baseball in his life when he tried out for the Reds six years earlier, wrestled the starting shortstop job away from incumbent Virgil Stallcup. Roy McMillan wasn't much of a hitter—he had just two hits in his first 52 at-bats in 1952—but boy-oh-boy could he pick it in the field. He was a natural on defense, and he made plays that others could only dream of. Leo Durocher declared him to be "the best defensive shortstop in the game today," and he quickly earned the nickname, "Mr. Shortstop."

He was also very durable, starting all but 39 games at shortstop from 1952–58, including 584 in a row at one point. He finished sixth in MVP voting in 1956 despite having hit just three home runs on a team that walloped 221 of them. He would also win the first three Gold Gloves for shortstops in the National League. That's how much respect people had for his defense.

In 1957, he made the cover of *Sports Illustrated*. The corresponding article declared him the best shortstop in the majors but had very little positive to say about the pitching staff. By 1960, the Reds staff had become such a problem that McMillan was shipped off to Milwaukee for pitcher Joey Jay.

McMillan was expendable because a 22-year-old Cuban named Leo Cardenas was turning heads at shortstop. Like McMillan, Cardenas was a light hitter, but he possessed a transcendent glove. His defensive prowess eventually earned him the nickname "Mr. Automatic" as well as four All-Star appearances (with a fifth as a Twin) and a Gold Glove in 1965. Of Cardenas, Si Burick of the *Dayton Daily News* wrote, "Cardenas has proved that he is almost the indispensable man. He makes the difficult play look routine; and he makes the routine play."

Cardenas held down the shortstop position for most of the 1960s, but once again the Reds were in desperate need of pitching. After the 1968 season, Cardenas was dealt to Minnesota for Jim Merritt, who would win 37 games over the next two seasons for the budding Big Red Machine. A year later, a lanky Venezuelan by the name of David Concepcion was all set to make the position his for nearly two decades.

When he came up, Concepcion was from the same mold as McMillan and Cardenas, great glove with a suspect bat. However, as time went by, Davey developed nicely as a hitter. From 1973–82, he batted .282 with an OPS that was just a tick over league average. Already the elite defender in the game—his five Gold Gloves were the most ever by an NL shortstop before Ozzie Smith came along—Concepcion held his own at the plate and became a key cog in one of the best offensive machines ever assembled.

After the longest consecutive tenure ever by a Reds player, Concepcion passed the reins to Cincinnati-native Barry Larkin who could do it all on the baseball field. Defensively he was graceful and athletic. At the plate his talents were diverse, enabling him to be an asset to the team just about anywhere in the batting order. Unlike his predecessors, Larkin wasn't a slap-hitter. He could hit the ball with authority to all fields, culminating in his 1996 season when he became the first shortstop in history to join the 30–30 club.

While McMillan, Cardenas, and Concepcion set the standard for defensive shortstops in the National League, Larkin helped revolutionize the position, paving the way for players like Derek Jeter and Troy Tulowitzki whose offensive contributions rivaled their defensive prowess. It was Larkin's complete game that eventually carried him into Cooperstown in 2012.

From 1952 until Larkin's retirement in 2004, these four players started 77 percent of Reds games at shortstop—easily more than any other foursome on a non-expansion team—and they started 47-of-53 Opening Days during that span. Together they were selected to 27 All-Star Games and won 12 Gold Gloves. The Reds have had 20 players start at least one game at shortstop in eight seasons since Larkin retired, including seven different starters on Opening Day. It may seem like forever since the Reds have had stability at shortstop but that's only because, for more than 50 years, stability was all that Reds fans knew at that position.

70 The 1957 All-Star Ballot Stuffing

A massive voter turnout in Cincinnati in 1956 landed five Redlegs on the National League All-Star starting squad. Ed Bailey, Gus Bell, Johnny Temple, Roy McMillan, and Frank Robinson were all having fine seasons by the standards of the day, and while there was some suspicion about the methods used to elect the five Reds players, there wasn't a great outrage over the outcome.

That wouldn't be the case a year later when the fans of Cincinnati outdid themselves.

Voting during the 1950s was handled via newspaper chains that had the infrastructure to handle a nationwide vote. In Cincinnati, it was the *Times-Star* who published the ballot in its sports section, collected and tabulated the votes in their offices, and sent the results to the commissioner's office. There was little or no regulation on how votes were collected and what standards needed to be met, which left a plethora of loopholes to be exploited. And that's exactly what Reds fans did.

The *Times-Star* promoted the voting, printing a ballot every day and conveniently listing the Reds starter at each position right next to the voting line. They encouraged readers to "vote early and vote often." The promotion was assisted by local radio station WKRC as well as the Burger Brewing Co., which printed and distributed 350,000 ballots.

When the first voting results were released, only three Redlegs (Bailey, McMillan, and Robinson) were in line to start, but that's mainly because the nearly 500,000 votes from the Cincinnati area had not been fully tabulated yet. By the time those last votes had been received—a total that was more than all other sections of the country combined—the Redlegs had a representative starting at eight positions.

Commissioner Ford Frick was not happy about the results, fearing that the team would not meet the approval of the fans across the country. After re-examining the votes, he determined that at five of the positions (catcher, second base, shortstop, third base, and left field) Redlegs were close enough nationally to be considered legitimate votes. However, he decided that the other three position players (George Crowe at first, Gus Bell in center, and Wally Post in right) were not representative of the national vote and the three were replaced by Stan Musial, Willie Mays, and Hank Aaron. Manager Walter Alston added Bell back to the team as a reserve, even though the Reds clearly didn't need anymore representation.

Former Reds GM turned National League President Warren Giles studied the vote and also declared that the outcome is not good for baseball. He added, "I hope the commissioner will find a way to make some adjustment. This doesn't carry out the intent of the All-Star Game as it now stands."

Frick did make some dramatic adjustments, taking the vote away from fans and putting it in the hands of players, coaches, and managers, where it stayed until 1970 when the vote was returned to the fans once again.

71 Build a Reds Library

Baseball is an entertaining game, but there is a lot of down time for fans between games. Even worse is the wintertime, a long and lonely time for a baseball fan when all there is to do, to steal a phrase from Rogers Hornsby, is stare out the window and wait for spring. It does not have to be that way. The winter is the perfect time to recapture memories of seasons gone by and learn stories of players and teams that may be unfamiliar to the average fan. The long storied history of the Cincinnati Reds lends itself to a variety of book options for any level of fan. Books that tell stories of the early days in the nineteenth century to books that recap some of the great world championship teams of recent times.

The original must-have history of the Reds dates all the way back to 1907. *Base Ball in Cincinnati: A History* by Harry Ellard is a detailed account of the early days of professional baseball by a journalist who happened to be the son of one of the founders of the Cincinnati club. Another early history of the Reds that carries on through the first half of the twentieth century is *The Cincinnati Reds* by Lee Allen, the one-time historian for the Baseball Hall of Fame. Allen artfully recounts nearly a century's worth of history, including details of the franchise's first two World Series victories. *The Cincinnati Game* by Lonnie Wheeler and John Baskin is as good as they come for a varied history of baseball in Cincinnati. And for a compilation of Reds history through the end of the twentieth century, there is no more valuable resource than *Redleg Journal* by Greg Rhodes and John Snyder. Told in a day-by-day format, the authors weave details of specific games with overarching themes throughout the book, giving a thorough, straightforward account of Cincinnati Reds history.

Rhodes, who is the official Cincinnati Reds historian, has collaborated on several books with other authors. *Reds in Black & White*, compiled with the help of Mark Stang, is hard to find, but the artistic work of the included photographs is second to none. Rhodes has also worked on several books with John Erardi, writer for the *Cincinnati Enquirer*. Their book, *The First Boys of Summer*, is an in-depth look at the origins and history of the 1869 Red Stockings. Their *Cincinnati's Crosley Field* is an indispensable history of the Reds home park from 1912–1970. *Opening Day* is a unique accounting of first-person stories from players about the most special of Cincinnati holidays. And *Big Red Dynasty* may be the finest history of the Big Red Machine ever put to paper.

If you are a fan of the Big Red Machine, there is no shortage of books available for your reading pleasure. One of the best and more recent ones is *The Machine* by Joe Posnanski, a history of how the 1975 team earned the name Big Red Machine. *Game Six* by Mark Frost and *The Long Ball* by Tom Adelman are stories about the cultural significance of that 1975 World Series.

The other most-written-about Reds team would likely be the 1919 squad, but mostly as a footnote in the details of the Black Sox scandal. *Eight Men Out* by Eliot Asinof is an enjoyable account of that story, though it is told mostly from the White Sox perspective. Mark Schmetzer's *Before the Machine* tells the tale of the 1961 Ragamuffin Reds and their surprise trip to the World Series. *The Wire-to-Wire Reds* by John Erardi and Joel Luckhaupt gives a season-long account of the 1990 world champions with a variety of stories from the players who were there.

If biographies are more your style, *My Life in Baseball* by Frank Robinson and *Catch You Later* by Johnny Bench are quality autobiographies. Pete Rose could fill a library with the biographies written about him, but two of the best are *Pete Rose 4,192* by John Erardi and *Hustle: The Myth, Life, and Lies of Pete Rose* by Michael Sokolove. *Born to Play* tells the tales of Eric Davis' life in baseball and overcoming cancer, and Tom Browning's *Tales from the Reds Dugout* is a humorous and thoughtful look at the left-hander's career.

Two classic baseball books that happen to involve the Reds are Jim Brosnan's *The Long Season* and *Pennant Race*. The former Reds pitcher gives insight into what life was really like for a ball-player years before the much more publicized *Ball Four* came out. And one of the best yet not very well known novels about baseball involves the 1869 Red Stockings. *If I Never Get Back* by Darryl Brock skillfully mixes time travel with baseball to make an enjoyable ride-along with baseball's original professional team.

Reds fans have no more excuses this winter when they are longing for a baseball fix. They need only pull a book off the shelf to get it.

72 Aroldis Chapman

On July 1, 2009, Albertin Aroldis Chapman walked out of the front door of his hotel in Rotterdam, Netherlands, got into the car of an acquaintance, and officially severed all ties with his homeland of Cuba. The decision to defect was not an easy one for the 21-year-old, but the lure of Major League Baseball was strong for the left-handed flamethrower and he could not resist.

Chapman was not a complete unknown when he defected from Cuba that day, but there were considerable question marks. Many people within the United States had a chance to watch him pitch for the Cuban team during the World Baseball Classic earlier that year, but he was obviously still raw. His fastball lit up the radar guns, reportedly touching 102 mph during the WBC, but

The Cincinnati Reds Cuban Connection

The Cincinnati Reds have a long history of Cuban-born players on their roster. In 1911, Armando Marsans and Rafael Almeida were the first Cuban players to get regular playing time in the big leagues, and both did it with the Reds. Dolf Luque first joined the league with the Boston Braves, but he became the game's first Latin star while playing for the Reds. The heart and soul of the Big Red Machine, Tony Pérez, is the only Cuban-born player in the National Baseball Hall of Fame. In the game's history, only the Washington Senators/Minnesota Twins franchise has had more Cuban players on its roster than these 26 who have played for the Reds:

Player	Years w/ Reds	Place of Birth
Armando Marsans	1911–14	Matanzas, Cuba
Rafael Almeida	1911–13	La Habana, Cuba
Mike González	1914	La Habana, Cuba
Manuel Cueto	1917–19	Guanajay, Cuba
Dolf Luque	1918–29	La Habana, Cuba
Pedro Dibut	1924–25	Cienfuegos, Cuba
Tommy de la Cruz	1944	Marianao, Cuba
Raúl Sánchez	1957, 1960	Marianao, Cuba
Vicente Amor	1957	La Habana, Cuba
Orlando Peña	1958–60	Victoria de las Tunas, Cuba
Danny Morejon	1958	La Habana, Cuba
Mike Cuellar	1959	Las Villas, Cuba
Leo Cardenas	1960–68	Matanzas, Cuba
Rogelio Álvarez	1960, 1962	Pinar del Rio, Cuba
Tony González	1960	Central Cunagua, Cuba
Joe Azcue	1960	Cienfuegos, Cuba
Cookie Rojas	1962	La Habana, Cuba
Tony Pérez	1964–76, 1984–86	Camaguey, Cuba
Chico Ruiz	1964–69	Santo Domingo, Cuba
Pedro Ramos	1969	Pinar del Rio, Cuba
Camilo Pascual	1969	La Habana, Cuba
Mike de la Hoz	1969	La Habana, Cuba
Tony Menendez	1992	La Habana, Cuba
Osvaldo Fernandez	2000–01	Holguin, Cuba
Aroldis Chapman	2010–12	Holguin, Cuba
Yonder Alonso	2010–11	La Habana, Cuba

Source: Baseball-Reference.com

Relief pitcher Aroldis Chapman throws against the Colorado Rockies in the eighth inning on Thursday, August 11, 2011, in Cincinnati. Chapman pitched a scoreless eighth inning, and Cincinnati won 2–1. (AP Photo/Al Behrman)

some scouts thought his secondary pitches were average or worse. Many also worried about his maturity level, since Chapman was seen several times barking at umpires about disagreements with the strike zone.

Nevertheless, talk immediately began that Chapman could receive the largest contract ever by a Cuban defector. Some speculated that teams might offer as much as $60 million for his services, with the Yankees and Red Sox considered to be the most likely winners in a bidding war. The Reds flew under the radar during the entire negotiation process, but when the deal was finally announced—five years, $30 million with an option—it was Cincinnati who came out on top. Some teams cried sour grapes and wondered how the Reds could take such a large risk with a small budget, but the Reds knew that Chapman was a rare talent that didn't come along very often. They also knew they could not simply wait around for things to improve. "When you look at the size of the market where we are in Cincinnati," general manager Walt Jocketty explained, "we have to take some bold moves from time to time to try and improve this franchise and make it better."

Chapman competed for a spot in the starting rotation during spring training in 2010, and while he was impressive, he was also still raw enough that the Reds decided to send him to Triple A in Louisville. He was up-and-down as a starter that year, but as the Reds got deeper and deeper into the playoff chase, it started to feel like Chapman could best help the team that season out of the bullpen. On August 31, he was called up and pitched in his first game in the big leagues, striking out the first batter he faced. Three-and-a-half weeks into his big-league career, Chapman wrote his name in the record books after throwing a pitch that was measured at 105.9 mph, the fastest pitch ever recorded. Opposing hitters were baffled by his velocity. "Even if it's a clear ball, you have to make up your mind so quick that it's hard to lay off," said the Padres' Chase Headley.

The Cuban Missile, as Chapman had become known to fans, stayed in the bullpen through the 2011 season. In May of that year, he hit his first major bump when his control disappeared. In four straight appearances, Chapman walked 12 batters and recorded a total of four outs in those games. The Reds cautiously put him on the disabled list and then had him rehab in Louisville. When he returned 41 days later, his control was much better, though he still had issues, and his stuff continued to dominate. That fall, the Reds decided that Chapman would move back to the starting rotation in 2012.

He spent the entire off-season preparing to be a starter, and by all accounts he was the best pitcher in camp during the spring. However, injuries to three key relievers forced the team's hand and Chapman was moved back to the bullpen. The left-hander did not allow an earned run until his 25th appearance of the season, by which point he was the team's closer. Despite a few hiccups along the way, Chapman put together one of the greatest seasons ever by a Reds reliever, even earning Cy Young Award consideration.

It's possible that one day Aroldis Chapman will find himself back in the starting rotation, but every year that passes with him posting mind-blowing numbers in the bullpen makes that transition less and less likely. Either way, as long as he continues to dominate big-league hitters like few others ever have, he will have earned that large contract, and then some.

73 Eppa Rixey

So many great baseball players have stories of what they almost became outside of baseball. For Eppa Rixey, it was a chemist. In fact, he nearly turned down a shot to pitch for the Philadelphia Phillies to pursue that goal. Umpire Cy Rigler saw Rixey pitch at the University of Virginia and went the extra mile to convinced the left-handed pitcher to take a major league contract with Phillies. Twenty-two years later, Rixey had the most wins ever by a National League left-hander.

When he was acquired by the Reds from the Phillies in 1921, he was still an unpolished pitcher. He had lost more than 20 games in two of his previous three seasons, and he was five years removed from his last winning record. The change of scenery did him some good as Rixey set a big-league record by allowing just one home run in 301 innings pitched in 1921. The following year he led the league in wins with 25 and innings pitched with 313⅓. Nevertheless, Rixey's success on the mound was not able to push the Reds over the top and into the postseason. The team finished second three times during Rixey's tenure, but they also finished fifth or lower in the eight-team league a total of eight times.

Rixey spent 13 seasons in all with the Reds, more than any pitcher other than Joe Nuxhall. He won 10 games in each of his first nine seasons with the squad, a streak that was only bested by Dolf Luque. His 179 victories with the Reds still stands today as the franchise record, and no Reds pitcher has come within 45 wins of that total since 1969.

A southerner with a thick drawl, Rixey was given the nickname "Jeptha" by sportswriter William Phelan. At 6'5", he was one of the largest pitchers in baseball during his era, but his height belied a certain finesse in his pitching style. He wasn't a power pitcher by any means, and by the time he joined the Reds the success he had built came from his ability to control his pitches with great precision. In his first seven seasons with the franchise, only three NL pitchers had a better walk rate than Rixey.

But it wasn't only the numbers that made Rixey an important part of Cincinnati history. It didn't take him long to become a valuable member of the community, working in the off-season selling insurance. In fact, the Eppa Rixey Agency that he set up in Terrace Park, Ohio, is still around today and is being run by his grandson, Eppa Rixey IV.

When Rixey retired after the 1933 season, he had 266 career wins, the most by a left-hander in National League history, a fact that was missed by most people until Warren Spahn passed that number with his 267th victory in 1959. Rixey, who had a very good sense of humor, appreciated Spahn breaking his record since it reminded everyone that he held the record in the first place.

The reminder may also have indirectly led to Rixey receiving the greatest honor a player can get. When Rixey visited the National Baseball Hall of Fame in 1959, he jokingly sent postcards to some friends saying, "I made it to the Hall of Fame... for only one day." However, four years later, Rixey was chosen by the Veterans Committee, who may have appreciated Rixey's wins record more now that it was broken. Rixey responded dryly with, "They're really scraping the bottom of the barrel, aren't they?" Rixey would never get the chance to see his own plaque—just four weeks after learning he was elected, he passed away suddenly from a heart attack at the age of 71. His widow and kids accepted his plaque for him that August, and Rixey remains to this day the only pitcher to wear a Reds cap in Cooperstown.

74 Sean Casey

Greatness is not always defined by what a baseball player does between the lines. Few have recognized that fact more than Sean Casey. That's not to say that Casey was not great on the field. He was a three-time All-Star. Six times he batted .310 or higher. He had three seasons of 40 doubles. He had three seasons with 20 home runs. Twice he drove in 99 runs during a year. He was a solid defender and a great hitter in clutch situations.

Yet those numbers don't capture the essence of what made Sean Casey one of the most beloved Reds players of all time. Known as "The Mayor," Casey's perpetual smile led you to believe that he never had a bad day. His ebullience permeated everything he did. Every day at the park, Casey would shake hands and share stories with everyone he saw, whether it was a teammate or an usher, the grounds crew or the general manager. Casey could spend five minutes with someone and make him or her feel like they have been friends with him for decades.

His affability is genuine, too. Some people can pat you on the back with one hand and stab you in the back with the other. Not Sean Casey. While with the Reds, he would frequently show up at Children's Hospital or Shriners Hospital unannounced and visit with kids just to brighten their days. Since his retirement, he has been actively fundraising for Miracle League fields to give kids with disabilities the chance to play baseball and be a kid. His passion for helping others goes to his core.

Reds broadcaster Marty Brennaman, who worked for 30 years with another kind-hearted and beloved man in Joe Nuxhall, had the highest praise for Casey. "In all honesty, [Sean Casey]'s the finest person I've ever known," Brennaman said. "I've never met a baseball player—never met an athlete—who is as nice, as good, and as giving as he is."

Of course, Casey's fantastic personality would not have as much impact if he weren't such a solid ballplayer, too. He was one of the top pure hitters in the NL during his career, thrice finishing in the top seven in batting average with two other top 20 finishes. His success was not a given, though. "I wasn't the five-tool guy, the guy you looked at and said, 'This guy is going to be the next

Joe Nuxhall Good Guy Award Winners

Every year the local chapter of the Baseball Writers Association vote for the Joe Nuxhall Good Guy Award. This award goes to the player who displays great character on and off the field, representing the kind spirit of Joe Nuxhall. These are the winners of the award for the Reds since it was first given out in 1991:

1991 Todd Benzinger
1992 Jose Rijo
1993 Tim Belcher
1994 Kevin Mitchell
1995 Bret Boone
1996 Jeff Brantley
1997 Joe Oliver
1998 Eddie Taubensee
1999 Sean Casey
2000 Steve Parris
2001 Dmitri Young
2002 Jose Rijo
2003 Austin Kearns
2004 Sean Casey
2005 Ken Griffey Jr.
2006 Bronson Arroyo
2007 Scott Hatteberg
2008 Aaron Harang
2009 Bronson Arroyo
2010 Scott Rolen
2011 Bronson Arroyo
2012 Bronson Arroyo

Source: Reds.com

big guy,'" Casey said. "I had no scholarship offers coming out of high school. I always felt I could hit and was going to make myself a great defensive player. I always believed I was going to play in the big leagues. I don't think a lot of other people did."

The fact that Casey was not a phenom kept him grounded and never let him forget where he had come from. Born in New Jersey, he grew up outside of Pittsburgh, which is where he still lives today. Even though he has that connection to his hometown, he still considers Cincinnati to be his home, as well. He returns to town regularly for fundraising and special events. In 2012, he came back to celebrate his induction into the Reds Hall of Fame after he was voted in by the fans who loved him. Casey returned the love in a heartfelt speech to the fans, thanking them for their support and calling the induction, "My biggest day in baseball." Fitting for a man who treated every day in the game like it was the most special one yet.

75 Johnny Cueto

To most Reds fans, Johnny Cueto the person is largely unknown. Born in San Pedro de Macoris, Dominican Republic, Cueto has kept most of his personal life private by requiring a translator for most interviews. Word around the clubhouse is that Cueto speaks broken English, but he speaks it well enough to communicate with his non-Spanish-speaking teammates. However, when it comes time for postgame interviews, Cueto usually works through a translator. He said it is so he does not mess something up during a rapid-fire question and answer, but it also seems like the right-handed ace likes that extra layer of protection between himself and the outside world. As his manager Dusty Baker explained, "He says he doesn't speak English? That's pretty convenient for him. Maybe you don't need to know him other than what he is doing because he is out there to pitch rather than be known."

Cueto anonymously moved through the Reds' minor league system after signing with the team as an amateur free agent in 2004. He was always in Homer Bailey's shadow as a prospect.

While Bailey was consistently rated as one of the top five or top 10 pitching prospects in all of baseball, Cueto was putting up better numbers at just about every level. Even though Bailey made his debut in 2007, it was Cueto who established himself in the starting rotation first, winning a spot with an outstanding spring training performance in 2008.

Cueto's debut was a memorable afternoon when the hard-throwing Dominican struck out 10 and allowed only one hit over seven innings pitched against the Diamondbacks. He was dominant at times during his rookie season, but at just 22 years old, he often showed signs of immaturity on the mound. He'd frequently fall into the trap of trying to strike everyone out, which in turn would run up his pitch count and limit his innings. He finished the year at 9–14 with a 4.81 ERA, which left fans wondering what they really had in him.

The 2009 season saw some improvement, but 11–11 with a 4.41 ERA was not all that impressive. Continued pitch inefficiency left him with only 171⅓ innings pitched on the year. It was a year later when Cueto started to put it all together. He struggled in April, but once the weather heated up, so did Cueto. From the start of May until the middle of September, Cueto was one of baseball's best pitchers, going 11–4 with a 2.99 ERA over 24 starts. During that time, the Reds also caught and passed the St. Louis Cardinals in the standings on their way to their first division title in 15 seasons.

The season wasn't without some problems, however. In a fight between the Reds and Cardinals on August 10, Cueto was pinned up against the netting behind home plate as the mob of players forced their way toward him. Panicked, Cueto started kicking with his cleats, landing blows on the back of pitcher Chris Carpenter and the face of catcher Jason LaRue. Cueto received a seven-game suspension for what the league called "violent and aggressive actions." He was also labeled a thug by many baseball fans outside

Johnny Cueto pitches in the sixth inning of a game against the Pittsburgh Pirates in Pittsburgh on Tuesday, May 11, 2010. Cueto pitched a complete-game one-hit shutout as the Reds won 9–0. (AP Photo/Gene J. Puskar)

of Cincinnati and even today is persona non grata for many in St. Louis. Cueto, as is his tendency, didn't talk much about the incident.

The right-hander turned things around—literally—in 2011. During that season, Cueto and pitching coach Bryan Price reworked his windup to keep him from falling off to the first-base side. In doing that, Cueto developed a Luis Tiant–like twist where he shows his backside to the catcher before uncoiling and hurling the pitch toward him. The windup allows for some deception, but mostly it keeps Cueto going toward home, which gives him more accurate control of his pitches. It's hard to argue with the results. Since the start of the 2011 season, Cueto has been among the league leaders in ERA, and he fell just short of the Reds first 20-win season since 1988 in 2012. Cueto was a leading contender for the Cy Young Award that season, but a couple of subpar outings toward the end of the year ruined his chances.

It remains to be seen whether Cueto will follow in the footsteps of another Dominican and be the ace of a world champion like Jose Rijo. That might be the one thing that finally makes him well known, but it won't be the only thing that makes him great.

76 Waite Hoyt

After a long successful career as a player that eventually landed him in the Hall of Fame, Waite Hoyt set the goal of becoming a radio play-by-play guy with the explicit desire of calling games for his beloved New York Yankees, whom he had played with for 10 seasons. Hoyt became fascinated with the role of the radio play-by-play man after hearing Graham McNamee call World Series games in the 1920s. He worked for several years doing a variety of radio shows and guest appearances, honing his craft, but there was still a bias against former players as play-by-play guys. At the time, teams typically employed professional broadcasters with booming voices and pristine elocution. Hoyt felt like the broadcasters' skills may have made them better speakers but not necessarily better for the listener.

"The athlete-announcers of today don't realize how tough we had it at first," Hoyt recalled years later, "because those so-called professionals who had preceded us had schooled the public wrongly. We had to break down all the misconceptions, the misinterpretations of rules, and the vernacular that our predecessors had interpreted according to their own whimsy."

Hoyt finally got an offer from WKRC in Cincinnati to call Reds games, and though he was skittish about coming to a seemingly dull town like Cincinnati, Hoyt felt like the job would allow him to get the experience he needed to make it back to New York for his dream job. Twenty-four seasons later, Hoyt retired as a Cincinnati institution, calling the Queen City "his town."

Success was not simple for Hoyt, but he worked hard to remove the imperfections from his technique and Reds fans eventually fell in love with his easy-going style. Hoyt faced a lot of challenges in the role, not the least of which was the poor play of the hometown Reds on the field. He spoke with such eloquence that fans forgot the team wasn't all that good. "Waite taught us you were allowed to be a baseball lover and still use words you had to look up in the dictionary," broadcaster Nick Clooney said.

The peak performance of a Waite Hoyt broadcast was a rain delay. Fans often might have listened to the game broadcast as background noise, tuning in and out as the action unfolded. But the moment there was a rain delay, they stopped what they were doing and gathered around the radio box for story time with Waite Hoyt. The old right-hander from Brooklyn, New York, was a master at spinning yarns about his playing days, and he had a seemingly unending basket full of stories, most about the great Babe Ruth, his teammate with the Yankees. "He would get halfway through a story and chuckle," Joe Hayden, founder of Midland Baseball recalled, "which meant he was leaving something out that did not belong on the air."

Hoyt's stories would range from humorous to poetic, and all the while he would be examining himself, his subjects and, in a way, the listener at home. "I would try to philosophize and level with the people," Hoyt said. "I just did the best I could, and that's all anybody can do."

Hoyt recognized his imperfections, but he never let them keep him from improving. In 1945, he missed several games because of a drinking binge that led to Hoyt being discovered on a sidewalk along Reading Road. Hoyt had been an alcoholic for years, but that moment was rock bottom and he joined Alcoholics Anonymous, a group he participated in for the next 40 years.

Hoyt stayed in the Reds booth until 1965 with his personal highlight coming in 1961 when he got to call the World Series between his new adopted team, the Cincinnati Reds, and his former team, the New York Yankees. Four years after retiring from the booth, he was inducted into the National Baseball Hall of Fame as a Yankee, but Hoyt never left his new home. He lived until the ripe old age of 84, passing away in his beloved Cincinnati in 1984. In 2007, Hoyt was honored along with Reds broadcasting greats Joe Nuxhall and Marty Brennaman, as the trio had their microphones retired by the Reds organization, signifying the importance of all three men to the history of the franchise.

77 Fred Hutchinson

When Fred Hutchinson started managing in the big leagues, he was nearly a month away from his 33rd birthday. Also, he was still a pitcher for the Detroit Tigers. Hutch was such a great leader that when the Tigers fired manager Red Rolfe midway through a disappointing 1952 season, his teammates fully embraced his ascension to the managerial role. Unfortunately, he was not able to pull the Tigers out of the gutter in his 2½ years in the position, and he was fired after the 1954 season. A year later he was brought into another franchise that was down on its luck, but in three seasons as the manager of the St. Louis Cardinals, Hutch could only get his team as high as second place once and he departed St. Louis near the end of the 1958 season.

The following year he was managing for the Seattle Rainiers when the Redlegs called him up to take over for Mayo Smith, who had been let go by general manager Gabe Paul. Hutch took over a team that was 10 games under .500 and led them to a 39–35 record the rest of the way. There was hope, but a shaky performance in 1960 and the death of owner Powel Crosley early in 1961 left doubts about Hutchinson's future. Those doubts were quickly erased as the Ragamuffin Reds took the NL crown with a 93–61 record before falling to the New York Yankees in five games.

Hutchinson's outbursts as a player and manager were legendary, but they were rarely directed at his players. For that, his players respected him. In fact, as former Reds pitcher Jim Brosnan wrote in his book, *The Long Season*, they admired him, which meant so much more. "The smile of Fred Hutchinson is a treasured one," Brosnan wrote. "His ball players vie hopefully for it. By playing well and winning, they earn it."

The Last Two Weeks of the 1964 Season

The 1964 pennant race is mostly remembered for the collapse of the Philadelphia Phillies during the last month of the season as they gave away an 11-game lead over the St. Louis Cardinals in the last 39 games of the year. What is often missed by those outside of Cincinnati is that the Reds actually caught the Phillies first.

When dawn broke on the morning of September 16, 1964, the Reds woke in fourth place, 8½ games behind the Phillies and 2½ behind the second-place Cardinals. Still rebounding from the decline in health of their manager, Fred Hutchinson, the Redlegs were amazingly about to put together one of the greatest stretch runs in team history.

Two wins versus the Cubs moved the Reds into third place and shaved a game off the Phillies' lead. A doubleheader split with the Cardinals two days later took off another half game, and when the Reds closed out the series win versus the Cardinals, they moved into a tie for second place, 6½ games back. That night they packed for an eight-game road trip, including three against the Phillies.

Leading into that series the Phillies weren't actually playing all that poorly. They'd won seven of their previous 11 and held a magic number of seven. That didn't stop the Reds from dominating the three games. John Tsitouris shut out the Phillies on six hits, and Chico Ruiz stole home in the sixth to score the game's only run in the first match. Frank Robinson led the offensive onslaught in the second game as the Reds pounded the Phillies 9–2. Vada Pinson's second home run of the third game, a three-run blast with two outs in the seventh, sealed the series sweep and the Reds left Philadelphia trailing by 3½ games.

Next the Reds played two double-headers in three days against the lowly New York Mets, winning all five games in the series. While that was happening, the Phillies were swept at home again, this time in four games by Milwaukee. By the end of Sunday, September 27, the Reds had won nine games in a row and 12-of-13. They controlled the National League by one game over the Phillies and 1½ games over the Cardinals.

Then the wheels fell off. The Reds came home to play Pittsburgh and couldn't score a run for two straight games, including a 16-inning pitchers' duel that the Pirates won 1–0. The Reds' NL lead was short-lived as the Cardinals leapfrogged them into first place with a three-game sweep of the Phillies, who now sat 2½ games back in third place. The Reds won the series closer against the Pirates and trailed the Cards by one game in the loss column with the reeling Phillies coming to town having lost 10 in a row.

Despite dropping the first game against the Phillies, the Reds did manage to tie the Cardinals again thanks to back-to-back losses by St. Louis to the Mets. However, a disastrous 10–0 loss on the final day of the season, coupled with the Cardinals 11–5 drubbing of the Mets, meant that for the second time in three seasons the Reds would win 90+ games and still have to watch someone else pop the champagne.

His Reds teams earned many smiles from their manager. In 1962, they won 98 games but finished in third place, 3½ games behind in the classic Giants-Dodgers pennant race of that year. An 86–76 season in 1963 meant fifth place for the Redlegs, but Hutchinson was optimistic about the team heading into 1964. That's when he received some of the worst news anyone can hear.

In January 1964, general manager Bill DeWitt announced that tumors found on Hutchinson's lungs, chest, and neck were malignant. The initial prognosis was grim, but after Hutch spent two months receiving treatment at home in Seattle, doctors were feeling good about the progress he had made. The normally fiery manager was somewhat subdued when spring training started, but it didn't take long for that to change as he was tossed from a spring contest just a week into camp. His team embodied his fire, and it played hard for its ailing manager. However, Hutchinson's condition worsened as the season progressed, and in late July, with his team sitting at 54–45, 3½ games out of first, the manager stayed in Cincinnati during a road trip to receive more treatment. He then managed through a 6–4 homestand before turning over the team to Dick Sisler for what would end up being the final time.

It had to be hard for the team to stay optimistic when its manager was suffering, but it kept playing hard, winning 12-of-16 and 12-of-13 over two different stretches. However, it wasn't meant to be as the team finished 92–70, a game out of first place.

By that point, Hutch was thin and the treatment was not going well. He consoled Sisler when the Reds fell short at the end of the season, and when he resigned in late October of that year, he told DeWitt that he hoped he would pick Sisler as his replacement, which DeWitt did. Hutch's condition deteriorated from there and on November 12, 1964, he lost his battle at the age of 45.

So great was the respect for this man among his peers that the following year, Major League Baseball created the Hutch Award in his honor, and each year since it has been awarded to the player who best exemplifies the fighting spirit and competitive desire of Hutchinson. It is an award that winners cherish more than just about any award a player can receive.

The Reds honored Hutch in 1965 by retiring his No. 1 jersey and inducting him into the Reds Hall of Fame. He is one of five managers to have taken the Reds to the World Series, and his .544 winning percentage is the fifth best in franchise history.

Perhaps Hutch's greatest legacy is the Fred Hutchinson Cancer Research Center in Seattle that was founded by his brother, Dr. William Hutchinson, after Fred's death. The Center today is one of the most prominent research centers in the world, saving thousands every year from the disease that took Hutch. His legendary fighting spirit carries on, even long after his passing.

78 Ewell "The Whip" Blackwell

As the Reds drifted through the war years of the mid-forties, slowly declining into mediocrity, Hall of Fame manager Bill McKechnie would occasionally stare off wistfully and dream of a pitcher he once managed named Ewell Blackwell. Coach Hank Gowdy described Blackwell to *The Sporting News* as "a great long strip of a whalebone with the pitching motion of a tarantula and a sidearm sinker that could break your bat. He had arms that hung clear down to here, and when he coiled up his right arm like a rattlesnake and then let it unwind, why, the ball he threw must've weighed 20 lbs." McKechnie felt that if his team could just have that sidearming right-hander back on his staff, he might be able to make something of it. The problem was that Sergeant Ewell Blackwell was in Europe fighting Nazis.

Blackwell made a brief, two-game appearance with the Reds in 1942 before he was sent to the minor leagues in Syracuse. He spent the next three years in the army, where he played for a variety of baseball teams both in the States and Europe. He was discharged in 1946 and finally got a chance to pitch for McKechnie again, going 9–13 with a 2.45 ERA for the sixth-place Reds, leading the league with five shutouts.

Despite the record, he quickly developed a reputation as one of the best pitchers in the league, making the first of six straight All-Star Game appearances that year. Fellow pitcher Schoolboy Rowe said of Blackwell, "That fellow is bad news for man and beast. He's got a fastball that drops so quickly you can't follow it…and he throws at you with that sidearm motion that makes you think of a buzz saw at your stomach." It was that sidearm motion that earned Blackwell the nickname "The Whip." As he flung his arm toward the plate, the ball zipped out of his hand with a snap of his wrist and batters were left helpless. "I realized my sidearm delivery was intimidating, and I took advantage of it any way I could," Blackwell once said. "I was a mean pitcher."

As a 24-year-old in 1947, The Whip demonstrated his full mastery of the mound, leading the league in wins with 22 against eight losses, complete games with 23, and strikeouts with 193. He finished second in the NL MVP voting to Bob Elliott and arguably should have won. He also nearly matched teammate Johnny Vander Meer's incredible feat of back-to-back no-hitters, nearly nine years to the day after Vander Meer pulled it off. On June 18, Blackwell no-hit the Boston Braves in a complete-game 6–0 victory. Four days later, he took the Brooklyn Dodgers into the ninth inning without allowing a hit before Eddie "The Brat" Stanky slapped a single to end Blackwell's bid for immortality.

The Whip's future looked boundless at that point, but his next couple of seasons were marred by arm issues, taking the snap out of his devastating sinker. He managed to spring back with quality seasons for miserable Reds teams in 1950 (17–15, 2.97) and 1951 (16–15, 3.44). He was the winning pitcher in the 1950 All-Star Game, pitching three shutout innings and inducing a double play from Joe DiMaggio to close out the NL's 5–4 14-inning victory.

He struggled terribly with his control during the 1952 season and was dealt midway late in the season to the New York Yankees for Jim Greengrass and others. He made six more starts over the next season and a half before retiring. He made a brief comeback in 1955 with the Athletics but only saw action in two games. He was an impressive pitcher with a short but very bright career, and in 1960 he was inducted into the Reds Hall of Fame.

79 Pete Rose Collides with Ray Fosse

It's possibly the most famous play in All-Star Game history. Or at least the most controversial.

Where one stands in judgment of the play says nearly as much about his opinion of the players involved as it does about the actual play itself. Was it dirty or was it simply hard-nosed, winning baseball?

It's an indelible image in many fans' minds. The National League had runners on first and second in the bottom of the 12th inning of a 4–4 ballgame. Cubs first baseman Jim Hickman lined a single to center field, and Pete Rose bolted around third base toward home plate. The hometown crowd at Riverfront Stadium roared to its feet as third-base coach Leo Durocher sprinted next to Rose down the third-base line.

As Rose reached about two-thirds of the way down the line, he appeared to get into position to do a patented head-first slide, but just at that time, catcher Ray Fosse moved just up the line enough to block Rose's path.

"I positioned myself where the throw was coming," Fosse said. "I knew I was up the line, so I intended to make a sweep tag. The next thing I knew, it happened. I had no warning."

Stumbling slightly as he trucked down the right side of the foul line, Rose felt Fosse left him "no recourse because there was no place to slide." He reached Fosse just before the ball did, blasting through the catcher with his left shoulder and tagging home plate with his right hand as the pair tumbled through the batter's box, clinching a 5–4 win for the National League.

Fosse, who was having a tremendous start during his first full season in the big leagues, sat up from the collision with what was

All-Star MVPs

Pete Rose's dramatic winning run may not have won him the MVP of the 1970 All-Star Game, but Reds have been frequent winners of the award over the years. In fact, the Giants are the only National League team that has more All-Star Game MVP winners than the Reds five. Here are those five:

1967—Tony Perez homers off Catfish Hunter in the 15th inning of a 1–1 game, giving the National League a 2–1 victory and the Reds their first Midsummer Classic MVP.

1972—Joe Morgan singles in the winning running off Dave McNally in the 10th inning to give the NL a 4–3 walk-off victory and take home the MVP.

1976—George Foster drove in a run in the first inning and then two more in the third on a home run off Catfish Hunter to win the MVP as the NL coasted to a 7–1 victory in Philadelphia.

1980—Ken Griffey nabbed MVP honors with two hits, including a fifth-inning home run to put the NL on the scoreboard and a seventh-inning single that eventually led to the NL's final run in a 4–2 victory at Dodger Stadium.

1982—Dave Concepcion's second-inning, two-run home run off future Hall of Famer Dennis Eckersley was the difference maker for the NL as the league won its 11th consecutive All-Star Game and 19-of-20.

diagnosed as a separated shoulder but turned out to be a fracture that was obscured in X-rays by massive swelling. Despite the injury, he did not miss any time, and while his power diminished—after hitting 16 HR in the first half, he hit just two the rest of the year—he still managed a .297 batting average and a .353 on-base percentage in the second half.

Rose, however, missed three games with a sore knee from the collision to start the second half, though the injury left no lasting effects. He ended the year with 205 hits to pace the NL, finishing seventh in MVP voting as the Reds won the NL West division by 14½ games.

It was a coincidence that these two men were involved in the play because just the night before they had gone out for dinner along with pitcher Sam McDowell and each player's spouse. In a time where there was no Home Run Derby, Fan Fest, or Red Carpet extravaganza, the players had plenty of time to hang out and talk baseball, which is what the pair did for much of the night before the game. Less than 24 hours later, they met again in a fashion that has linked together two names in the annals of All-Star history.

Some have criticized Rose's hard-nosed play as excessive in what was simply an exhibition game. Others hold up the game as an example of what made Rose great a never-ending desire to do whatever it took to win. Either way it was certainly one of the most exciting moments in All-Star history and the first truly memorable moment in Riverfront Stadium's young history.

80 Reds on the Radio

Technology has changed the way fans experience the game of baseball today. Go to any picnic during the summer and you are likely to find a fan staring at his or her smartphone, checking for updates on the game. If they subscribe to MLB.tv, they may actually be watching the game. Every second of every game is available at our fingertips, and if you miss it, just watch the archive later.

For decades, however, there were only two ways to follow the action of a baseball game live. You could see it in person, or you could listen on the radio. The Reds' first broadcast came in 1924 when Eugene Mittendorf called play-by-play of Opening Day for a game that was simulcast on WLW and WSAI in Cincinnati. It was the only game broadcast over the airwaves that season. In fact, for the next three seasons, the Reds only allowed Opening Day to be broadcast, this time with WLW owner Powel Crosley doing play-by-play. Crosley would purchase the Reds less than a decade later. Finally in 1929, the Reds allowed WLW to broadcast 40 games with Bob Burdette on the mic. Harry Hartman became the primary play-by-play guy in 1931, working for three seasons before Larry MacPhail called upon an unknown broadcaster named Red Barber to take the mic. Barber stayed with the Reds for five seasons before following MacPhail to Brooklyn and building a Hall of Fame career as a play-by-play maestro.

In 1942, four seasons after finishing his Hall of Fame playing career, Waite Hoyt took over the play-by-play duties and did not let go for 24 seasons. Hoyt saw the Reds through some lean years in the late forties and early fifties, often as the only voice on the broadcast. But he managed to keep the games interesting and when that was impossible, he was always able to fall back on stories of his playing days with Babe Ruth and Lou Gehrig.

Joe Nuxhall joined the broadcast team in 1968, three years after Hoyt retired. Nuxie would work his first six years with Jim McIntyre and Al Michaels before a poofy-haired fancy boy from North Carolina took over the play-by-play duties in 1974. Marty Brennaman and Joe Nuxhall would work 30 seasons together as the only voices on the Reds radio broadcast, calling some of the biggest moments in franchise history. In an era where televised games were still only a once-a-week occurrence, Marty and Joe became synonymous with Reds baseball. Brennaman's straight-shooting willingness to be critical when things were bad was a perfect foil to Nuxhall's invincible fandom.

Eventually Nuxhall's age and health forced him to cut back on the number of games he worked, and by 2007 the team had brought in a new former pitcher to sit in the chair next to Brennaman. Jeff

Brantley, known affectionately as "The Cowboy," has been Marty's main play by play partner for six seasons, but the broadcast has also been joined off and on by Marty's son, Thom Brennaman, former big leaguer Chris Welsh, and longtime Louisville play-by-play man Jim Kelch, giving the Reds what just might be the largest broadcast team in history.

Today, Reds games can be heard on local radio stations from as far north as Fostoria, Ohio, and as far south as Pensacola, Florida. Of course, fans could just watch the game on their iPhones, but every now and then it's nice to have the crackle of an AM radio tell you the story of the game, just like it did years ago.

Heinie Groh

Most studies of the history of the game agree that Heinie Groh was the finest defensive third baseman of the Dead Ball Era. During that time, third base was one of the most critical spots on the field because hitters utilized the bunt much more frequently, trying everything they could just to get on base. Having a good fielding third baseman was essential to a good defensive team, and Groh was the cornerstone to some very good Reds teams in the late teens and early twenties. "I'd get in front of that ball one way or the other," Heinie said, "and if I couldn't catch it, I'd let it hit me and then I'd grab it on the bounce and throw to first."

For all of the praise that Groh received for his glove, what history most remembers him for is his bat. The diminutive Groh, who was listed at 5'6" in some publications, had contact issues when he came up. His efforts to get better resulted in his famous "bottle bat." As historian Lee Allen wrote in his excellent book,

The Cincinnati Reds, "Groh decided he needed a bat with plenty of hitting space. But the big bats that he would have liked to use were unsuited to him because he could hardly swing them. So he started cutting down the size of the handle, until the bat was light enough for him to swing. One day a teammate shouted, 'Hey, Heinie, what are you using, a bottle?' and there it was. The handle was only about 6" long, but the bat weighed 41 ounces."

The unorthodox bat served him well as did a unique batting stance that had Groh standing way up in the front of the box, crouched down with his feet pointed at the pitcher. His miniscule strike zone made Groh an on-base machine, and his tremendous bat control with such a large piece of lumber helped him to become one of the league's best hitters.

When Groh came to the Reds in a deal with the New York Giants that turned out to be tremendously lopsided in Cincinnati's favor, he had not yet established himself as a hitter. Originally a second baseman, he moved to third base in 1915 and quickly made himself known as one of the game's greats. With a complete game on both offense and defense, Groh was arguably the best player in the National League from 1915–19, leading the NL in doubles and on-base percentage while ranking fifth in batting average and eighth in slugging during that span.

The world champion 1919 Reds were equally adept at both run prevention and run scoring due in large part to Groh's play on both sides of the ball. Batting third most of the season, Groh led the league in OPS and led the Reds in home runs and runs scored all while playing outstanding defense at the hot corner. The Reds topped the White Sox in the World Series, though it was later revealed that the Sox agreed with gamblers to throw the series. Groh, like many of his teammates, believed it didn't matter. "I think we'd have beaten them either way," he said years later. "That's what I thought then, and I still think so today."

He played two more seasons with the Reds, but a contentious holdout over a contract dispute prior to the 1921 season convinced the Reds and Groh that they needed to part ways. A deal was worked out to return Groh to the Giants, but commissioner Kenesaw Mountain Landis stepped in and vetoed the deal, fearing "an unhealthy situation if a dissatisfied player could dictate his transfer to a strong contender before he agreed to sign a contract." A disgruntled Groh remained a Red and grumpily played out his remaining contract. You'd never know how upset he was from the results though as he batted .331/.398/.417 in 97 games. When the season was done, the deal with the Giants was consummated and Groh left the Reds after nine fantastic seasons.

Despite his excellent career, he never received much of a shot at the Hall of Fame from the baseball writers. However, he was elected to the Reds Hall of Fame in 1963. His accomplishments at the hot corner still hold up today as some of the best in Reds history. In the words of Greg Rhodes and Mark Stang from their book, *Reds in Black & White*, "Unless your all-time Reds team has Pete Rose at third base, Groh still deserves the accolade today."

The 1995 Reds

From 1991–2012, the Reds won a total of three playoff games, all of them coming during the 1995 postseason. Yet somehow the 1995 Reds squad remains a largely forgotten unit. It was a weird time for baseball. The O.J. Simpson murder trial still held America's attention for most of the summer. Coming off a strike in 1994 that canceled the postseason, many fans were disinterested in the game, and those who were interested still had to depend on a limited number of televised games to see the action.

The Reds had been one of the best teams in baseball when the strike hit in 1994. They lost outfielder Kevin Mitchell to Japan during the strike, but they replaced him with Ron Gant, who was returning from an ATV accident that had blown apart his knee. Gant, who hit .276/.386/.554 with 29 home runs and 88 RBIs was very productive in the middle of the 1995 lineup. He was joined by a breakout season from Reggie Sanders, who was arguably the Reds' best player that year even though shortstop Barry Larkin won the NL MVP. Sanders batted an impressive .306/.397/.579 with 28 home runs and a team-leading 99 RBIs, just missing 100 RBIs because of the shortened 144-game schedule.

Larkin—who was one of three remaining players from the 1990 world champions, along with Hal Morris and Jose Rijo, when the season started—made himself known on the national stage with an impressive .319/.394/.492 batting line while playing Gold Glove defense. He was the anchor for manager Davey Johnson's lineup, that finished second in the NL in runs scored behind the Coors Field–inflated Colorado Rockies.

Led by reclamation project Pete Schourek, the Reds pitching staff was solid, though injury-riddled, throughout the year. Schourek went 18–7 with a 3.22 ERA, finishing second in the Cy Young Award voting to Greg Maddux. After one-time ace Jose Rijo went down with a nearly career-ending elbow injury, general manager Jim Bowden added Mark Portugal and David Wells to the rotation just before the trade deadline. The pair joined left-hander John Smiley (12–5, 3.46) to give the Reds a formidable playoff rotation as the Reds easily won the NL Central by nine games.

The offense and pitching were clicking as the Reds easily swept through the Los Angeles Dodgers in three games. The Reds scored 22 runs in those three games and five different players each homered once, including the franchise's only postseason grand slam off the bat of Mark Lewis to put away the Dodgers in Game 3. Feeling confident, the Reds were all set to face the NL East champion Atlanta Braves, who had just beaten the wild-card Rockies 3–1.

A disappointing crowd of just more than 40,000 fans showed up to watch Game 1 of the NLCS in Cincinnati. Pete Schourek was masterful through eight innings, shutting out the Braves on four hits while striking out eight. The Reds could only manage one run though, and when Schourek surrendered back-to-back singles and a fielder's choice to lead off the ninth, the game was sent into extra innings, where the Braves eventually won in the 11th inning 2–1. The Reds offense failed to come through with men on base throughout the game, hitting into a postseason-record five double plays.

The Game 1 loss set the tone for the series as the Reds offense could only muster five total runs in the four-game sweep by the Braves. The goat of the series is often hung on Reggie Sanders, who went 2-for-16 with 10 strikeouts, but the offensive blame should be spread around as starters Bret Boone, Ron Gant, Benito Santiago, and Hal Morris all batted .231 or worse. Only Barry Larkin, 7-for-18, managed any success against the impressive Braves pitching staff, but it wasn't nearly enough to dig his team out of the hole.

After the 1995 season, manager Davey Johnson was replaced with Ray Knight, whose style did not sit well with the team. Ron Gant left via free agency and David Wells was traded to Baltimore, leaving them with a team that struggled to make it to .500. It would be another 15 seasons before the Reds would make it back to the postseason, an unexpected drought that somehow still has not made the 1995 team any more memorable.

83 Tom Seaver

It does not take many fingers to count the number of future Hall of Famers who were traded mid-season while still in their prime. In the last 50 years, that list only includes Orlando Cepeda in 1966, Tom Seaver in 1977, and Rickey Henderson in 1989.

Seaver, who had been the ace of the New York Mets staff for a decade, fell into the Reds lap in 1977 because of a contract dispute. Actually, calling it a contract dispute is putting it mildly, as in reality it was an angry fight between pitcher and front office that spilled over into the media. Seaver was frustrated that the Mets were making no effort to pay not only him but anybody under the new free-agent rules. He saw the high-paying deals that other pitchers of his caliber were getting around the league, and he wondered why the Mets weren't willing to pay him the same. Chairman of the Board M. Donald Grant attacked Seaver in the press, and everything escalated from there. Eventually a deal was agreed upon, giving Seaver a three-year extension with pay comparable to his peers. But before the deal was signed, Dick Young of the *New York Daily News* blasted Seaver for jealousy he had toward Nolan Ryan. Fed up, Seaver called off the deal and demanded a trade. Without any leverage, Mets general manager Joe McDonald dealt Seaver to the Reds on June 15 for a package of players headlined by pitcher Pat Zachry.

Manager Sparky Anderson was elated with the deal. Years later, he explained, "Seaver was a joy to have around. He is such a bright young guy that his weird sense of humor almost seems out of character." The right-hander gave the Reds a legitimate ace that they were missing after Don Gullett left for the New York Yankees in free agency. Seaver was impressive in his first season with the Redlegs, going 14–3 with a 2.34 ERA in 20 starts, but his presence

Pitcher Tom Seaver winds up to deliver a pitch against the Montreal Expos in Montreal on June 18, 1977. It was Seaver's first start with the Reds since being traded to the club from the New York Mets just days earlier. (AP Photo)

Reds No-Hitters

There have been 15 complete game no-hitters thrown by Reds pitchers. This does not include the 10 innings of no-hit ball thrown by Jim Maloney on 6/14/1965 where Maloney allowed two hits in the 11th inning and the Reds lost 1–0. It also does not include the performance by Johnny Klippstein (seven no-hit IP), Herschel Freeman (one no-hit IP), and Joe Black ($2\frac{1}{3}$ no-hit IP) where the no-hitter was broken up with two outs in the 11th inning. Both games had once been recognized by MLB as no-hitters but are no longer.

Here are the 15 no-hitters thrown by Reds pitchers:

Charles "Bumpus" Jones	10/15/1892 vs. Pittsburgh
Ted Breitenstein	4/22/1898 vs. Pittsburgh
Noodles Hahn	7/12/1900 vs. Philadelphia
Fred Toney	5/2/1917 at Chicago (10 innings)
Hod Eller	5/11/1919 vs. St. Louis
Johnny Vander Meer	6/11/1938 vs. Boston
Johnny Vander Meer	6/15/1938 at Brooklyn
Clyde Shoun	5/15/1944 vs. Boston
Ewell Blackwell	6/18/1947 vs. Boston
Jim Maloney	8/19/1965 at Chicago (10 innings)
George Culver	7/29/1968 at Philadelphia
Jim Maloney	4/30/1969 vs. Houston
Tom Seaver	6/16/1978 vs. St. Louis
Tom Browning	9/16/1988 vs. Los Angeles (perfect game)
Homer Bailey	9/28/2012 at Pittsburgh

was not enough to help the team overcome a seven-game lead by the Los Angeles Dodgers and the Reds finished the season 10 games behind the NL champs.

Seaver was very good again in 1978, going 16–14 with a 2.88 ERA, but once again the Reds fell short of the Dodgers. The right-hander achieved a personal highlight that season on June 16, nearly one year to the day after he was traded to the Reds. On that day, Tom Terrific pitched the only no-hitter of his career, shutting out the St. Louis Cardinals 4–0. Seaver had three times prior with the Mets taken a no-hitter into the ninth inning, including a perfect game in 1969, only to lose the bid. Finally, with the Reds he was able to finish one off, giving the franchise its 13th no-hitter in history.

The Reds ace was impressive despite some injuries during the 1979 season, winning 14 of this last 15 decisions to carry the Reds into the playoffs for the first time in three years. Seaver surrendered two runs over eight innings in his only NLCS start, but the Reds fell, both in that game and the series, to the eventual world champion Pittsburgh Pirates.

Arm troubles put a damper on his 1980 season and Seaver went 10–8 with a 3.64 ERA, the highest of his career to that point. He bounced back with an outstanding 14–2, 2.54 ERA strike-shortened season in 1981, but the Reds were left out of the playoffs because of a split-season rule to adjust for the shortened schedule. Seaver's best season also butted up against Fernandomania, as Dodgers rookie Fernando Valenzuela just edged out the future Hall of Famer's best shot to become the Reds' first Cy Young Award winner.

The 1982 Reds were atrocious, losing 101 games while Seaver suffered through the worst year of his career, putting up a career-high ERA of 5.50 and a career low in wins with five. By that point, the Reds were ready to part ways with the 38-year-old, and Seaver left via a trade back to re-sign with the Mets. In all, Tom Terrific spent 5½ seasons with the Reds, posting a 75–46 record, the fifth best winning percentage in team history. In 2006, he was voted into the Reds Hall of Fame by the fans, 14 years after entering the Baseball Hall of Fame with the highest vote percentage ever at 98.8 percent. Just another feather in the cap of perhaps the greatest pitcher to ever put on a Reds uniform.

84 Bid McPhee

It is not uncommon for great players to be forgotten to history, especially when they played in an era with sporadic media accounts and shoddy historical records. Occasionally, those players are rediscovered for their greatness, and if they are lucky enough, their greatness is recognized by someone who makes sure that it's never forgotten. John Alexander "Bid" McPhee is one of the lucky ones whose rediscovery led to enshrinement into the National Baseball Hall of Fame, never to be forgotten again.

It wasn't clear from the get-go that McPhee would wind up as one of baseball's immortals. After a brief stint with pro ball in Iowa, Bid became a bookkeeper and was quite certain that would be his career path from then on. After playing some ball again in Akron, Ohio, he was picked up by the Cincinnati Red Stockings in the newly formed American Association, but McPhee still had doubts that baseball was something he'd do long term. His first game with the Red Stockings left even more doubt for the second baseman.

Bid had a particularly bad day in the Red Stockings' 10–9 loss in the franchise's first game ever. Riding home on the streetcar afterward, McPhee overheard a conversation by some fans who didn't recognize the player in his street clothes. "That stiff they played on second base today made me sick," one of the crowd said. "What's his name? McPhee? Yes, that's it. He ought to have stayed in Akron. He might be a good bookkeeper, but he is a rotten ballplayer!"

The conversation didn't help the youngster with the doubts he had about his baseball career, but he stuck with the game and even though he only hit .228 that season, he was an important part of the Red Stockings' American Association championship, the only title the team would see during McPhee's 18-year career.

What eventually made McPhee a star was the move to overhand pitching by the American Association in 1885. The change meant hits were more rare, and so teams turned to speedsters to produce runs and leaned on strong defensive players to help prevent them. This perfectly suited McPhee's game.

McPhee is credited as the all-time stolen bases leader in Reds franchise history with 568 thefts. That number is somewhat deceptive as players in McPhee's day were credited with a stolen base when they advanced an extra base on a hit or an out. That fact should not diminish the value of McPhee's speed whatsoever. He was still one of the most prolific base runners of his era, posting the fourth highest stolen base total for the years spanning his career.

Defensively, Bid had few rivals at second base. He led the league in fielding percentage nine times and was frequently at the top of the leader board in putouts, assists, and double plays, all while steadfastly refusing to wear a glove like some of his contemporaries. When McPhee finally relented and wore a glove after a finger injury, he set a fielding-percentage record of .978 that stood for nearly 30 years.

The dapper gentleman with the handlebar mustache who spent all 18 of his seasons with the Reds was known in Cincinnati as "an honest man and the best second baseman in the world." He was famous for his sobriety at a time when drinking was the norm for most ballplayers. When *The Sporting News* erroneously reported McPhee's death in 1932, a friend of Bid's wrote to the paper to point out its error, stating that McPhee was "one of the finest players and most perfect gentlemen the game has ever known."

McPhee finally did pass into 1943 at the age of 83. Fifty-seven years later he was inducted in the National Baseball Hall of Fame by the Veterans Committee. His election reminded many in the Reds community of his greatness, and he was elected to the Reds

Hall of Fame in 2002. To this day, he still ranks in the top five in Reds history in hits, runs, triples, RBIs, walks, and stolen bases.

85 Woulda, Shoulda, Coulda

Did you know that Babe Ruth could have played for the Cincinnati Reds? It's true. As part of an agreement with the minor league Baltimore Orioles, the Reds could choose any two players off their roster to play for Cincinnati in 1914. The man making the decision for the Reds, Harry Stevens, was not much of a talent scout and he completely overlooked Ruth, who was a pitcher for the team. Instead he chose outfielder George Twombly and shortstop Claud Derrick, neither of whom brought much to the Reds. A more keen eye could have changed the fortunes of two franchises.

Twenty-two years later, the team had a deal in place to acquire Ruth as a player-manager, but the Yankees refused to let the Bambino out of his contract. Alas, the Babe never played for the Reds, but he is just one of a handful of great players the Reds just missed out on or gave up on too early. Every franchise has players who they wish they had not given up. Here are a few that came back to haunt the Cincinnati franchise.

In 1900, the Reds drafted a 19-year-old pitcher named Christy Mathewson from the minor league Norfolk squad. Mathewson was not long for the Reds as they soon traded him to the New York Giants for Amos Rusie. While Rusie had been great at one time, he only pitched in three games in Cincinnati. Mathewson went on to win 372 games for the Giants and was a member in the initial Hall of Fame class in 1936. Mathewson did eventually come back to the Reds in 1916 as a player-manager. He only pitched one game for the squad, an unimpressive victory, but more importantly his management helped the Reds build toward their eventual championship in 1919 under manager Pat Moran.

In December 1934, the Reds purchased the contract of prospect Johnny Mize from the St. Louis Cardinals on a conditional deal. They were impressed by what they saw, but a late spring groin injury was determined to require surgery and the Reds were leery about spending money on someone who wasn't a sure thing. The team sent Mize back to the Cardinals and a year later, after having the surgery, he made the big-league debut to what would turn into a Hall of Fame career. Mize led the NL in OPS three times and home runs four times, finishing in the top three in MVP voting three times. The Reds were a very good team during the early part of Mize's career, but they could have been a dynasty with his bat in the lineup.

More than four decades later, the Reds had a deal in place to acquire 1971 AL Cy Young Award winner Vida Blue from the Oakland A's for rookie outfielder Dave Revering and $1.75 million. The deal was nixed in January 1978 by commissioner Bowie Kuhn on the grounds that the amount of cash was excessive and that the deal was not good for the competitive balance of the league. Blue would have packed a powerful 1-2 punch with Tom Seaver on that 1978 squad that finished second to the NL pennant-winning Dodgers. Unfortunately for Reds fans, a subsequent deal could not be worked out, and Blue was instead dealt to the Giants two months later.

Blue's teammate with the Oakland A's, Rollie Fingers, also could have been a Red at one time The deal never happened because Fingers refused to shave off his trademark handlebar mustache to comply with the team's no facial hair policy and instead chose to retire. Seven years later, the Reds had a chance to draft another future Hall of Famer and came very close to doing so, but at the last minute they decided to draft Chad Mottola instead of Derek Jeter. Every team passes up on an eventually great player at some point, but by all accounts, the Reds decision to go with Mottola was made right at the bell, leaving Jeter available for the Yankees with the very next pick.

During the 2006 Rule 5 draft, the Reds shrewdly acquired super-talented but often injured Josh Hamilton via the Chicago Cubs. Hamilton had been a number one overall pick at one time, but injuries and drug abuse left him as a big question mark. Despite never playing above AA, Hamilton wowed the baseball world with his performance in 2007. The Reds needed pitching and dealt the outfielder to the Texas Rangers for Edinson Volquez following the season. At first it looked like the deal would work for both teams as Volquez won 17 games for the Reds in 2008 and Hamilton led the AL in RBIs. Volquez fizzled though while Hamilton flourished, making the All-Star team every year since the trade and winning the 2010 MVP with the Rangers. The Reds have had success since the deal, but who knows what they would have accomplished with Hamilton in the lineup.

History is full of "what-ifs" and every team has a doozy of a deal that they regret, but it's still hard not to imagine what could have been if any of these deals had worked out in the team's favor.

86 Pete Rose's 44-Game Hit Streak

For all of his foibles, one thing was certain about Pete Rose—the man could hit. In his first 15 seasons in the big leagues, he racked up nearly 3,000 hits, nine times topping the 200-hit plateau. However, in 1978 he was 37 years old, and even though he'd passed the 3,000-hit milestone in May, some were starting to wonder if Rose's time in the game was winding down. He hit .227

in the 36 games after his 3,000[th] hit, one of the worst slumps of his career. For most players, it's what you start to expect at the age of 37. But for Pete Rose, age was just another number. As his manager Sparky Anderson liked to remind everyone, "In Pete's mind, he still thinks he's a 20-year-old."

That 20-year-old inside of Rose broke out on June 14, 1978, with two singles, and for the next month-and-a-half pundits stopped wondering if Pete Rose could still hit. Instead, they were wondering if he could be stopped.

Rose followed up that two-hit game with hits in nine straight games, including multiple hits in five of those nine. It was still a meager streak at that point, but it was a familiar show to his manager. "When Pete gets a couple of hits, he goes for three," Anderson pointed out. "He gets three, and he shoots for four."

By the All-Star break, Rose's hit streak was up to 25 games and his batting average was finally back over .300 for the first time since late May. Three days after the break, a first-inning single extended the streak to 28 games, passing Edd Roush and Vada Pinson for the longest hitting streak in Reds history. At this point he was only halfway to Joe DiMaggio's record 56-game streak, but the national media was starting to take notice. Rose was unflappable, though.

"Guys talking to me all the time doesn't bother me," he explained. "And it's not gonna jinx me. I'm still the guy there swinging the bat."

Asked what it would take to keep the streak going, Rose showed that he still had a sense of humor about the situation, saying that he "would have to get a hit every game."

A seventh-inning single off former teammate Pat Zachry on July 24 tied Rose with Tommy Holmes for the longest hitting streak in the National League since the turn of the century, but Rose still wanted to top the NL record of 44 games set by Wee Willie Keeler in 1897. Rose would match that record a week later with a single in the sixth inning off Braves knuckleballer Phil Niekro.

The streak wouldn't make it into August though as Larry McWilliams and Gene Garber combined to hold Rose hitless for the first time in 45 games. The end of the streak didn't come without some drama however as Rose lined hard to third baseman Bob Horner in the seventh inning off Garber. Had the ball been a few feet in either direction, Rose might have extended the streak a little further. He managed one more at-bat in the ninth, but the submarining Garber got Rose swinging to end the game and the streak.

Rose still holds the NL record for longest hitting streak with Keeler at 44 games, although one could argue that Rose's path was much harder given that in Keeler's day a foul ball was not considered a strike. Had Rose had that luxury, it's possible he may not have struck out versus Garber in the ninth of that final game.

All told Rose hit .385 during the 44-game hit streak, raising his season batting average by 49 points in the process. He had 18 multi-hit games during the streak. Six times during the streak he got a hit in his final at-bat of the game to extend the streak. Probably most important for Rose was that the Reds were 26–18 during his streak, cutting the lead of the first-place Giants from two games to ½-game in the span.

Rose finished the year with 198 hits, falling just short of what would have been a record-breaking 10th season of 200 hits, a record he'd break the following season. Yet most importantly for the prideful Rose was that he put to rest any doubts that, even at the ripe old age of 37, he could still collect base hits as well as anyone in the league.

87 Johnny Bench Night

It's hard to believe that a mid-September game could be a memorable one for a team that was in last place, 17 games out of first, and had already been eliminated from playoff contention four days prior. The 1983 Reds were coming off the franchise's first 100-loss season and were struggling to avoid a second consecutive season of 90+ losses for the first time in nearly 50 years. All of that negativity did not keep more than 53,000 fans from making the trip to Riverfront Stadium to celebrate the greatest catcher the game has ever seen.

Johnny Bench won over Reds fans with his incredible combination of offense and defense at the hardest position on the field. He held on to their hearts with his charisma and charm. Well-spoken and thoughtful, Bench was one of the mouthpieces of the Big Red Machine, a recognizable star not just in Cincinnati but around the country.

By 1983, the years behind the plate had taken their toll on Bench. He started more games at third base and first base than catcher that year. In fact, Bench did not make a single start at catcher until August 6. By that point, he had already announced his plans to retire at the end of the season. The Reds in return had scheduled a celebration for one of their greats, announcing that Johnny Bench Night would be held on September 17.

The Reds rolled out the red carpet for the event. A 45-minute pregame ceremony was emceed by Marty Brennaman and local TV personality Bob Braun, both wearing tuxedos. Bench's parents and family were in attendance, as was former Yankee catching great Bill Dickey. Sparky Anderson, who was managing the Detroit Tigers at the time, sent along a heartfelt taped message to one of his favorite players he ever managed. Even President Ronald Reagan participated via a congratulatory telegram.

After a four-minute standing ovation, Bench gave a speech prior to the game, thanking the fans for their love. "I have tried to be the very best ballplayer that I could," Bench said, "for my family, for my friends, and for everybody who paid to get in this park." He closed the speech by telling the fans in attendance, "I appreciate you, and I'm going to try like hell to play good for you tonight."

Always one with a flare for the dramatic, Bench gave fans a special treat that late-summer night. After a first-inning walk versus Houston Astros pitcher Mike Madden, Bench came to bat in the third inning to face Madden one more time with a man on first base. The crowd buzzed every time Bench came to the plate that night, but after an 0–1 pitch on a check-swing, they erupted into applause when he launched a no-doubt home run into left field, the 389th bomb of his major league career. Bench thrust his finger into the air in excitement three times as a he rounded the bases as if to say, "That one's for you, fans." When he reached the dugout he gave a slight shrug of the shoulders in disbelief. He had turned an already special night into an unforgettable one for everyone involved, but that's what great players do.

Bench led off the fifth inning with a single but was erased on a double play. His night came to an end after a seventh-inning fly out as Dann Billardello replaced Bench at catcher, marking the final time he sported the tools of ignorance in a major league game. Johnny Bench Night would be his last start in the big leagues, but it's hard to imagine a more fitting finish for a great player. Even though the Reds lost 4–3, everyone in attendance left the park happy about what they had just seen.

88 Pat Moran

As a player, Pat Moran wasn't much. He played in all or parts of 14 seasons, mostly as a backup catcher, only twice playing in more than 100 games in a season. He never hit particularly well, which is what kept him out of the lineup. But he could handle a pitching staff like no one else. It was that fact that got Moran into coaching, first as a pitching coach and then as manager of the Philadelphia Phillies. An intelligent ballplayer, Moran's best baseball skills translated well to the managerial role. First he helped develop pitcher Grover Cleveland Alexander into one of the game's best. Then in 1915, through some shrewd deals, he pulled a burgeoning Phillies team into the World Series for the first time in franchise history. They lost to the Boston Red Sox, and two years later Phillies owner William Baker sabotaged Moran's roster by selling off Alexander and Bill Killefer, leaving his manager with a shell of a team. Moran was later fired at the end of the 1918 season.

The firing would end up being fortuitous for Moran as a Reds team that was on the upswing found itself in need of a manager as Christy Mathewson was in Europe doing war exercises. Moran signed on with the Reds and immediately made a couple of critical deals. First, he traded outfielder Tommy Griffith to Brooklyn for first baseman Jake Daubert. The 35-year-old Daubert was a good hitter and had a couple of fine seasons with the Reds, solidifying the top of the batting order. Moran also picked up two pitchers off waivers who would play major roles for the 1919 squad. Slim Sallee was a good pitcher for the New York Giants, but when he came to the Reds, he was excellent, leading the team with a 21–7 record and posting a 2.06 ERA. Ray Fisher added some extra depth to the staff, going 14–5 in 20 starts for the Reds. Moran also moved seldom-used Dutch Ruether, who the Reds had acquired two years prior, to the rotation and he responded with a 19–6 record and a team-leading 1.82 ERA.

The 1919 squad had all the markings of a Moran-coached team. It led the league in pitching and defense and sported a surprisingly good offensive squad, too. It easily won the National League pennant with a 96–44 record and took home the team's first World Series title in eight games over the Chicago White Sox, who were later labeled the Black Sox for allegedly throwing the Series. No longer the story of that Series, Moran, like everyone associated with the Reds, was left to argue that the Reds would have won the Series even if the White Sox had played it straight.

One of the few players' managers of the era, Moran had a mutual trust with his players. When center fielder Edd Roush alerted Moran that pitcher Hod Eller had been approached by gamblers, Moran called Eller into his office. The manager looked his pitcher in the eye and asked him for the truth. When Eller admitted that he had been approached but told the gambler that "if he didn't get damn far away from me real quick he wouldn't know what hit him," Moran believed in his player but told him, "One wrong move and you're out of the game." Eller showed no signs of impropriety as the Reds easily won game eight and the Series.

The situation was a prime example of what made Moran a great manager. As he explained, "As a leader, it is my business to give orders, and these are always carried out. Not by the 'mailed fist' method, as I do not believe in that style, but as one friend to another. The players carry them out because they have confidence in me."

Moran would manage the Reds for four more seasons, twice finishing in second place. However, alcoholism had been a problem for years. After the 1923 season, there were reports that Moran had begun drinking even more heavily and had taken ill. He still came to spring training, but it was too late and he passed away on

March 7, 1924. The cause of death was determined to be Bright's Disease, a kidney ailment, yet many believe that Moran's years of drinking may have been the primary culprit. He only managed the Reds for five seasons, but his .564 winning percentage is third best all time for any Reds manager with at least 500 games, and he's one of four managers in team history to ever win a World Series.

89 Frank McCormick

For many Reds fans, Frank McCormick is likely the best former Reds player of whom they've never heard. He has been overshadowed in Reds history by more well-known teammates like Ernie Lombardi, Johnny Vander Meer, and Bucky Walters, and he is less familiar than some lesser first basemen from franchise history like Ted Kluszewski, Sean Casey, and Lee May. McCormick was a precise contact hitter with some power, and if not for a late start to his career, he may have had a shot at Cooperstown.

Nicknamed "Buck," McCormick was one of the largest players of his day, standing at an imposing 6'4" and weighing 200 lbs. He grew up playing sandlot ball in New York and was forced to travel to tryout camps when he decided that he wanted to play pro ball. The Reds liked what they saw in 1934, and McCormick hit so well in the minors that year that the team brought him up to the big leagues for a cup of coffee in September. For a while that looked like it might be Buck's only shot as he languished in the minors for two seasons before making the team out of spring training in 1937. The right-hander spent three weeks in the majors before being sent to Syracuse where he again toiled until mid-September. When the Reds recalled him to the big leagues, McCormick went 7-for-9 in a doubleheader his first day back and didn't stop hitting for the next three years.

Essentially a 27-year-old rookie, McCormick finally got a full-time starting job in 1938. He swatted hits all over the field, leading the NL with 209 knocks and finishing second with 40 doubles. He only hit five home runs that year, but he still drove in 106 runs, good for fourth in the league. He finished third behind teammate Ernie Lombardi with a .327 batting average, which added up to a fifth-place finish in MVP voting when Lombardi took home the hardware.

By this point, the Reds were establishing themselves as a power-house of the National League, and as the fourth hitter, McCormick was tasked as the team's primary run producer. Buck certainly produced in 1939, establishing career highs for batting average (.332), on-base percentage (.374), and slugging percentage (.495), while once again leading the league with 209 hits as well as in RBIs with 128, all while striking out a mere 16 times the entire season. His incredible ability for contact established McCormick as one of the two best first basemen in the NL along with the Cardinals Johnny Mize, but once again Buck fell short in the MVP voting, finishing fourth to teammate Bucky Walters.

The Reds won the NL pennant in 1939 but were toppled by the Yankees in the World Series. They'd repeat as NL champs the following year due to another great season from McCormick. The burly first baseman led the NL in hits for a third straight season and also paced the league with 44 doubles. He finished seventh in average and second in RBIs, which was finally enough for voters to hand him his only MVP award, just beating out Mize. McCormick wasn't particularly effective in the World Series, but it didn't matter much as the Reds pitchers and timely hitting from team-mates snatched the title from the Tigers in seven games.

McCormick reportedly injured his back in 1941, requiring a brace during that whole season. His power tailed off for a couple of seasons before a big resurgence in 1944 when he hit a career-high

20 home runs and drove in 102 RBIs. He played one more year with the Reds before he was sold to the Phillies. In his eight full seasons with the Redlegs, he batted .300/.350/.438, averaging 176 hits, 35 doubles, and 99 RBIs. His success with the team earned him the honor of being among the first class of inductees in the Reds Hall of Fame in 1958. His 149 career strikeouts is the fewest in the modern era by a Reds player with at least 4,000 career plate appearances—that's fewer than Adam Dunn had in his first 580 career plate appearances.

90 Have a Day, Art Shamsky!

Art Shamsky is a legend to many fans of the New York Mets for the role he played on the 1969 Miracle Mets, but the greatest game of his career came as a member of the Reds. And it wasn't even a game that he started.

On August 12, 1966, the Reds were playing the Pirates at Crosley Field in a game that was back and forth from the get-go. When Shamsky entered the game in the top of the eighth inning as part of a double-switch, the Pirates were leading 7–6 and the teams had already combined for six home runs and five lead changes. The lean youngster with dark hair first strode to the plate in the bottom of the inning with Dick Simpson standing on first base and launched a bomb into deep right field, catapulting the Reds into the lead with just three outs remaining for the Pirates hitters.

But pinch-hitter extraordinaire Jerry Lynch blasted a one-out dinger in the top of the ninth—the 18th and final pinch-hit home run of his career—tying the game at eight and dragging both teams into extra innings.

Willie Stargell joined the home run parade in the top of the 10th, giving the Pirates a one-run lead. But Shamsky delivered again in the bottom of the inning with a solo-shot of his own. The 11th inning saw the Pirates push across two more runs on a Bob Bailey double. Bailey had already hit two home runs in the game. Shamsky would not let his Redlegs go that easy. After Johnny Edwards managed to squeak out a two-out walk in the bottom of the inning, Shamsky delivered his third shot of the night, another deep blast into the right-field moon deck.

The game carried to the 13th before the Pirates were able to plate three runners. As luck would have it, Shamsky was due up fifth when the Reds came to bat, and a lead-off single by Chico Ruiz had many fans thinking that the impossible just might happen again. Unfortunately, Tommy Helms struck out looking and Leo Cardenas grounded into a game-ending double play, leaving Shamsky standing in the dugout waiting for another chance.

The 24-year-old Shamsky became the only player to hit three home runs in a game he didn't start, and he's also the only player to hit three home runs in the eighth inning or later of the same game. All three of his blasts either tied the game or gave the Reds the lead, making his performance one of the most clutch hitting displays in the history of baseball.

"If you are in the groove, you can hit anyone," Shamsky said afterward. "I was just lucky to hit any of these home runs. This was one of those days when everything I did was exactly right. But I don't think I was a star of the game because we lost."

Despite being in the groove, manager Dave Bristol did not have Shamsky in the lineup the next day either as the Reds won 11–0 in a rain-shortened match versus the Pirates. When Shamsky finally did see the field again, it was as a pinch hitter two days after his monstrous feat. And what did he do? You guessed it, he launched another two-run home run into the seats to give the Reds a 2–1 lead in the seventh inning, making Shamsky the only Reds player to hit home runs in four consecutive plate appearances, which is also the major league record.

Still unable to crack the lineup, Shamsky had a chance to break that record the following day when he pinch-hit in the eighth inning versus the Dodgers, but he only managed a single in that at-bat, breaking his streak.

Shamsky went on to hit 21 home runs in that 1966 season, second most on the team, but a low batting average and an inability to hit left-handed pitching left him as a platoon player for most of his eight-year career and he never hit more than 14 home runs in another season. But for one day, he did something that's never been done before or since.

91 Attend the Reds' Hall of Fame Gala

Baseball has been a date-night destination for sports fans for decades, but rarely is there an opportunity for fans to get gussied up and have a nice meal while celebrating America's pastime. Every other year, when the team elects new members to its Hall of Fame, the Cincinnati Reds give their fans the chance to do just that at the Reds' Hall of Fame Gala, an experience that is unlike any other during the baseball season.

The night starts with drinks and hors d'oeuvres as fans and honored guests gather. A silent auction is set up for collectors to bid on items such as autographed baseballs, bats, and jerseys or unique photographs of players for display. Even if you are not one to bid on such items, there is usually plenty of fun stuff to view and discuss.

When the time comes for the event to start, guests gather in the beautifully decorated reception hall. A main stage is set up in the front of the hall with giant video screens so that everyone can see. The beauty of this event is in the subtle baseball themes throughout. From the baseball bat centerpieces on the tables to the replica power stacks flanking each side of the stage, every Reds fan will feel right at home even if he's not used to the formal setting.

The atmosphere for the night is typically light-hearted and sentimental. The event celebrates both the current players as well as the all-time greats from throughout the franchise's history. Fans get to see interviews with some of their childhood favorites in a relaxed atmosphere. The camaraderie and respect that the players have for each other is on full display, and the stories that they tell will take you back to the days when you watched in awe as they raced around the diamond. And rest assured that if Lee May or Eric Davis has a microphone in his face, you'll be laughing hysterically.

Another treat of the night is that many of the tables where the fans sit have a current or former player sitting at them. This is a unique opportunity for fans to talk one-on-one with a player and learn about them not just as an athlete but as a person. This makes the event a one-of-a-kind experience that is difficult to duplicate anywhere else. Add in a delicious meal and open bar, and fans are left with little doubt that the team has spared no expense to make the evening memorable for everyone in attendance.

But the highlights of the evening are always the men that are there to be honored with their induction into the Reds Hall of Fame. Highlight videos flood you with memories of the greatness the player displayed on the field, and the stories from teammates and family members often show a side of the player you've never seen before.

Speeches from the players themselves can be even more revealing. In 2012, Reds fans heard from the normally reserved Dan Driessen and saw a proud family man who was truly touched by the gesture of the Hall of Fame induction. Fans were also treated to a speech from Sean Casey that topped most stand-up comedians for laughs per minute.

These are just a few of the highlights of an event that every Reds fan should try to experience at least once. Each Gala has some surprises that are special unto itself, so no two Galas are exactly alike. Even if you can only make it once, it will be one of the most memorable nights you have as a Reds fan.

92 Adam Dunn

The longest home run ever hit at Great American Ball Park might still be floating down the Mississippi River if not for some driftwood on the banks of the Ohio River. In the days before the party boat rested atop the hitter's eye in center field, Adam Dunn launched a satellite into orbit over that hitter's eye, over an exterior wall for the park, and on to Mehring Way below, an estimated 535' from home plate. From there the ball trickled down into the Ohio River where it found its final resting place among some driftwood on the bank.

"You know the Paul Bunyan legend?" teammate Sean Casey laughed. "He's building the Adam Dunn legend. He's so strong maybe he can help push boulders around and build a dam or something. If a flood is coming, they can use him to stop up the river. He could probably grab those 5,000-lb. boulders and pick them up with one arm."

Only 24 years old, Dunn had already established himself as one of the greatest, young power-hitters the game has ever seen. This prodigious blast was the 107th of his career in just his 451st game.

No Reds player had ever hit so many home runs in so few games to start a career. The 46 home runs that Dunn would eventually hit in that 2004 season were the 10th most in a season by a player age 24 or younger.

Standing at 6'6" and listed at 285 lbs., it's hard to imagine how Adam Dunn had been recruited to play quarterback at the University of Texas. In fact, he had enrolled in the college and planned to play baseball in the summer and football in the fall until the Longhorns also signed phenom Chris Simms to play the quarterback position. Realizing that his path in baseball might be easier, Dunn dropped out of college and focused on baseball full-time.

Dunn moved quickly through the Reds minor league system. In 2001, he hit 32 home runs as a 21-year-old in only 94 games. He was called to the majors that July and put on an impressive power display, hitting 18 doubles and 19 home runs in 66 games. He also demonstrated a patient eye at the plate along with a high propensity for strikeouts, facts that would lead him to become one of the greatest "Three True Outcomes" players of all time. In that 2004 season when he hit 46 home runs, he also drew 108 walks, but the only category that he led the National League in was strikeouts. His 195 whiffs that year broke the major league mark of 189 set by Bobby Bonds in 1970.

Dunn would go on to lead the league in strikeouts the next two seasons, as well, something many fans were unable to overlook despite the fact that Dunn led the team in home runs, walks, and RBIs each season. As often is the case, Dunn, the Reds' best offensive player, was blamed for many of the team's shortcomings as the Reds never posted a winning record during the Big Donkey's eight seasons with the club. While Dunn was hardly innocent in the team's failures—his poor defensive play was a contributing factor to the Reds consistently poor showing in runs allowed—rarely was the supporting cast deep enough for the Reds to ever really be considered contenders.

Dunn was eventually dealt during the 2008 season to the joy of some fans and to the sadness of many others. His 270 home runs with the Reds are the fourth most in franchise history, and his four straight 40-home-run seasons has never been duplicated by a Reds player. He is also sixth all time in walks and third in strikeouts, impressive rankings for a player who's not even in the top 20 all-time in games played. But that's the legend of Adam Dunn for you, a three true outcomes hero.

Adam Dunn bats against the New York Mets in a game on July 19, 2006, in Cincinnati. (AP Photo/Al Behrman)

93 The Only Woman Ever to Bat in a Major League Game

The enthusiasm for night baseball did not subside quickly in the Queen City. Two months after the first night game, Crosley Field played the sixth night game in big-league history and saw its largest crowd ever, including a spunky nightclub entertainer who quickly made a name for herself.

Crosley Field's maximum capacity was about 26,000, and the team saw somewhere around 19,000 to 23,000 for the previous five night games, but a stifling traffic jam kept many locals and out-of-towners from reaching the park by game time on July 31, 1935. In the interim, the ballclub oversold capacity by as much as 10,000. By the time all of the late arrivers made their way into the park, many were forced to stand on the field behind a makeshift rope corral.

"The park was loaded," Reds left fielder Babe Herman recalled 50 years later. "The fans were all over the field. You couldn't see the game from the dugout."

As many as 12 rows of fans stood along the foul territory, forcing managers and players in the dugouts to request updates from fans as their views of the playing field were often blocked. The hubbub from so many on the field led to multiple delays, including one that forced umpires to threaten a Reds forfeiture if fans did not behave.

In the mass of people on the field was a "pretty young blond dressed in red." Some reports say Kitty Burke, a 20-year-old local performer, was angered by not being able to see the field. But as she explained it, "What burned me was Ducky Wucky Medwick, the St. Louis left fielder."

Burke had gotten into a shouting match with Joe "Ducky" Medwick, the Cardinals 23-year-old left fielder, after Medwick scored a run to put the Cardinals up by two over the hometown Reds.

"Medwick, you can't hit anything," she brashly yelled at the Cardinals All-Star.

"Yeah, you can't hit anything yourself," he hollered back.

Fuming, Burke decided to prove her worth. During an injury delay, and with Herman on deck, Burke ducked under the rope and made her way onto the playing field.

As Herman later recounted, "This blond says to me, 'Babe, give me your bat.'"

"I said, 'What do you want with it?'"

"I want to go to bat."

"I said, 'Go ahead.'"

Since there was already a delay on the field, home plate umpire Bill Stewart played along, recommending to pitcher Paul "Daffy" Dean to throw the young lady a pitch. Burke was determined to stand in there at home plate all night if that's how long it took her to hit one.

Dean lobbed a floater over the plate, and Burke slapped it down toward first base. The pitcher managed to field the ball and tag first base before Burke could scoot down the line. Despite protestations from Cardinals manager Frankie Frisch, the out did not count against the Reds, and Burke ducked back under the rope and disappeared into the hysteria of the crowd.

After the game, Herman commented, "It was the first time a woman ever pinch-hit for me."

He eventually did take his at-bat that inning, swatting a run-scoring double to help the Reds snatch a victory in 10 innings—one of the few bright spots in an otherwise dismal season.

Soon after the game, Burke went on to work the burlesque circuit. Taking advantage of her sudden fame, she billed herself as, "The only woman ever to bat in a major league game."

94 Check Out a Reds Minor League Affiliate

It's hard to admit but sometimes the big-league product of the Cincinnati Reds isn't all that fun to watch. The fact is whether because of injuries, poor talent, or an evil curse from an enchanted wizard, there are years when the Reds aren't pennant contenders. Fret not, loyal Reds fan there are still options for you to cheer the future Reds stars today.

About 90 minutes southwest of Cincinnati lies Louisville Slugger Field, home of the Louisville Bats, the Reds' Triple A affiliate since 2000. The Bats have been Western Division champs five times since becoming a Reds affiliate, including three straight titles from 2008–10. Typically, teams use Triple A as a holding spot for replacement players you might see in the big leagues at some point during the year. However, it's not uncommon to watch quality prospects in Triple A if they play a position that is already occupied in the big leagues. For instance, Bats fans saw a lot of Yonder Alonso, Todd Frazier, and Juan Francisco in recent years as all three players had to wait their turn (or for a trade) to get to the majors. The close proximity of Louisville to Cincinnati makes for a fun trip for local fans looking for a baseball fix, especially when the Reds are on an extended road trip.

If you are a Florida resident or on a vacation in the Sunshine State, check out the Pensacola Blue Wahoos, the Reds' Double A affiliate. The Blue Wahoos are fairly new to the Reds' fold, pairing up with the franchise in 2012, but they've already seen some great talent take the field in players like Billy Hamilton, Daniel Corcino, and Donald Lutz. Double A baseball is a good chance to learn about the future stars of your favorite franchise before any of your friends. Highly talented players will often skip from Double A straight to the majors, but even those who spend time in Triple A tend to spend much more time in Double A.

West Coast Reds fans can catch the Bakersfield Blaze, the Reds' high-A affiliate. The Blaze play in the California League, which is a well-known offensive environment, so if you are a fan of high-scoring games, they are one to check out.

The Reds' low-A affiliate is just up the road from Cincinnati in Dayton. Like the Louisville squad, the Dayton Dragons have been part of the Reds franchise since 2000. Fifth Third Field in Dayton is a beautiful park famous for holding the longest consecutive sellout streak record for professional sports. A 2012 poll of Midwest League players picked Dayton as the favorite place to play, in large part because it is packed with an enthusiastic crowd on a nightly basis.

If you're the type of fan who likes to get in on the ground floor with prospects, then you have two choices for trips to plan. The Billings Mustangs have been the rookie ball affiliate for the Reds since 1974, easily lapping the tenure of any other affiliate. That history has meant that many of the great Reds players of the last 30 years have passed through Billings, Montana, at some point. From Tom Browning to Reggie Sanders to Aaron Boone to Joey Votto, fans in Billings have gotten to see some very good players get their feet wet over the years. Billings is a long way from Cincinnati, and rookie ball is a long way from the majors, but you never know what future star you might see there.

The Reds also have a rookie league team that plays in their spring training facility in Goodyear, Arizona. The Arizona League is mostly an instructional league with very little fanfare. However, the games are still real and the players are still trying to make their mark and if you ever catch them in action, you might be lucky enough to see a future big leaguer long before any fans have heard his name.

Reds Fall One Game Short in 1999

Heading into 1999 with three consecutive losing seasons, the Reds were building with an eye toward 2002 and the opening of a new ballpark. There wasn't much hope for success during the '99 season. At least, that was the case until general manager Jim Bowden received a call from Kevin Towers. The San Diego Padres GM offered up Greg Vaughn, who was coming off a 50–home run season. Bowden thought it was too good to be true, that Towers would want a pile of the Reds most-coveted prospects to get the deal done. But that wasn't the case. Towers wanted Reggie Sanders, who made about $2 million less than Vaughn. Once he got approval from the Reds' brass to increase payroll, Bowden pulled the trigger.

Always the promoter, Bowden remained low key about the deal, making no promises about a championship, though he did say, "Who knows? We might win a little quicker than people thought."

It sure didn't look like much had changed after the trade, except maybe the removal of the team's no facial hair policy to appease Vaughn and a change in ownership in April as Marge Schott quietly sold off her majority share of the franchise. The team started out 14–18, and fans figured it would be relegated to another season pulling up the rear in the National League Central. That's just when things started to get interesting.

The Reds reeled off a 16–4 stretch that included an eight-game win streak and a record-setting 24–12 victory in Colorado highlighted by a three-home-run game from Jeffrey Hammonds. A slight stumble through interleague play was followed by a 10-game win streak that put the Reds in first place by a half game. It was the first time the team had been alone in first place at any point in the year since the end of the 1995 campaign.

The team headed into the All-Star break tangled up in a pennant race with the preseason favorite Houston Astros. Offensively, it was being carried by young first baseman Sean Casey. The 24-year-old led the team in doubles and RBIs at the break and was second in the National League with a .371 batting average, garnering his first All-Star selection. He was joined at the All-Star Game by a reju-venated Barry Larkin, who was healthy and having one of his best first halves in years. The team wound up scoring the most runs in modern franchise history with 865, and Vaughn led the team with 45 home runs, the most since George Foster in 1977, and 118 RBIs, the most since Dave Parker in 1985.

The second half started slowly, and the Reds fell to 3½ games back of the Astros. The team showed its resilience with a 20–8 stretch, closing the gap back to a half-game. Proving itself to be a team of hot and cold streaks, the Reds fell four games back despite a 10–1 stretch starting Labor Day weekend. With only 17 games remaining, it looked like the Reds' best shot at the playoffs would be the wild card, where they sat 2½ behind the New York Mets. But another hot stretch, this time a six-game win streak, coupled with a stumble by the Astros, actually saw the Reds leading the NL Central by a game on September 28.

Unfortunately, that was the final bright spot of the season. The team dropped three in a row, handing the NL Central back to the Astros in the process. They still could clinch the NL wild card with a win on the last day of the season and a loss by the New York Mets, but when the Mets won on a 2–1 walk-off wild pitch while the Reds sat through a five-hour 47-minute rain delay in Milwaukee, they knew that they had no choice but to win. And win they did behind a third-inning home run from Vaughn, who had become the undisputed team leader. The Reds and the Mets

The No Facial Hair Policy

It is often believed that the Cincinnati Reds' traditional no facial hair policy dated back to the team's founding, but that could not be further from the truth. In fact, the original 1869 Red Stockings had five players with facial hair, including captain Harry Wright, who nearly had more hair on his face than he did on his head.

The origin of the policy that so many fans remember actually dates back to the 1960s. Bob Howsam was a brilliant baseball man, but he was also very conservative when it came to baseball's traditions. He wanted his players to look clean cut and ready for business. So in 1967, when he joined the franchise as the team's general manager, he instituted the famous policy, along with strict standards for uniforms. Howsam knew exactly how he wanted his players to look, and his rules enforced that.

For more than 30 years, there were no exceptions to the policy, either. In 1985, Rollie Fingers declined a chance to continue his career with the Reds simply because the rule would require him to shave his famous handlebar mustache. Jeff Reardon, who coincidentally had passed Fingers as the all-time saves leader the year before, shaved the beard he had worn for 14 seasons when he signed with the Reds in 1993. It didn't matter who the player was, the policy was strict.

It was not until 1999 that the policy changed when a strong outcry from media and fans convinced owner Marge Schott to remove the rule so that newly acquired Greg Vaughn could keep his goatee. Players rejoiced at the decision and many immediately set about the act of not shaving. The rule, at one time a defining trait of the organization, remains but a memory today.

were tied for the NL wild card, meaning a one-game playoff in Cincinnati the very next day.

Exhausted, the Reds got home from Milwaukee early the next morning. They came out flat as Steve Parris gave up a two-run home run to the second batter of the game. That's all Mets starter Al Leiter needed as he held the Reds to two hits, not even allowing a runner to reach second base until the ninth inning. The Reds' surprising season came to an end with a 5–0 beating, leaving them just short of the postseason despite winning 96 games.

96 The Only Reds Team to Lose 100 Games

It's really not that hard to make the 1982 Cincinnati Reds look good on paper. They had two future Hall of Famers (Johnny Bench and Tom Seaver) and three other future Reds Hall of Famers (Dave Concepcion, Dan Driessen, Mario Soto). They had a three-time member of the 20 HR/50 SB club, Cesar Cedeno. They had a young phenom in Paul Householder who had destroyed Triple A ball the year before. They also had some great names—Wayne Krenchicki, Larry Biittner, and Rafael Landestoy—and some great characters like Brad "The Animal" Lesley.

Naturally, they stunk.

Actually, stunk is putting it lightly. The 1982 Reds were the worst Reds team in at least 45 years, and given where they had come from, they might be the worst team ever. For instance, the 1982 team won 61 games, dropping 101 for the year. The year before, it won 66 in a schedule with 54 fewer games. The 1982 Reds produced the franchise's first losing season since 1971 and only its third since 1961. The team hadn't finished with a winning percentage less than .400 since 1945, and it hadn't finished in last place since 1937.

From 1956–81, no National League team had more wins or a better winning percentage than the Cincinnati Reds. They say it's always darkest just before the dawn. For the Reds, it was darkest immediately after midday.

So what went wrong? It started with general manager Dick Wagner's decision to tighten the purse strings and deal some of his higher-priced players. Outfielder Ken Griffey Sr. was moved to the New York Yankees. George Foster was dealt to the Mets. Dave Collins left via free agency, and Ray Knight was traded for Cedeno, who it turned out was on the downside of his All-Star career.

The future Hall of Famers, Bench and Seaver, had very un-Hall-of-Fame-like seasons. Bench hit just 13 HR and had 38 RBIs, both career lows for a full season. Seaver (5–13, 5.50 ERA) had easily the highest ERA and fewest wins of 20-season career.

The Reds offense scored the fewest runs in the NL. Driessen led the squad with 17 home runs, and his 57 RBIs matched Cedeno for the team lead. Both Cedeno and Concepcion had solid batting averages but not much else. Rookie Householder failed to live up to the hype, hitting .211 with 11 doubles and nine home runs in 456 plate appearances.

While the offense was a disaster, the pitching was at least mediocre. Mario Soto (14–13, 2.79) set the franchise record for strikeouts with 274. Bruce Berenyi's 9–18 record distracted from a respectable 3.36 ERA. Closer Tom Hume finished seventh in the NL in saves, heading up a bullpen that posted a decent 3.14 ERA. Ultimately, though, the run support was pathetic, and this team was one of only two teams in the last 65 years to have five pitchers with 13 or more losses on the year.

The 1983 Reds followed up the '82 campaign with another last-place finish, but things would start to turn around for the franchise a year later when a deal for Pete Rose brought a new manager and new hope for a proud franchise.

97 Chris Sabo

Raised in a blue-collar family the son of a plumber, Chris Sabo learned early to play hard and not toot his own horn. He was never much for flashy play, but he was intense and when he showed up in Cincinnati, he reminded many of the city's favorite son, Pete Rose. In a city that worships hard-nosed, high-energy players, Sabo quickly became a star.

It was an unlikely rise to stardom, though. Sabo had a solid but unimpressive minor league career. By the time he earned his way onto the Reds' roster in 1988, he was 26 years old, a little older than the typical prospect. He was given the starting job during his rookie year when the regular third baseman, Buddy Bell, was shelved with an injury. Sabo came out swinging, hitting .340 in his first 13 games. The city fell in love with his crew-cut hairdo and his now iconic Rec-Spec sports goggles. His look earned him the nickname "Spuds" based on his resemblance to a popular pooch pitchman of the day. At 5'11", 185 lbs., Sabo was not a big man,

Reds Rookies of the Year

The first Rookie of the Year award was given in 1947 to Jackie Robinson. The Reds' first winner came nine years later. Since that time, only the Dodgers have had more Rookie of the Year winners than the Reds. These are the seven Reds who won the award:

1956 Frank Robinson
1963 Pete Rose
1966 Tommy Helms
1968 Johnny Bench
1976 Pat Zachry
1988 Chris Sabo
1999 Scott Williamson

Andy Van Slyke of the Pittsburgh Pirates is tagged out by Chris Sabo after trying to reach third on a fly ball hit by Barry Bonds during the NLCS game on October 5, 1990. The throw was from the Reds' Paul O'Neill. Calling the play is umpire Jerry Crawford. (AP Photo)

but he played with such heart that he made anyone believe that it could be them down on that field.

By mid-May, his average was at .284, but Sabo showed a little bit of pop (11 doubles and six homers in 34 games) and a little bit of speed (14 stolen bases in 16 attempts). He got really hot in early June and batted .361/.414/.597 from the third of that month 'til the All-Star break, earning himself a selection to the All-Star Game, where he was used as a pinch runner. He batted just .216 in the second half of the season, but his 40 doubles and 46 stolen bases were enough to convince voters to give him the NL Rookie of the Year Award.

Sabo continued to work hard and build his game. With the help of manager Lou Piniella before the 1990 season, he turned himself into a power hitter, launching 25 bombs and garnering his first of two All-Star Game starts. A man of few words and little flashiness, Sabo continued to drive his old Ford Escort years after he made it to the majors even though the car frequently broke down.

That's not to say that Sabo didn't have pride. During the Reds' celebration of their World Series title in 1990, Sabo stepped to the mic on Fountain Square and addressed the now vanquished Oakland A's, who, despite being swept, still told everyone they were the better team. "They can say what they want," he shouted to crowd of 20,000. "We got the ring. We got the money. We got everything!"

Another quality season followed by a couple of down years in 1992 and 1993 left Sabo at a crossroads with the franchise when free agency arrived. Sabo wanted to stay with the Reds, but the team did not make him a competitive offer in his eyes. "They said all along they'd like 25 Chris Sabos; now it sounds like they don't even want one," he said. "I'm not bitter. I wanted to ride in a World Series parade with the Reds again."

He left for Baltimore in free agency and battled injuries for two seasons, spending time with the Orioles, White Sox, and Cardinals. He came back to the Reds in 1996 to try to recapture the magic, but a balky back made it difficult and Sabo only appeared in 54 more games before retiring after that season. His career was relatively short but exciting, leaving an indelible impression on many fans and leading to his induction into the Reds Hall of Fame in 2010.

98 Cy Seymour

Since 1893, there have been two players to pitch in at least 100 games in the big leagues and accumulate at least 1,500 hits. One of those is a player named Babe Ruth. The other was a much lesser known turn-of-the-century player known as James "Cy" Seymour. The left-hander from Albany, New York, started his big-league career as a pitcher with the New York Giants. And truth be told, he was a pretty good one. In 1898, he was 25–19 with a 3.18 ERA and he led the league with 239 strikeouts. During a three-year span, he led the NL in both strikeouts and walks, and though his wildness might have been a factor in forcing Seymour to leave the pitcher's mound, the explanation given was "dead arm," a general term given to many vague pitching injuries of the day.

While Seymour was a pitcher, he also started playing some outfield, more out of need than because of the identification of some hidden talent. He acquitted himself well at the plate, and when it was clear that he was no longer effective on the mound, a permanent move to the outfield was the obvious step. He hit well for a season-and-a-half with John McGraw's Baltimore Orioles before coming to the Cincinnati Reds midway through the 1902 season.

Seymour became a hitting star in Cincinnati, batting .340 for the remainder of the 1902 season. The following year he batted .342, good for fifth in the league. He was one of seven NL hitters to bat better than .300 in 1904, hitting .313, good for third in the batting race. Only fifth NL hitters outhit Seymour over the three season span from 1902–04. One of those was Honus Wagner, who led all NL hitters with a .344 average during those three years. He would be Seymour's only competition for the batting title the next year.

In 1905, Seymour had one of the finest seasons ever by a Reds hitter. That season he led the league in hits, doubles, triples, RBIs, total bases, slugging percentage, and OPS. But as it was for the century afterward, batting average was the glamorous title that every hitter longed to capture. The only player standing in Seymour's way was the three-time batting champ, Honus Wagner. The two entered the final day of the season with Seymour up by .011 points and their teams facing off in a double-header. The crowd, numbering more than 10,000, seemed to be more interested in the hitting of the two men rather than the outcome of the games. According to reports, "Cheer upon cheer greeted the mighty batsmen upon each appearance at the plate and mighty cheering greeted the sound of bat upon ball as mighty Cy drove out hit after hit. The boss slugger got 4-for-7 while Wagner could only get 2-for-7."

Seymour captured the batting title that day, the first in franchise history. His .377 average is still the highest all time by a Reds player, and no Red has come within 20 points of that number since. A modern metric known as Wins Above Replacement (WAR) rated Seymour's 1905 season as the best by a Reds player in the first 72 years after the team returned to the National League. It still ranks as 10th best all time in franchise history.

Cy would only play 79 more games with the Reds before he was purchased off the team by the New York Giants. In approximately four seasons worth of games with the team, he batted .332, which is the highest career average for any player with at least 1,000 plate appearances for the franchise. It was on the strength of that batting average that Seymour entered the Reds Hall of Fame in 1998.

221 Home Runs in a Single Season

In the 11 seasons from 1945–55, the Cincinnati Reds weren't quite the laughingstock of the National League—that titled belonged to the Pittsburgh Pirates—but they were close. The Reds won just 44 percent of their games in that span, never once crossing over the .500 mark for a season and never once finishing above fifth place.

It was with that context in mind that one could say the success of the 1956 Cincinnati Redlegs came out of nowhere. That statement, however, is a bit misleading since the Reds were second the National League in runs in 1955, and they had a team that was a touch better than league average at preventing runs. The 1955 team ended up being one of the unluckiest teams in Reds history, finishing nine games under its expected record based on the run differential. That's not to say they should have been a contender, but had they won the 84 games their run differential suggests, 1956 would not have seemed so out of place.

But history is what it is, and the 1956 Redlegs made quite a bit of history for the franchise. The Redlegs were an offensive juggernaut, becoming the first team in franchise history to lead the National League in runs scored, outpacing the rest of the NL by more than 50 runs. How did they do it? By mashing the ball. The Redlegs tied a major league record in 1956 by hitting 221 longballs, 40 more than the franchise record they had set just a year prior.

The leader of the offensive onslaught was a 20-year-old rookie from Beaumont, Texas, named Frank Robinson. Robinson tied the National League mark for home runs by a rookie with 38 and led the NL in runs scored with 122. He easily won the league's Rookie of the Year Award. Robinson also led the NL in hits by pitch, a statistic he'd lead the league in seven times during his career. His 20 HBP in 1956 was more than half the total of any other team in the NL, and the Reds set a franchise record with 51 HBP on the season.

Robinson may have been a major driver of the Reds offense, but he was hardly a lone cog in the machine. Sluggers Wally Post and Ted Kluszewski contributed 36 and 35 bombs a piece, tying a mark for most hitters with 30+ home runs in a season. They nearly broke that mark if not for a late-season slump by Gus Bell that left him with 29 home runs. Ed Bailey set the franchise record for most home runs by a catcher with 28, and three other players added double-digit taters to give the Reds eight players in all with 10 or more home runs, another franchise record.

The Redlegs increased their scoring output as well as their run prevention and as a result, they not only improved their expected record over 1955, but they improved their actual record, winning 91 games. It was the most victories by the franchise since they won 100 games and the World Series in 1940. They were in the pennant race from start to finish, even leading the NL by 1½ games at the All-Star break. That lead quickly slipped away two days after the break, and the Redlegs never found themselves in first place again the rest of the year. Ultimately, manager Birdie Tebbetts's club finished in third place, two games back of the Brooklyn Dodgers.

Many of the records set by the 1956 Redlegs have long since fallen due in large part to the homer-happy days of the 1990s and early 2000s. And it would be another five years before the Redlegs could get themselves back into the title hunt, but the 1956 season remains a special one for many fans because it signaled that the days of the also-ran Reds were numbered.

100 The Stowes

Who is the greatest player in Reds history? That question will always be up for debate. What is undeniable is that whoever it is, Bernie Stowe or one of his sons, Mark and Rick, has a story about him. The first family of the Reds—the Stowes—have been part of the organization for nearly 70 years. In 1947, the visiting clubhouse boy at Crosley Field fell ill. The Reds' clubhouse man, Chesty Evans, asked 12-year-old Bernie Stowe, a friend of the batboy, if he could do the job. In 1953, he was selected to be the batboy for the National League All-Stars. By 1968, Stowe was named the Reds' clubhouse manager and the rest is history.

"You get lucky," Stowe recalled to Hal McCoy of the *Dayton Daily News*. "I was so young at first and I always thought they'd get rid of me. Then as time went on I was older than the players. Some of them even trusted me enough so that when they went on the road they let me use their cars."

In the nearly 150 years of Cincinnati baseball, it's hard to imagine that there is a more respected man than Bernie Stowe. The next former player to say a bad thing about him will likely be the first, and that respect is often extended to his two sons, Rick, who is now the home clubhouse manager, and Mark, the visiting clubhouse manager at GABP.

The clubhouse managers become like family members to many of the players. Spending eight months out of the year, seven days a week with the guys will do that. The friendships that have developed between the Stowes and some of the players they take care of are deep.

Big Red Machine manager Sparky Anderson credits Bernie Stowe with keeping him humble during his highly successful run in the 1970s. It started with day one when Stowe approached the new manager and said, "Let's get one thing straight. I was here before you got here and I'll be here after you're gone, so don't give me any crap."

There are few people who get Hall of Fame catcher Johnny Bench as choked up as Bernie Stowe. "Every day, he walked through this clubhouse trying to make our lives so much easier and better for us," Bench said. "We've all been honored and blessed throughout all our careers to have known this man, and to have his sons take over his legacy is also very special."

At an event honoring the retirement of Bench's No. 5, the Reds great recognized Bernie directly with the gift of a painting and two round-trip tickets to Las Vegas. Gifts to the Stowes from players have been numerous throughout the years. Some of the more publicized ones were a silver Mercedes given to Rick from Barry Larkin when the future Hall of Famer retired. Rick, who joined the Reds clubhouse crew in 1983, had been with Larkin his entire career and the two had a deep bond. The clubhouse staff also received a new golf cart from Aaron Harang a few years later, helping them to more easily do their jobs around the park.

When Great American Ball Park opened in 2003, the Reds surprised Bernie and his boys by naming the home clubhouse in his honor. In 2008, Bernie was awarded the Powel Crosley Jr. Award for his lifetime of service and dedication to the franchise. Even 65 years after his first job with the Reds, Bernie still shows up occasionally to clean cleats and help out around the clubhouse that is now being run by Rick. For most in the organization, it's hard to imagine it any other way.

Sources

Books

Erardi, John G., and Gregory L. Rhodes. *Opening Day: Celebrating Cincinnati's Baseball Holiday.* Cincinnati, Ohio: Road West Pub., 2004.

Erardi, John G., and Joel Luckhaupt. *The Wire-to-Wire Reds: Sweet Lou, Nasty Boys, and the Wild Run to a World Championship.* Cincinnati, Ohio: Clerisy Press, 2010.

Frost, Mark. *Game Six: Cincinnati, Boston, and the 1975 World Series: The Triumph of America's Pastime.* New York: Hyperion, 2009.

Posnanski, Joe. *The Machine: A Hot Team, a Legendary Season, and a Heart-Stopping World Series: The Story of the 1975 Cincinnati Reds.* New York: William Morrow, 2009.

Rhodes, Gregory L., and John G. Erardi. *Big Red Dynasty: How Bob Howsam & Sparky Anderson Built the Big Red Machine.* Cincinnati, Ohio: Road West Pub., 1997.

Rhodes, Gregory L., and John Snyder. *Redleg Journal: Year by Year and Day by Day with the Cincinnati Reds Since 1866.* Cincinnati, Ohio: Road West Pub., 2000.

Smith, Daryl Raymond. *Making the Big Red Machine: Bob Howsam and the Cincinnati Reds of the 1970s.* Jefferson, North Carolina: McFarland & Co., 2009.

Newspapers/Magazines

The Sporting News
Cincinnati Enquirer
Cincinnati Post
Dayton Daily News
Sports Illustrated

New York Times
Los Angeles Times
Toronto Star
Tuscaloosa News
St. Petersburg Times
Boys' Life
Baseball Digest

Websites
Reds.com
Baseball-Reference.com
BaseballProspectus.com
FanGraphs.com
HardballTimes.com
SABR.org
WaiteHoyt.com
LatinoSportsLegends.com
baseballinwartime.com
crosley-field.com